Encountering
CHINA

New Zealanders and the People's Republic

Encountering
CHINA

Edited by
Duncan Campbell & Brian Moloughney

MASSEY UNIVERSITY PRESS

新

人

地

事

轉

Contents

Encountering China | **11**
Chris Elder

初 Beginnings

Kwantung Guest House: Canton | **23**
Hone Tuwhare

Scoria, Loess, Silt: Reflections on the Human
Geologies of South Auckland and North China | **25**
Lewis Mayo

Speaking Half-truth to Power | **33**
Chris Elder

Muldoon Meets Deng, Autumn 1980 | **39**
Nick Bridge

The Canton Trade Fair, 1977: Pages from a Diary | **43**
Leo Haks

Finding China: Relationships and Myself | **50**
James Ng

Images for Sages | **56**
Diana Bridge

China, 'A Tired Old Country'?
The Dangers of Group Thinking | **67**
Michael Powles

Inside China as an Outsider | **74**
John McKinnon

Māori Business Relationships with China | **82**
Mavis Mullins

人 People

A Haunted Taste | 96
Jacob Edmond

Finding Dr Li Lairong:
Pioneer of New Zealand–China Science Co-operation | 104
Tony Browne

Madame Sun Yat-sen's Apple Pie for Pudding | 111
Mary Roberts-Schirato

Vic Wilcox, the People's Republic of China
and the New Zealand Communist Movement | 118
Kerry Taylor

Learning from Dai Qing | 125
Pauline Keating

Poets in Exile: Yang Lian and Gu Cheng in Auckland | 133
Hilary Chung

Hong Kong Revisited | 136
John Needham

A New Kiwi Chinese Celebrates 50 Years of Relations | 142
Bo Li

Where Shi Le Used to Hunt | 147
Michael Radich

Lost in Shanghai | 153
Alison Wong

地 Place

The Temples of Xi'an | **160**
Margaret T. South

'The Earl of Zheng Overcame Duan in Yan':
China's Past in Our Futures | **165**
Duncan Campbell

Stages of Enlightenment | **173**
Amanda Jack

Song Dynasty Dragon Kiln Revival | **179**
Peter Holmes

Return to Liangzhu | **187**
Wen Chin Powles

Reflections on Being a Foreign
Student in Shanghai in the 1980s | **195**
Rebecca Needham

1989: Beijing Under Martial Law | **202**
Brian Moloughney

Winter (Season of Baby Mandarins, Apples):
Spring Onion Oil Noodles 葱油拌面 | **208**
Nina Mingya Powles

Urumchi and the World in 2004 | **212**
Joe Lawson

Chengdu: 12 May 2008 | **218**
Andrew Wilford

事 Occasion

Memories of a Polisher in Beijing | **224**
Phillip Mann

Whakawhanaungatanga | **231**
Meng Foon

The Poll Tax Apology and Reconciliation | **239**
Esther Fung

1989 Matters | **246**
Brenda (Englefield) Sabatier

Crossing the 'Chinese Bridge' | **253**
Thomas Nicholls

Where It All Started: The Class of '06 and
the First China Field Study Course in Beijing | **260**
Xiaoming Huang

Poets on Yellow Mountain | **267**
Murray Edmond

10,000 Lights Across the City 万家灯火: Lantern Festivals
and Their Role in New Zealand–China Relations | **275**
James To

Making Friends: A China Journey Spanning 30 Years | **283**
Garth Fraser

Revisiting China for the First Time | **291**
Jason Young

轉 Transformations

Crows, Ducklings and Kiwis: New Zealand in Chinese Minds | **298**
Paul Clark

Two Decades of Development Work in West China | **304**
Dave Bromwich

Myths of Dumplings, Business and
International Relations: Is it Time to Demystify? | **311**
Hongzhi Gao

Understanding Grandmother's Buddhism:
Lessons for Respecting the Beliefs of Others in China | **318**
Amy Holmes-Tagchungdarpa

Bridges and Rainbows:
Teaching Chinese Students in New Zealand | **326**
Ellen Soullière

Between Imaginaries:
Interconnections of a Samoan New Zealander with China | **335**
Ashalyna Noa

They Aren't Going to Take My Organs, Mum | **339**
Adam Osborne-Smith

Middle Kingdom, Middle Earth, My Adventure | **347**
Luke Qin

Reflections of a NZUSA Delegation Visitor, 1971 | **354**
Philip S. Morrison

A Young China-watcher's Take on a Changing China | **361**
Alex Smith

About the Contributors | **368**

Acknowledgements | **385**

Index | **387**

Encountering China

CHRIS ELDER

The fiftieth anniversary of New Zealand's establishing formal diplomatic relations with the People's Republic of China is unusual among diplomatic occasions. Most commonly, relationships between countries develop organically over time, but in this case the Joint Communiqué signed in New York on 22 December 1972 set the scene for a whole new beginning. It provided the springboard for a multifaceted relationship that has come to occupy a central place in New Zealand's external dealings, and in the perceptions and the experiences of many individual New Zealanders.

This collection sets out to provide a patchwork built up from the memories, the experiences and the emotional responses of some of those who have been caught up in different aspects of the two countries' interaction over the past 50 years. It offers 50 at 50 — 50 contributions centred on the period 1972 to 2022. The perspective it provides is a New Zealand one, leavened on occasion by the insights of those whose lives have spanned both countries. It makes no claim to be comprehensive, or definitive in any way. It stands simply as a record of how certain people have regarded certain aspects of the relationship at one time or another in the 50 years since the establishment of relations.

It would of course be simplistic to suggest that New Zealand's links with China have sprung up only in the past 50 years. Modern research has revealed ancient DNA links back to North Asia among these islands' first inhabitants. The earliest trade contacts date back more than 200 years — not a long time in the annals of China, but pre-dating New Zealand's existence as a nation. Māori were closely involved in those early contacts, just as iwi enterprises engaged with China today are flourishing. Appropriately, *Encountering China* takes as its starting point the response of the poet Hone Tuwhare to his opportunity to come face-to-face with China as part of a Māori workers delegation in 1973, which visited within a year of recognition.

Sojourners, and later settlers, came to New Zealand from China in numbers from the time of the 1860s gold rushes. In early years, they were subject to hostility and discrimination. In this collection, James Ng takes that period as his starting point in reflecting on his family's acclimatisation, while Esther Fung provides a coda to the transgressions of many years in her account of the process leading to a formal apology for past injustices.

It is true, nonetheless, that the agreement signed in 1972 paved the way for a substantial expansion of contacts between two countries which had spent the previous 23 years largely ignoring one another's existence. It allowed the establishment of a range of official frameworks for inter-action and co-operation, it provided a way forward for linkages between institutions and interest groups in the two countries, and it created the conditions that would promote familiarity and inform judgement going forward. 'If understanding between the two countries is still not all that it might be,' New Zealand's first ambassador to China grudgingly recorded at the end of his three-year term, 'it is at least better than it was.'

The New Zealand government somewhat unconvincingly sheeted home its long-delayed decision to recognise China to the fact that 'China has now re-entered the mainstream of world affairs'. That being the case, the official announcement noted, it was 'logical and sensible for New Zealand to recognise the People's Republic of China and enter into normal relations with it'. 'Normal relations', the Joint Communiqué made plain, included establishing embassies in each other's capitals. Cash-strapped New Zealand would just as soon have left the next step in abeyance for a few years, but was brought around by China's intimation that recognition without reciprocal representation would not, in its view, amount to recognition at all.

Inevitably, this compilation includes the recollections of some who, as diplomats, worked to support New Zealand's political objectives in China. John McKinnon reviews that process from three different points in time, while Michael Powles struggles with the discovery that those supposedly better informed often are not. The relationship has been buttressed by a remarkable series of high-level visits in both directions, lending some credence to the perception that New Zealand has been seen as sufficiently small and non-threatening to provide a proving ground for senior Chinese leaders. That such visits have not been without their perils, particularly in the early days, is attested by the accounts of Chris Elder and Nick Bridge.

It is chastening to recall the level of ignorance in New Zealand about China at the time of recognition. 'One sight is worth a hundred descriptions' (百聞不如一見), according to a Chinese proverb, but not many New Zealanders had had the opportunity for even one sight. (One of the few who did, Philip Morrison, here describes a student trip in the lead-up to recognition.) People-to-people contact was largely in the hands of the small and left-leaning New Zealand China Friendship Society; party-to-party contact the preserve of Victor Wilcox and his associates in the Communist Party of New Zealand (CPNZ). Neither commanded a large hearing within New Zealand. Press reporting about China was filtered through a small coterie of Western journalists in Beijing, and a larger but not necessarily better-informed press corps in Hong Kong.

China, for its part, had not advanced much past the condition signalled in the 1602 geographical treatise *Yueling guangyi* 月令廣義, in which a world map showed an indeterminate mass roughly corresponding to New Zealand's geographical location with the notation 'few people have been to this place in the south, and no one knows what things are there'. In the early 1970s, the best authority on what things were there was to be found in the pages of the CPNZ's *People's Voice*, which, as Chinese diplomats discovered when they arrived in Wellington, was not as authoritative as all that.

The half-century that has passed since the establishment of a formal relationship between China and New Zealand has seen major changes in both countries. China has become confident and outward-looking in its international dealings, to the point where it has come to vie with the United States for global influence. It has accepted Deng Xiaoping's mantra that 'to grow rich is glorious', launching a programme of economic growth that has delivered a previously-unknown level of prosperity to its people and turned China into a vital engine of international economic growth. A number of the contributions reflect aspects of this process, not always without regret: 'I cannot help but feel,' notes Phillip Mann, 'that something has been lost in the mad rush for economic prosperity.'

New Zealand, for its part, has over time shifted to a worldview that brings China into much sharper focus. In 1973, just a year after this country recognised China, Britain entered the European Economic Community. New Zealand was moved a step away from the country that had traditionally provided its foreign policy lead, at the same time as it faced major constraints on access to what had always been the biggest market for its goods. Little more than a decade later, it lost its main security guarantor when the United States withdrew from co-operation under the ANZUS Treaty. History has increasingly given way to geography, as New Zealand has sought new partnerships and new markets. China is central to that process, not just in its own right, but also because it is itself committed to building enhanced relationships with its Asian neighbours, and more distantly the islands of the Pacific, the countries that lie to its near south, and to New Zealand's near north.

In the 1970s, prospects for trade with China were not generally seen as very bright. Total two-way trade in 1972 amounted to $8.2 million. In 1973, then Trade Minister Joe Walding urged upon his Chinese counterpart the notion that there could be a vast improvement if only everyone in China took milk in their tea, but even the genial Mr Walding was not overly hopeful. Leo Haks, an early attendee at the Canton Trade Fair, found the prospects underwhelming: 'an educational holiday with work thrown in, and very little at that'.

How things have changed. The dilemma New Zealand now faces is how to avoid overdependence on the Chinese market, which in the year to June 2021 accounted for 31 per cent of total New Zealand goods exports, while China provided 20 per cent of this country's imports. That dilemma is based on a perception that economic dependence could be used as a bargaining chip or weapon in cases of political disagreement. Other countries' experiences suggest that this is not a baseless fear. Potential overdependence is an element in the relationship that needs to be managed in a carefully considered way, but it has not so far been sufficient to diminish the attraction of a stable and lucrative trading relationship with the main economic player in our region.

Educational exchanges were an early fruit of recognition, and remain a major contributor to bilateral understanding. In New Zealand a special programme, the China Exchange Programme (CHEP), was set up in the 1970s to manage the process. Its success is reflected in the contributions in this book of a number who were its beneficiaries. CHEP allowed Mary Roberts-Schirato to eat apple pie with Rewi Alley in Beijing; it launched

Duncan Campbell on the path of scholarship that allows him to draw lessons for today's China from a text more than 2000 years old.

CHEP, and subsequent opportunities to study Chinese language and culture in-country, have most commonly been built on interest and knowledge sparked by earlier study in New Zealand. That being the case, it is all the more worrying that, at the end of 50 years, interest among New Zealand universities in providing China-related courses appears to be on the wane. Few universities now offer courses on Chinese history, and only one offers Classical Chinese. Postgraduate work in any field of Chinese studies is generally taken up only by students who are themselves from China. Looking ahead, it is hard not to be concerned that New Zealand tertiary institutions are largely failing to provide the base that will generate enthusiasm among their students to learn more about China.

To lament the predominance of Chinese students in postgraduate Chinese studies is in no way to imply criticism of their contribution. They, and all the others who have come to New Zealand from China to undertake study — all the way from basic English language courses to those working in different fields at the highest postgraduate levels — have contributed greatly to bilateral understanding. By their very presence they have helped to normalise the relationship; on their return to China, they have helped to counter the seventeenth-century plaint that 'no one knows what things are there'.

Importantly, New Zealand has been enriched over the past 50 years by those — students and others — who have chosen to take up permanent residence in New Zealand. Their presence in New Zealand has offered a window into Chinese culture, and Chinese social norms, that has done a great deal to broaden the perspective with which New Zealanders regard their giant neighbour. Bo Li has become a successful businessman who moonlights designing stamps for New Zealand Post to mark the Lunar New Year; Hongzhi Gao teaches marketing into China, while warning 'it is dangerous to be focused only on trade'.

In his contribution, former Gisborne mayor and now Race Relations

Commissioner Meng Foon describes how he has gone about building links with China: 'It's all about relationships, face-to-face.' For many New Zealanders, people-to-people relationships are the bedrock of their association with China. That is reflected in what a number of contributors have chosen to highlight: Amanda Jack, 'a goat farmer's daughter from Kaukapakapa', being tutored on the intricacies of Peking Opera; Garth Fraser, holding on to friendships even while being subjected to Cultural Revolution-style criticism for his temerity in questioning opaque financial practices at Rewi Alley's old school at Shandan.

There is an odd symmetry about the beginning and the end of the 50-year period. Its beginnings came at the end of a time during which New Zealand kept China at arm's length, essentially because of the United States' unwillingness to treat with it. It ends at a time when the United States and China are once again at odds, and the stand-off between the two presents a difficult balancing act for small nations such as New Zealand.

China does not always present itself in a sympathetic light. It is perceived to be heavy-handed in the way it deals with national minorities within its borders, in its administration of the 'one country, two systems' approach to Hong Kong, even in its apparent attempts to influence the behaviour of Chinese people resident outside China. At the same time, it has demonstrated a growing and at times unwarranted assertiveness in its dealings with other countries. It is a measure of the degree to which such behaviour gives rise to dismay that some potential contributors to this volume have opted not to do so, either because of their profound disagreement with aspects of Chinese policy, or because of fear of repercussions for themselves or others should they speak freely.

Encountering China encompasses as many points of view as there are contributors. For Friendship Society president Dave Bromwich, it is 'policy filtering down from Beijing' that provides the environment for successful development work. Support for Beijing's policies is less apparent in the contributions of Brian Moloughney and Brenda Englefield-Sabatier, both of whom write about events during the city's time under martial law in 1989, events that in Moloughney's experience left the ordinary people of China with 'a sense of incomprehension, anger and sadness'. Joe Lawson describes his experience in Urumchi, 'a city where different worlds tumbled alongside each other'. Amy Holmes-Tagchungdarpa contributes a gentle discussion of Buddhism, in particular that practised by Tibetan communities. A teacher, she places her faith in the young, who 'often have unique talents for respecting the beliefs of others and for cultivating tolerance, benevolence and care'.

Where to from here? Tolerance and care, and perhaps benevolence as well, will be needed as New Zealand as a nation, and New Zealanders as individuals, go forward in managing a relationship that has become too complex to be capable of easy solutions, and too important to be left to chance. Jason Young, reflecting on often formulaic academic discussions, argues strongly for continued engagement in that setting: 'we should take every opportunity to present and hear alternative views and attempt to resolve issues'. In a broader context, Alex Smith writes of the prospect of 'uneasy personal compromise' that has for the time being deflected her from a China career path.

There is, Smith points out, no singular China, and no way of knowing what it will look like in the future. Michael Radich makes the same point. 'I have long been unsure I believe in anything called "China", but am grateful, all the same, for a life spent grappling with many things travelling under that name.' The past 50 years have seen New Zealand launched on a path of engagement with the 'many things' that make up China. If the experiences of that period, reflected in the contributions to this book, are no certain guide for what lies in the future, they may at least offer some context for the way ahead.

Imposing an appropriate structure on the many-sided offerings has presented a challenge. Simple chronology did not seem to meet the need, especially since many pieces range over a considerable period of time. It was perceived, however, that contributions tended to coalesce around three broad themes: people, place and occasion. These themes seemed focused enough to provide the possibility of a degree of coherence, while still being sufficiently capacious to accommodate a range of differing approaches. It was evident, too, that for many contributors the experiences described had proved transformational. Hence the adoption of a final section that might point towards an eventual arrival at some sort of resolution, without venturing to suggest what this might look like.

Throughout this anthology, the font employed for Chinese characters, whether full-form or simplified, has been standardised. In light particularly of the time period covered here, the editors have chosen, however, to respect authorial preference in terms of both the system of Romanisation used (for the names of people and places, for instance), and, more generally, of a range of other referents: China or People's Republic of China or PRC, New Zealand or Aotearoa, Chinese Communist Party (CCP) or Communist Party of China (CPC), and so on.

Encountering China has been put together by an editorial group composed of Pauline Keating (organiser), Duncan Campbell, Paul Clark, Chris Elder, Maria Galikowski, Brian Moloughney, James To, Andrew Wilford and Jason Young, working under the auspices of the New Zealand Contemporary China Research Centre, housed at Te Herenga Waka Victoria University of Wellington. The editors' thanks are due to all who have contributed, and to the others whose contributions have not been able to be included for reasons of space and balance.

初 Beginnings

In 1973, soon after the establishment of diplomatic relations with the People's Republic of China, the Communist Party of New Zealand helped organise the visit to China of a 'Māori Workers' delegation. The delegation included (from left) the trade unionists Timi Te Maipi and Willie Wilson, Hone Tuwhare, Miriama Rauhihi of the Polynesian Panthers and Tame Iti, representing Ngā Tamatoa. Like most visitors at this time, the delegation travelled to China from Hong Kong by train, and spent their first night at the famous Kwantung Guest House in Canton. TAME ITI

Kwantung Guest House: Canton

HONE TUWHARE

All the way from the border and in the roomy
air-conditioned train, I try sleep. Impossible:
my neck hurts with the swivelling.

The vastness with the colours changing, banded
geometrical and curving off, make lonely the figure
nearby of a peasant with a black and wide-fringed

hat, and another further away with a water buffalo.
With my eyes seduced by the miracle of thousands of
reclaimed *mou* of red earth burgeoning, I wondered,

thinking in terms of a paltry million or two, where
on earth are all the people? Expecting, I suppose,
to see them burst from the ground like

People's Militia units with crimson flags pulsing
in the wind. Now at day's end, I try to sift
impressions. My sifter breaks down: the City laughs.

I'm overwhelmed by the size of my bedroom suite.
Below my window on the second floor, and through a
long thin island of Saliu trees, palm and decorative

shrub, I can see large chunks of coal, glinting in
the rain and banked up along an eight-foot-high
concrete wall. A pathway between doesn't divide,

but unites the scene in an incongruous way. From the
kitchen below voices of varying intensities float up
human and near. I lift the phone and ask for a beer.

Canton: City of workers — and bicycles. Teeming; alive,
and set firmly into a dynamic base built painfully by
their heroic predecessors and revolutionary patriots.

But Canton is a city as drab as any other on a wet
day: with this notable exception. There are no
bill-board advertisments for Coca-Cola, Dutch Shell

And Exxon petroleum products. Instead, a poster high
and as wide as a building, flaunting a brigade of
coal miners surging. But night has slipped a marker

in closing the Day Book. Tiny lights burning
intermittently among the leaves of the Saliu trees
fade and re-appear. *What are they?*

I fight sleep remembering only the urgent bus and
truck horns blurting, underlining proletarian forms
and priorities. I think of Yellow Flower Hill

and the shattered bones of seventy-two revolutionary
martyrs buried there. At least they sleep easier now.
For I am startled by these wide-awake thought-shifts

occasioned by the newness and press of contrasts.
Like the Saliu trees and black coal gleaming: visually
unlike, and with thousands of years between them:

But indistinct, like fire and hammer-blow.

Scoria, Loess, Silt: Reflections on the Human Geologies of South Auckland and North China

LEWIS MAYO

'History is about you.'
— Richard T. Phillips, remarks in a tutorial for 'China Since the Opium War', University of Auckland, 1982

'During Cambrian times the New Zealand region was part of the continental sea floor off East Gondwana and not surprisingly our trilobites and brachiopods show a very clear East Australian–East Asia relationship. Favourable ocean conditions and land–sea relations enabled these shallow-water organisms to have easy contact between these three areas, which were much closer together then. This same Australia–China affinity continues through the Palaeozoic among these shelly fossils, but the Chinese relationship gets weaker. Some barrier to migration between New Zealand and China must have been developing, and we believe that barrier to have been a widening and deepening sea as moving plates carried the two regions further apart.'
— Jack Grant-Mackie, in Graeme Stevens, Matt McGlone and Beverley McCulloch, *Prehistoric New Zealand*, Auckland: Heinemann Reed, 1988, p. 20

Five scoria cones — Māngere Mountain, Puketutu, Waitomokia, Pukeiti, Ōtuataua and Maungataketake — appear on the map of the volcanoes of the Māngere–Ihumātao district in E. J. Searle's *City of Volcanoes: A Geology of Auckland*. To these five scoria cones geologists nowadays would add the one in Māngere Lagoon, recently restored as a part of the attempt to recover something of the local landforms broken down by quarrying and land transformation in the decades between the 1860s and the present.

The map of Māngere–Ihumātao referred to above appears in the second edition of Searle's book, published in 1981; a year of considerable moment in the history of Aotearoa New Zealand and in my own life, where the conflicts over sporting contacts with apartheid-era South Africa precipitated more profound and public political division than in any subsequent period in the history of the country.

As it happens, 1981 was also the year in which the Chinese Communist Party and the Communist Party of New Zealand, both founded in 1921, celebrated their sixtieth anniversaries, anniversaries that took place at significant points of transition in the history of both parties. The Chinese Communist Party was for its part engaged in shifting its economic and political programme away from the class-struggle paradigm which had rhetorically dominated in the era of Mao Zedong. The Communist Party of New Zealand (CPNZ), having sided with China in the Sino–Soviet split in the early 1960s, had at that stage repudiated not only the incumbent leadership of the Communist Party of China, but the whole legacy of Maoism, which, it declared, was simply a form of 'bourgeois nationalism'.

The first edition of Searle's book on Auckland volcanoes was issued by Paul's Book Arcade in 1964, the year of my birth and the year in which the same publisher brought out Hone Tuwhare's first poetry collection, *No Ordinary Sun*. Tuwhare spent part of his childhood in Māngere in the mid-1930s, when his father was working on Chinese market gardens there, and was thus, while young, an inhabitant of the scoria, tuff, basalt and silt landscapes that Searle's map depicts. Beginning his apprenticeship as a boiler-maker at the Ōtāhuhu railway workshops in 1939, he joined the New Zealand Communist Party in 1942. Tuwhare moved into a different segment of South Auckland's volcanic landscapes — the one depicted in the map of the volcanic deposits in the Ōtāhuhu–Manurewa district in Searle's book. There, in addition to scoria, basalt, tuff and ash, are found Pleistocene-era silts, sands and peats and recent alluvium — silt in the non-technical sense of 'fine sand, clay, or other soil carried by moving or running water and deposited as a sediment on the bottom or on a shore or flood plain'.

Beneath the scoria cones and basalt lava flows that make up Ngā Kaoua Kohora/Ngā Kapua Kohuora/Crater Hill in Papatoetoe, part of the Ōtāhuhu–Manurewa volcanic zone mapped by Searle, lies what is known as the Underground Press Cave. It is so named because the cave was used in 1940 to print *People's Voice*, the newspaper of the Communist Party of New Zealand, a publication which was at that stage banned because of the Party's opposition to the Second World War. Here, South Auckland's political history intersects directly with its geomorphology. New Zealand communists, active in South Auckland in the 1930s and 1940s because of its identity as an industrial area, took advantage of the geology of the region and the possibilities it provides for underground operations.

When the party shifted to support for the war effort following the invasion of the Soviet Union in 1941, its publications became legal again and were edited by R. A. K. Mason, a party member, poet, and friend and mentor of Hone Tuwhare, someone whose intellectual and emotional involvement with China is well known.

At the time that these events were taking place, the Chinese Communist

Party had its headquarters in the Loess Plateau in Northwest China, where its leaders forged the organisational, political and cultural frameworks that they would deploy when assuming power in 1949. For many outsiders who have experienced them in the modern era, the landscapes of the Loess Plateau have an almost overwhelming force. Their aridity, coupled with their stark contours — treeless and often completely devoid of vegetation — leaves an extraordinary impression on someone encountering them for the first time, as I did in 1985–86. The yellow loess of Northwest China, a soil made up of particles of fine grade deposited on the land over the centuries by the wind, and to a lesser extent by water, seems, to the untrained observer at least, a kind of antithesis to the dark, moist volcanic earth found in Māngere, Ihumātao and other parts of South Auckland.

The human geologies — the geological structures which shape and are shaped by human cultural action — of North China and South Auckland seem to be in polar opposition to each other. If South Auckland is in New Zealand contexts frequently associated with poverty, that poverty does not arise from the inability of its soil to nourish its population, but from experiences of dispossession and displacement associated with colonisation and industrialisation. If the Loess Plateau is in Chinese contexts habitually associated with poverty, it is because overtaxed soil and lack of rainfall mean that the area cannot produce enough food to support the people who live there. While South Auckland and North China were both targets of twentieth-century communist revolutionary mobilisation, the outcomes of that mobilisation, unsuccessful in South Auckland and successful in North China, seem to have much to do with the very different human geologies in both places. The social and geological realities symbolised by scoria and loess appear to be radically dissimilar.

Perhaps no cultural document from the era after New Zealand and the People's Republic of China established formal diplomatic relations in 1972 conveys the effect of the landscapes of the Loess Plateau on an outsider with as much power as Chen Kaige's 1984 film *Yellow Earth* (*Huang tudi* 黄土地), a film that had its first major public screening in New Zealand in 1987. That film sits between the official celebrations of two very different visions of China. The first is the official celebrations of the achievements of the Chinese communist revolution as an uprising of workers and peasants that led to massive improvements in production and in the material conditions of China's farmers and workers — a set of propaganda images now regarded as generally false, if not as monstrous pieces of misrepresentation. The second is the official celebrations of the achievements of market-led economic reform of the Deng Xiaoping era and afterwards, whose deregulatory unleashing of individual economic energies were seen as, if not inspiring, at least paralleling the actions of liberalising regimes in New Zealand in the years after 1984.

Yellow Earth is set in 1939; that is, in the same period in which the CPNZ was engaged in the political mobilisation work in South Auckland described above. In the film, a young communist soldier travels to exceptionally impoverished parts of the Loess Plateau region in northern Shaanxi to collect folksongs that can be used by the communist forces in their war of resistance against Japan. The harshness of the landscape and the poverty of the local people are depicted with great force through camera work that emphasises the emptiness of the physical environment, by acting in which emotion is communicated with extreme understatement and with limited dialogue, and through a soundtrack that relies heavily on silence punctuated by singing and by music whose diversity of styles helps to create the sense of a plurality rather than a unity of viewpoints. In place of a picture of the Party leading the people to the radiant future is a much more uncertain and ambivalent representation of China's modern history.

It is difficult to escape the impression that the loess landscapes of *Yellow Earth* are intended as a metaphor for a country historically worn out and beset by problems that a socialist revolution had been unable to resolve. Given that the Chinese Communist Party's heroic account of its own past focused heavily on its years in the Loess Plateau in the 1930s and 1940s, the bleakness of the world which *Yellow Earth* depicts can hardly be coincidental. Rather, this arid and impoverished vision seemed (and seems) to be a rebuke to the Party, reflecting the sense of exhaustion experienced by the generation of educated people born with the revolution and battered by the political upheavals of the late 1960s and early 1970s.

The idea of loess symbolising a China which is culturally sterile, eroded and impoverished finds its corollary and overt expression in the 1988 television documentary *River Elegy* (*He shang* 河殇). In this six-part documentary, the Yellow River — choked with silt that originates in the Loess Plateau (an area that *River Elegy* portrays as the ultimate source of a culture incapable of change) — is holding China and its people in a state of subjection and backwardness.

This depiction came as a shock to the small number of New Zealanders — including myself, an enthusiast for the Maoist cause from the age of 10 or 11 onwards — who had embraced the Chinese socialist revolution as a harbinger of a new kind of society in which manual and mental labour would be joined together in a political and cultural world defined by shared commitment to a radical conception of human equality. Instead, the vision of a North China whose culture was weighed down by the sediments of a history from which it could not escape, as projected by *Yellow Earth* and *River Elegy*, was profoundly disconcerting, not least because it seemed to reflect what millions of Chinese people had actually experienced in the decades of Maoist radicalism.

In the 1980s, those who had dreamed of a Maoist revolution in South Auckland and elsewhere in Aotearoa New Zealand started to seem like naive dupes of a propaganda apparatus that now began to appear more and more transparently false; or, worse still, as people who had blithely ignored or even sanctioned human suffering on an enormous scale. More modest aspirations for personal economic and social betterment, above all those of hardworking business and home owners, began to look more worthy of respect than the grandiose claims about revolutionary working-class solidarity advanced by those depicting themselves as waging war on the conformist and materialistic culture of the bourgeoisie.

The depiction of loess and silt as a sedimentary historical burden weighing down upon China, which one finds in the work of critical liberal intellectuals in that country, emerged in the 1980s. In the past two decades this bleak vision has given way to a celebration of the historical bonds that link the Chinese nation to its native soil, historical bonds that are seen as validated by the economic and political might of the People's Republic.

Meanwhile, scoria and the other constituents of South Auckland's volcanic landscapes and their human geologies seem to have recently been bound up with a quite different kind of historical politics. In the struggles over the disputed land at Ihumātao, the defence of the scoria, basalt and silt structures that form the human and geological environment in the South Auckland volcanic zone, seen in Searle's maps, has been advanced as the goal pursued by all sides, but with the strongest claims being lodged by SOUL (Save Our Unique Landscapes), the chief opponents of the proposed housing development in Ihumātao.

The histories of land seizure, racism and industrial expansion that have shaped South Auckland in the years since the annexation of the area by Pākehā in the 1850s and 1860s can be juxtaposed against the histories of cultural contact and engagement, in which Chinese South Aucklanders

31

have had a central place. The calls by South Auckland communities to preserve and restore the old volcanic landscapes, eroded by decades of quarrying and broader commercial expansion, seem to invoke a desire for human geologies that are structured by something other than simply the dictates of economic reason.

How far these developments will parallel or diverge from those in the loess and silt landscapes of North China is something that those interested in the intersections between the histories of China and Aotearoa New Zealand might find interesting to contemplate.

Speaking Half-truth to Power

CHRIS ELDER

In April 1976, New Zealand Prime Minister Robert Muldoon (as he then was) paid a state visit to China. He was taking up an invitation that had originally been extended to his predecessor, Labour Prime Minister Bill Rowling. His decision to do so was welcomed as signalling a bipartisan acceptance of the new relationship that had been established with the People's Republic of China.

Among the questions to be considered in the lead-up to the visit was what role might be assigned to Rewi Alley, the veteran revolutionary who had by then lived in China for 47 years. Alley was a figure of some standing in China, and was seen by many in New Zealand as the embodiment of long-standing links between the two countries.

Unfortunately, those who held this positive view did not include most members of the National Party, who viewed Alley as a dangerous subversive who had undermined New Zealand interests at the time of the war in Korea, and had continued on the same perverse path thereafter.

Rewi was by then 78 years old, and in indifferent health. The embassy suggested it would be a gracious gesture if the prime minister were to call on Alley at his home in the compound of the Chinese People's Association for Friendship with Foreign Countries (the old Italian Legation).

Prime Minister Robert Muldoon and Thea Muldoon stand either side of Premier Hua Guofeng (centre front) before the state banquet in Muldoon's honour, 29 April 1976.
CHRIS ELDER

Mr Muldoon was not attracted to the proposal, but did agree that Alley could be invited to attend a small reception to be held at the embassy. (The reception was intended to allow the delegation to meet embassy staff and other New Zealanders resident in Peking, by no means a large number.) The ambassador, Dick Atkins, had added to the guest list a few foreign representatives closely associated with New Zealand interests: the ambassadors of Australia, Canada, Japan and the United Kingdom, and the head of the United States Liaison Office.

By the time the New Zealand delegation arrived, Dick had arranged these dignitaries into an informal reception line, so they would each have a chance to meet the prime minister before he mingled with other guests. At the front of the line, he placed New Zealand's veteran revolutionary, Rewi Alley.

On being introduced to Alley, an apparently discomforted Muldoon growled, 'I've heard a lot about you.' Rewi replied with some spirit: 'I've heard a lot about you, too.' That was the beginning of an extended and apparently amicable conversation which took up a good part of the hour allocated to the gathering. Dick Atkins, uncomfortably aware of the senior representatives waiting their turn, did his best to shepherd the prime minister down the line, but Muldoon persuasively indicated that he had no wish to be so shepherded. 'I'll have your job, mate', he explained.

The official schedule called for departure from the embassy to the Great Hall of the People for a signing ceremony to amend the New Zealand–China Trade Agreement concluded in 1973. A state dinner would follow. At the time set for departure, Mr Muldoon, by this time circulating among the guests, showed no disposition to be hurried. His mood was sombre. He was tired. He resented having been taken away from an interesting conversation, and being fobbed off with a group of people whom he assessed as being no more than the foreign equivalents of Ministry of Foreign Affairs cookie-pushers. A glass or two taken on his way around the room had sharpened, rather than diminished, his sense of grievance. In the words of P. G. Wodehouse, if he was not actually disgruntled, he was far from being gruntled.

After some delay, however, the prime minister did indicate to his ambassador that he was ready to go and sign the agreement. This gave rise to another difficult moment, because, as everyone had thought the prime minister understood, there was no intention that he should be the one signing. The original agreement had been set in place by the two countries' trade ministers, and so it was, in Chinese eyes, inappropriate that a prime minister should stoop to amending an agreement concluded at a lower level. It was explained to Mr Muldoon that his role would be to stand in the background and nod approvingly while the ambassador appended his signature.

The prime minister, who clearly felt he had been made subordinate to diplomatic fiddle-faddle enough for one day, announced that if he was not doing the signing, he would not be going to the ceremony. When this uncompromising approach had been kicked around a little, he softened enough to ask if 'the other bloke' was going to be there ('the other bloke' being Premier Hua Guofeng, with whom he had been locked in bilateral talks earlier in the day). It had not occurred to any other of those present that the premier might not make himself available for a formal occasion involving his opposite number and guest. That being the case, no one had sought a direct assurance from the Chinese side that Hua would be there. Accordingly, no one was in a position to provide the prime minister with the cast-iron assurance that he was now demanding as a precondition for his own participation.

At this point, things got murky. An ashen-faced Dick Atkins sought out the most junior and least offensive of his diplomatic staff, and requested him to telephone the Chinese Foreign Ministry, the Waijiaobu 外交部, in order to obtain the required assurance. The unfortunate Second Secretary Elder (for it was he) could see some flaws in this plan. The first was that the Foreign Ministry was notorious for never answering the phone (of which there appeared to be only one in existence). The second was that it was doubly certain not to be answered after 5.30pm, when Cultural Revolutionary convention dictated the workday should end — and by now it was 6.45pm. The third was that even if by some miracle someone did pick up the phone, the odds were that Elder's Chinese would not be up to conveying the urgencies and niceties of the situation.

A quick assessment of the atmosphere within the official delegation, however, suggested that the time was not right to air these objections. Accordingly, the hapless second secretary made his way to the embassy switchboard and dialled the number on record for the Waijiaobu. The phone at the other end rang (a surprise in itself). And rang. And rang. Then, remarkably, it was picked up. 'Wei?' said a disembodied voice. The situation was explained, the question asked. A long pause. Then 'Meiyou ren.' (没有人 'No one here.') At the other end of the line, the phone went down with a sharp, irretrievable click.

What to do? The only possible expedient seemed to be to report back fully and honestly to the ambassador and the prime minister. Second Secretary Elder returned to the reception hall. He squared his slight shoulders and approached his superiors. 'I have spoken to the Foreign Ministry,' he said. 'Hua Guofeng will be at the ceremony.'

The signing went ahead on schedule. Prime Minister Muldoon and his Chinese counterpart were both on hand to witness a great step forward in Sino–New Zealand relations. Ambassador Atkins never asked about the phone call. And, at least until the next incident, peace and tranquillity reigned once more within the prime minister's delegation.

Muldoon meets Deng, Autumn 1980

NICK BRIDGE

When Deng Xiaoping got back into power, Prime Minister Muldoon instructed that he wanted to meet him the following year, and that, as a lead-up, three of his senior ministers would make visits to China. The Chinese signed on, and so the New Zealand Embassy had visits by Brian Talboys, Duncan MacIntyre and George Gair to plan for. All three were most agreeable individuals. The visits kept us busy and broadened the relationship as only ministerial visits can. Some posts rarely receive ministers. It can make for a quiet assignment. In my nearly five years in Delhi as high commissioner, we got two! Both were junior ministers.

Each of these three lead-up visits was enjoyable. Deputy Prime Minister Talboys brought with him a business delegation of about 20. Duncan MacIntyre, Agriculture, was as relaxed as ever when he came a few months later; and in typically good voice at the traditional embassy party on the last night of the visit. He hadn't much enjoyed the two official banquets in the Great Hall of the People, the welcoming one and New Zealand's return one two nights later. They were, as usual, stilted, formal affairs.

But it was George Gair, Minister of Health, who stole the show. His small delegation was a couple of hours late arriving at Peking's old and ailing airport. On arrival, we were disconcerted to see Mrs Gair's right arm in gleaming white plaster and a sling. She'd slipped over on Canton airport's treacherous marble floor. The Chinese doctors had quickly treated the fractured arm. Her unfortunate pain apart, it was an appropriate if bizarre start to the health minister's visit.

Health issues were to continue to take centre stage during the visit, albeit in some rather unscheduled and unexpected guises. The next day, as a special treat, the delegation attended open-heart surgery performed under acupuncture at the leading hospital. The first secretary at the embassy was John McKinnon, destined to be New Zealand's ambassador to China twice over in the 2000s. He was, and still is, very tall, at around six feet three. He fainted in the operating theatre, poleaxing to the floor and cutting his head open rather badly. Meanwhile, back at the embassy, one of the New Zealand staff cut herself on the guillotine as she topped and tailed papers for the minister. She was cared for by medical staff at the British Embassy, next to ours. Like Mrs Gair, she had her arm placed in a sling.

That night at the Chinese welcoming banquet in the Great Hall, our delegation brought the house down as it entered, half covered in bandages. Both health ministers discarded some of their texts, and instead revelled in the misfortunes and the way that the Chinese had so generously and skilfully treated them. It set the scene for a good Muldoon visit.

The prime minister came in beautiful, late-summer weather. Although he rather spoilt it, at the outset, with a remark at a press conference after a long day's discussions with China's brand-new premier, Zhao Ziyang. Zhao had, to everyone's expert surprise, been appointed just two days before. The Brits and Americans had immediately given us full biographies of this relatively young man who was far from the advanced age of some of the Long March veterans still in high positions.

Zhao was pretty impressive in what was his first meeting as premier. He had mastered his briefs, and when in any doubt about something would quietly refer to his papers or his officials before replying. When Muldoon emerged from the talks, he was surprised and delighted to see on the steps of the Great Hall the full corps of the Peking foreign press correspondents, some of them justly celebrated, waiting to ask him about this new man, Zhao. The New Zealand prime minister spoke admiringly about his counterpart, but said that he'd put a reservation over Zhao's health and stamina. Consternation and pressing requests for elaboration ensued. Muldoon, who was apparently referring to the fact that Zhao had occasionally mopped a sweating face, dug himself in a little deeper before wisely halting proceedings. The international wire services reported overnight what the New Zealand leader had said.

The next morning at the Great Hall, Muldoon had his all-important meeting with China's supreme leader. Deng came into the cavernous meeting room, exuding his magnetic and seemingly personable power. Muldoon stood up to be greeted. Deng got straight to his point: 'I gather you have some reservations about my premier' was his brusque greeting. Muldoon explained that there seemed to have been a misunderstanding and apologised for any confusion. It was an historic moment, did Deng but know it: it was the only political apology Muldoon ever made.

The visit went well after that, and the whole year, as had been planned by Muldoon, set the tone for the largely constructive relationship that has followed ever since. There is probably some truth to the view that China has occasionally used the relationship with our tiny country as a toe into Western waters in the early years of its relations with Western governments.

On a personal level, for me Muldoon's visit was to have positive consequences. There was an incident that most unexpectedly sent my standing with our Chinese staff sky-high. The delegation had gone down to Fujian, and I was left in charge back in the capital. They took with them a strange contraption that the PM's press secretary, Gerry Symmans, had brought with him. It contained at its heart a secure telephone link so that Symmans and others could, if necessary, talk with Wellington without the Chinese listening in. We christened it the Thunder Box.

The day after they had left, I was relaxing in my first-floor office tidying up some of the visit's loose ends, when we received a cable from the PM's private office in Wellington asking the embassy to inform Muldoon that the chairman of his own National Party had gone public in demanding that he step down. Apparently, the opinion polls had turned against him and his dictatorial ways. A second unclassified cable gave the texts of the morning's relevant front-page articles.

This clearly was a situation tailor-made for the Thunder Box. I rang the secret number and was surprised to get through to Symmans some two thousand miles to the south. However, he could barely hear me. So I relayed the news in a loud voice. 'Louder, Nick!' he shouted back. So I shouted the various headlines: 'Chapman says Muldoon must go.' 'Muldoon is finished.' 'The people turn against Muldoon.' 'Time for a new leader.' I ran through the key points from the papers. Finally, Symmans thanked me and I walked over to my open windows, overlooking the embassy forecourt and garden. It had been a bit stressful, and I welcomed the fresh autumn air. Forty years ago, Peking still had some of it.

Looking down, I was surprised to see half a dozen of our Chinese staff standing below and looking up at my windows. They looked equally surprised, stunned in fact, and I realised that, hearing my loud voice from downstairs, they had gathered outside under my windows to hear what I was saying more clearly. I went down. They looked at me with apprehensive respect. They had never heard anything like it. Clearly here was the leader of an emerging New Zealand coup, or, at the least, one of its leaders. It took a few days and the return of my ambassador for their reverence to ease.

The Canton Trade Fair, 1977: Pages from a Diary

LEO HAKS

Established in 1957, the Canton Trade Fair (now the China Import and Export Fair) is held twice a year, during spring and autumn, in the southern Chinese city of Guangzhou. In the years before the establishment of diplomatic relations between Aotearoa New Zealand and the People's Republic of China, the fair offered New Zealand importers a rare opportunity to travel to China to source whatever products they thought might sell at home. For many, attendance at the fair was their first occasion to visit China; many, also, became regular attendees. The fair remains the largest such event in China.

Monday, 18 April 1977

The train journey from Kowloon to Sham Chun [Shenzhen] on the Chinese border led us through the rugged hillside of the New Territories, relatively uninhabited and arid. Train stops some five times on the way towards its destination, some 1.5 hours after departure; here we have to wait for our passports which had been collected and sent to Guangzhou for visa clearance. Passports arrived at 10.30. Then the walk from British to Chinese soil, quite an experience. Uniformed people all around, quite gay with their green uniforms and red trimmings, broad smiles and courteous attention. Elaborate immigration procedures.

Eventually, we reached our destination for now, the waiting room.

A huge hall with white cloth draped sofas and easy chairs. Beautiful mountain-scape paintings. Instructions that nobody can hear keep being piped through. No one listens, everyone is anxious. Tea, in fine variety, is served.

After lunch, back to the waiting room where I collected a memorial issue on Chairman Mao in Malay. Very well done and a welcome addition to my collection. Into the train at 1.05pm. Beautiful it was, fully air-conditioned, two people only next to each other. Loud music all the way. Couldn't quite follow all of it but I liked the marches. The train was smooth, not unlike the feel of beer in your throat. It is good beer indeed.

Everything highly organised, like an army of children under the patronising eye of the old mistress who could cope so effectively so long as all went according to plan.

Tuesday, 19 April 1977

Good start to the day and what a day. At last we were off to the Fair; my God, never seen the like. Literally miles of halls with every conceivable and unconceivable merchandise, from frozen and canned fish through to colour TV sets, investor jewellery, arts and crafts (mostly awful) some very cheap and worthwhile. (You can see here what margins there *must* be in that trade.) Piles of boxes with jade, carpets, textiles in all varieties, from ordinary plain linen shirts to the finest handmade lace handkerchiefs. There were all sorts of medicines and essential oils (we bought eucalyptus oil), books, all sorts of sportswear, etc.

Fantastic to see all the buyers getting involved with the products. They become the people they really are, no more fancy suits and showing off. It is for that reason suits and ties are completely out. Some buyers even go in their tee-shirts and sandals. It is a beautiful night.

Then of course the sellers. In uniform to a man (and woman). Showing off, I thought. The sellers were never alone, rarely with two, mostly with three, four or even five. One does the talking, the others just sit and do some writing. What really goes on, no one knows. No formalities, no niceties, straight to the point and out you go. In most cases, you have to wait and stick your head into the little room where they sit, preceded in by your visiting card, which will be taken and you'll be told that either please come back in five days at 8.30am, or please wait five minutes. We had both. And all the time they neither smile nor get upset if people get too pushy. These people must do yoga or something. In the Western sense of doing trade (or anything for that matter), this total control is unthinkable. As a result, one can neither like nor dislike them. They accept nothing at all, do not even allow you to light their cigarettes, which all of them smoke all the time very noticeably. Very specialised in their field they are indeed.

We walked into one office which sells essential oils and the man quoted us Cost, Insurance, and Freight (C.I.F.) Singapore prices without referring to anything but his memory. No bargaining. They know much more than they pretend to. Tea by the gallons, cigarettes on the house. Next office two floors up, three buildings away, same story. None look associated with their trade. All negotiations I was involved with were handled by men; women always present (almost always anyway). It was a Fair indeed, like a fun fair where people push and shove to get rid of their money. In a way, as if it was their last chance to do so ever.

11.30am lunch break

Lunch. Buffet or sit-down-and-get-served style. We took the former. A huge table with no less than 100 different dishes. Stunningly beautiful for ¥6.00 each. Well done in all respects. After lunch Telex to H.Q. Have to punch your own tape and ask for a connection, four Telex rooms, sounds like BBC connections to all over the world.

By the time we had our Telex done it was 2.45pm so rush back for the balance of the day's work. Completed by 4.30pm. Once done, left for private shopping. Bought nothing, too tired (dog tired) and nothing really took my fancy. Back to hotel at 5.30pm; bags collected, had a long hot bath.

Dinner we had at a 'Muslim' restaurant. This meant Chinese food minus pork. We had steamboat; the best I ever had in an extraordinary place. Ground floor for the local people, dirty, crammed and plain food. Upstairs to the left, for second-raters, traders from Hong Kong and Macao; to the right for first-raters like us! We had booked as it gets busy. When we arrived we were led to a table with a magnificent bouquet of flowers which was removed as soon as we were properly seated to be used for the next VIPs! Took a taxi there but wanted to walk back. No way; when we paid the bill we were told that our taxi was on the way to drive us back. Pity. Had a little walk around the hotel when we saw trolley buses stopping. It was the end point. Buses were new, clean and well looked after. Then it happened. A bus drove up, then suddenly two people ran behind it, grabbed a rope each and pulled the connecting arms down. Bus without power came to a slow standstill. Arms were transferred to another set of overhead lines for the return journey. Why manually? I don't know. People strolling down the streets. Mainly couples. Rather reserved. One couple necked a bit.

Wednesday, 20 April 1977

Less hectic day. Did my own first negotiation. The most difficult part of attending this Fair is to get to meet the people concerned, once that is done it is easy meat. Did see some women negotiate and also saw Chang successfully negotiate a lower than quoted price. Had another excellent lunch. Food the way I imagined the way Chinese food should be. Just out of this world. The restaurant was an old one using ivory chopsticks with their pre-revolution name engraved on them. Hard bargaining for a pair resulted in a [blank] and a promise that they may exchange a pair for a new pair. A new pair at the Fair and in the shops are around ¥30.00 per pair. I bought an old pair for ¥22.

Intended to go to the ceramic museum but was misdirected to the ceramic wholesale market. Away from the Fair. It was in an old building, full of ceramics, wood cuttings, etc. They didn't allow me to buy a piece but directed me to the antique shop. In both places, as well as in two book shops that I went to, there was no electric light. People were buying their things by candles, kerosene lamps and torches. Street lighting at night is very sparse indeed and the vehicles only use side lights. Quite dangerous indeed. The drivers rely on their horns to get noticed, hence an enormous noise all night long. No private car ownership that is noticeable. Only taxis (to carry Fair participants) and a few motor scooters, three-wheelers taking five or six passengers. Took photos of the poster of the 'Gang of Four'. Tried to get some but failed. Streets look like Kathmandu minus the cows. People look at you as if from outer-space, especially in remote areas like the ceramics place. Taking pictures of the Gang of Four poster had me a crowd of at least 100 around me and I had to (nearly) run. They do say they understand you when they don't; annoying, more so as they get angry when you show they don't. They really had me think I went to the ceramics museum. Blessing in disguise.

Thursday, 21 April 1977

One thing for sure, bonsai is well in. Saw many not only in the hotel, but in several shops where people were buying them. Beautiful ones. Must be an old habit. People handle them with great respect and love.

Management is poor really. Our toilet keeps overflowing and, in spite of people having come several times to repair it, once you pull the chain, same problem. Laundry very poor. The carpets on the staircase haven't seen a brush for months. I suggest there is no supervisor or management so there is no-one to give instructions. Have started to smoke.

Went to ceramic museum this morning. A Ming-period fort five storeys high located on a hill, beautiful building fully decorated with period roof decorations including tiles. Walls 10 ft thick. Ceramics on display included one or two samples of all ages, ranging from late Stone Age until what is produced today. Some beautiful Tang funeral houses (some nine of them). Altogether, well worthwhile a visit. Many schoolchildren there, taking down notes like reporters taking down a speech of importance. Was there before opening, explored the surroundings and found several people doing their exercises. Really moved me a lot. Took one roll of film of one old man who was as beautiful as ever I saw one. If no other pictures turn out well, please let those be good (he did Tai Chi exercises).

10.00pm

Awful thing this evening: a cable from Singapore arrived addressed to Republic of China. Got a long decline and a note that read: 'THE NAME OF THE DESTINATION COUNTRY OF YOUR MESSAGE IS WRITTEN WRONG STOP THE NAME OF OUR COUNTRY IS PEOPLE'S REBUBLIC OF CHINA (OR ABBREVIATED AS CHINA) STOP PLEASE ADVISE THE SENDER TO PAY MORE ATTENTION LATER STOP. How embarrassed I felt. Apologised like mad.

Went for a long walk this evening early. Came across a school, shabby looking, outside of which little girls were doing their gymnastics. Unbelievable somersaults with twist quite flawlessly. They were about ten years of age. Took some pictures which they loved. I loved them loving it. Walked on to find yet another lot of anti-Gang of Four posters. Lots of pictures, black and white this time. Only two rolls of colour left. Awful shame. Seems funny to me, only saw Gang of Four posters near places frequented by foreigners. Coincidence?

Chang took local friends to dinner tonight. They tell him inside information. Like an explanation for the bad services in the hotel. The staff are all young sons and daughters of high-up officials. Better than having to do practicals in the field. Corruption?? Who knows.

Dinner alone. Fantastic roasted duck soup with orange, quail's eggs with fresh mushroom and lettuce, pig kidney with bamboo shoots and pork ribs. What a feast.

Went back to the antique shop to buy some more old chopsticks to make it six pairs in all. The lights were working again, looked quite different. Blackouts must happen regularly judging by the ready-to-hand candles and kerosene lamps.

At the traffic lights schoolgirls or students assist the policemen and the lights in controlling the traffic. They stand with four or five in a row, the one nearest the centre of the road with the red flag. Very efficient. Didn't like to have pictures taken. Did do so nevertheless, but not the way that I would have liked to.

Saw the places people live in too. Appalling, no larger living room than 8 x 10 feet, badly lit at that. There sure is poverty on a large scale. In addition, coming home and blowing my nose, what came out was black as coal. Some buildings must have been real fancy when new. Now they are decrepit and not cared for. A cry for past glory. Yet things seem to work, the workers smile; it is the people we are in touch with who don't. Would so much like to speak their tongue and get lost amongst the people for some months. I see red flags flying from where I now sit. Much sign of turbulence in my mind. Do not know what really they stand for. Do I want to?

Chang is going back next Saturday. I plan to stay for another four or five days more.

It really is an educational holiday with work thrown in, and very little at that.

Finding China: Relationships and Myself

JAMES NG

I am a Chinese New Zealander of the fourth Cantonese 'Gim Shan' generation.[1] My generation was the first to transition from sojournism to settlement here, and I witnessed the accompanying change from discrimination to citizenship. Until the mid-twentieth century, we Cantonese had looked back to China as our lodestone in terms of culture, wealth accretion and patriotism. Our 'home' villages commonly became rich because of the savings sent or taken back from New Zealand to China, and we supported the strongest political force at the time in China, the Kuomintang Party, and later government, in its modernisation efforts and its opposition to Japanese imperialism. Our China-focused patriotism peaked in the Second World War, when I was a child.

Then, in the post-war period, our sojourner world drastically altered with the gross weakening of the Kuomintang, the victory of communism in China and, simultaneously, the New Zealand government's encouraging of our Cantonese minority to settle permanently here. The establishment of the People's Republic of China (PRC) in 1949 meant a temporary though

---

1 The term 'Gim Shan' (or 'Jin Shan' in Mandarin) means 'Gold Mountain', and here refers to the Cantonese migrants with a link back to the Otago and West Coast goldfields.

harsh severing of our links with China. But despite becoming New Zealanders, I and others like me could not ignore our Chinese side, especially when facing the universal question: 'Who am I?' However, in my own efforts to integrate and assimilate into general society, and at the same time to establish a career and bring up a family, my Chinese side was in the main temporarily put aside.

I had no need to become involved in China-related politics. Accordingly, I had no contact with the Taiwanese Kuomintang Embassy except once, when, in 1971, I spoke at an art gallery opening sponsored by their last ambassador to New Zealand. Nor did I have any contact with the succeeding PRC Embassy until 1978, when Dunedin doyen Hugh Sew Hoy brought the ambassador to visit me. There followed sporadic contact, and then the unexpected invitation in 1984 to the National Day celebrations in Beijing.

While attending this, I was particularly impressed with the big National Day parade starting on the dot. I was checking my watch when the loudspeaker and guns boomed, and in that instant I knew that China was on the path of modernisation. Another major impression for me was the huge banquet for 3000 guests in the Great Hall of the People, which ran efficiently and without a hitch.

Subsequently, I began writing my book *Windows*, and, to research my background, I made three visits to my ancestral village in Guangdong, twice in the 1980s and once in 1997. On the 1985 trip, I accompanied a TVNZ team, who were filming an episode for the *Legacy* series, on the settling of New Zealand. I was deeply moved by my grandfather's grave, although less affected by our house now being occupied by strangers. Our burnt-out tower, ruined investment shop, and the impoverished environs affected me only superficially, and I seemed to feel more curiosity than anything else. By my third village visit, the countryside had improved economically. A little later, my grandmother's burial site was found. She had had a hasty second burial, and my first cousins and my siblings and I completed her grave.

Also in the 1980s, my wife and I went on two of the New Zealand China Friendship Society's annual China tours (one of which I headed), and on both of these tours I met Rewi Alley. The society tasked each tour leader with taking a big carton of marmalade, Marmite and other New Zealand edibles to Alley, and he responded with an afternoon tea for the tour party. Upon our first meeting, he told me that what was still needed to strengthen the integration of the Chinese into New Zealand society was more history and social accounts of our minority group.

Richard Walls, the Dunedin mayor, and Murray Douglas, his CEO, then invited me in 1996 to accompany them, together with interpreter Jean Chen, to Shanghai, to negotiate the Shanghai–Dunedin sister-city relationship. Clearly, the Shanghai negotiators had read up on Dunedin and Otago, but had missed the fact of the Chinese (Cantonese) gold-seekers' presence by invitation in the province from 1865, and were also unaware that modern Dunedin had very good relations with some 2000 New Zealand Chinese (principally Cantonese) residents.

We three New Zealanders assured them that the Dunedin Chinese could help with any Shanghai visitors, that there were good places for Chinese food (one of their questions), and that the general community would welcome young Shanghai students to our city. Dunedin's Chinese goldmining history and the valued contemporary Dunedin Chinese presence were the clinching points, and, from then on, staff from Shanghai's Foreign Affairs unit, Sister Cities unit, Chamber of Commerce, the Shanghai Museum and, in due course, the Shanghai Construction Decoration Group became our friends.

Murray Douglas, who had overseen the building of a Chinese garden in Hamilton, sowed the seeds in my mind of constructing a commemorative Chinese garden in Dunedin. So when the city council asked me to chair and organise China Week as the first event of Dunedin's sesquicentennial anniversary celebrations in 1998, I put forward the idea of a south-China-style garden for the city, to widespread public approval. The city council's

James Ng (front row, second from left) and members of a New Zealand China Friendship Society tour with Rewi Alley (front row, third from right) in front of Rewi's Beijing home, winter 1985. JAMES NG

senior gardener, Mick Field, and I chose the site, a very capable committee was formed, and one of the members, Alex Tang, secured the fine services of Auckland Chinese architect Bruce Young, who drew the basic outline of the garden. We also linked up with the Shanghai Museum for essential additional help.

Later in the year, I handed over chairing the garden committee to Peter Chin (who carried the project over long years to completion) when Murray Douglas asked me to chair a New Zealand Shanghai Trade Fair proposal, alongside John Christie, CEO of the Otago Chamber of Commerce, and Dr Cheung-Tak Hung, managing director of Zenith Technology Corporation. We three altered the function to a more or less Otago Shanghai Trade Match, which was deemed worthwhile and proceeded to a repeat Trade Match in the next year. Around the same time, I founded the Dunedin Shanghai Friendship Association.

The late 1990s were the acme of my involvement with China, and I subsequently had little engagement with modern China; instead, I returned to a focus on New Zealand Chinese history. However, I did write a letter to the local *Otago Daily Times* giving my own version of events to balance a Christchurch newspaper report on a minor demonstration against Jiang Zemin's 1999 visit to New Zealand, held outside the city's banquet venue for the president. More recently, during Winston Peters' first stint as foreign minister (2005–2008), Beijing sent an investigator to New Zealand, and he spoke to, among others, foreign affairs experts and Chinese New Zealanders to ascertain the real feelings of New Zealanders towards China. I gave him my positive opinion of the New Zealand–China relationship.

My last China trip was as a member of a Dunedin delegation attending the opening of the New Zealand Pavilion at the 2010 Shanghai World Expo.

(The invitation to attend had been extended by the head of the pavilion, Phillip Gibson.) During that trip, I said my last face-to-face farewells to good friends, including Fu Fenghao and Yu Pengnian from Shanghai's Foreign Affairs unit; Professor Tan Yufeng and wonderful Lucy Liang (interpreter) from the Shanghai Museum; Yang Zhihua, Zhao Jiandong and Pang Guojing from the Chamber of Commerce; and Zhang Hongxing, head of the Shanghai Construction Decoration Group. I missed seeing Xu Zhaochun of Foreign Affairs, who had sadly passed away, Sun Xiyuan of the Shanghai Friendship Society for Sister Cities, and Hu Jianzhong, Secretary of the Museum.

Mr Hu had been the prime mover on the Shanghai side in terms of support for the Dunedin Chinese garden. When Malcolm Wong and I took him to Central Otago, he was visibly moved by the Chinese miners' graves; he understood then why we wished for a Chinese garden, and upon his return to Shanghai he approached the mayor, a schoolmate of his, and championed our cause from that point on to completion. On a personal note, around 2008, Mr Hu demonstrated his friendship for my wife and me, and signalled his impending retirement by taking us to a boutique restaurant which served delicious Taiwanese wagyu beef. He did the same with Peter Chin and Malcolm Wong.

All my China contacts — whether officials, interpreters or ordinary folk — were good, reasonable, often generous people. None discussed politics with me. I was asked about my Christian faith once, with the result, I think, that trust in me was enhanced. Only one person ever made a personal request, to help his daughter. Everyone I worked with gave me maximum commitment, with good humour, and they largely embodied the five Chinese qualities I have taught my own family to maintain, alongside the duties and high standards of New Zealand citizenship: family cohesion, family ambition, respect for elders, an emphasis on education, and the fostering of a long-term perspective.

Images
for Sages

DIANA BRIDGE

Towards the end of the eighties, when I was teaching at Hong Kong University and completing a dissertation on the beginnings of regulated verse in the Chinese poetic tradition, I found myself writing poems. At first it seemed that they had pushed up in some kind of competitive relationship with the lyric verse in which I was absorbed. All the same, those shoots were the beginning of a writing self.

Somewhere in the transition between Hong Kong and Wellington they vanished, and only a line or two ever surfaced again. I had to wait until we were living in India to make an unambiguous crossing from scholarship to poetry. But I have come to see that without the intensive reading of the 'poems on things' that were the topic of my dissertation, and of a much wider swathe of classical poetry, there might never have been poems in my own language.

Not only the repertoire but the style of my poems was influenced by a poetic tradition that is spare, compressed and allusive. I credit it as well with contributing what stringency I am able to bring to bear in constructing and refining them.

The poems are presented in the order in which they were written.

Images for sages

a character surfaces on West Lake,
its neat bars slotted like
a grave plaque into grass ripples.
I ask the waves to freeze —
only for a moment —
and let meaning through.

And if they did
could I read what is
strung across a landscape,
holding the edges of a world to order,
centred, symmetrical,
border-fixed and square?

Though they say, and I know,
the process is otherwise,
once in a lifetime when the sage
is laughing, you may turn your head
quickly and catch the spin
of image into sign.

from **Talking to the songs**

(iv)
Some say you may be
line upon line Gertrude Stein
stopping short each time
of syntax.

You exist between the cypress boat
and the man who sits wave-
tossed in its cradle.

You are out of reach
and your gap is the reason
for singing.

(from *Landscape with Lines*)

Fragment, Dunhuang

In this sandscape
the space between lines
is as precise as
the space between waves

or the lines of the robe
of the saint which
he spends his days
retracing, stroking

the soft ochre
onto a body
he will later ask
her to buy.

(from *Landscape with Lines*)

Looking at porcelain

Thrown   whole   against a wall
the character   *porcelain*
splintered into   blue and white shards
   once brush strokes
magnified   so large   spaces assert themselves
independent as solids   they contradict
emptiness   reach   into   enveloping air
the fluid we live in   its turbulence
pooled   and   ordered
into peace

Projected on a screen   dividing first attempts
rustic and charming   from the genuine article
heated to perfection   our eyes swim in glazes
new   as the tenth century
combings   incisions   rakings
of the pearl and green skin
bodies archetypal   splashed or moulded
   examples so rare
 they   like the emperor   will never
be seen   again

Situate someone   out of context   watch them
separate   verticals   elongating
behind glass   the nodes and sticking points
   of character   curios   reassembled
in the exhibition halls and bookshops of museums
   your daughter   framed
among cases of   spaced   bowls
  her elegance   a foil to
      the perfection of bases

(from *Porcelain*)

Diana Bridge (second from left) during a visit to the Buddhist caves in Dunhuang in 1980, with a fellow student from the Central Academy of Fine Arts 中央美術學院, a friend from her days at SOAS University of London and a local guide. DIANA BRIDGE

Pond

1

All winter I have harried the pond
with restless visiting.

As rain beats like drummed lament
on the glass roof and a fan worries

the edge of sight, I remember something
missed. How buds on the Chinese lake

that June rose from leaves like these,
to take on the shape of stupas — each

pleated bulb closed like a cone on hope.

2

The lotuses have flown,
acquired visas and migrated

to the middle of this pool.
Here they huddle, like with like.

Precarious, unrooted; community
is all. Their sons and daughters

rise on curving stems,
turning the plates of their small-featured

faces to the light, as if to music.

(from *Red Leaves*)

Dream sound

She dreams sounds clear as stitches on her province's
embroideries. Duck-squawk, as ducks walk on broadening

feet from the countryside into the town. Next thing
the whole city tastes it, the coming of winter —

duck and preserved egg stew. Sounds of the Sichuan
seasons enter her dreams. They quarter her émigré years.

Taking leave of a friend

at first you want connectives, reach like anyone for 'as',
your only chance, you think, of seeing how things stand;

or how they might have stood for him, that is, the poet,
for whom the Chinese word lay open. They,

the trained and the knowledgeable, have their own bridges.
Listen, they say, to the white waters that wind around

the east part of the city, its outer rampart thrown
across a range of hills; or that same mountain range —

it might be green, was sometimes blue — crossing
the straddle of those northern walls. Feel the palindromic

pull of the furniture as Li Bo is saying goodbye.

*

Once they part, with but one prop, a rootless orphan weed,
on this journey of ten thousand miles,

you will have to leave the tight determined weave
of your own tongue, its forward plunge, behind.

Now there is nothing that binds the floating clouds
to a wanderer's thoughts, the sinking sun to

that yearning for your friend. On the great plain
of the unknown the Chinese word has turned on its side.

In this strange place, with the day slipping down
out of sight and the clouds always changing the sense,

you glimpse a glue between lines. The double life
of a cloud, that's how the poet sees it; he always has.

And if they are reliable, your guides, you will have run up
in the slyness of the space between two words

against the largest measures. But to end, we're back
to the small animal moment. Hands sign a parting.

He goes from here. It's the horses that neigh.

(from *Aloe*)

Note: I draw here on a poem by Li Bai (701–762), the title of which, in Ezra
Pound's translation, is 'Taking Leave of a Friend'.

from Morning mist, Karori

1

The world outside my window has fallen away,
reduced to a shifting triangle of roof, a whale-back
of hill and the verticals of headless trees in the hidden
square of the back garden. Like islands floating in sea,
you cannot guess their distance. Even the near camellia,
which is sharpest and least strange, defies perspective.
The scene keeps on re-forming as a soft estranging mist
winds through it, like one of those most inward of adagios
seeking repose. Objects await some more than momentary
assembly — you might find it in an album leaf by Ma Yuan,
the painter who returned to space its parity with solid form.
Like the viewer who looks out from a terrace, I am drawn
by boundless mists into a Promised Land, one which
starts in the mysterious occluded present, the way
a rainbow starts in nearby hills or a rear garden,
before it leads us upwards and beyond.

(from *In the Supplementary Garden*)

Encountering *The Book of Change*

Reach for what's at hand. It is always what you want.
Aphorisms froth in the tea this morning.
Here is another, a poet's warning.
Seamus Heaney delivers it: beware late Auden,
let in the sparkling polyvalent water of the image,
let go of labouring after truth — as if it issued
from the mantic sections of *The Book of Change*.

I hardly know what's meant by image there. A little self-
sufficient stand of lines throws up some architecture
in the heavens, an archetypal element of earth:
mountain, or pit. I see, not pictures, but a clue to name;
a broken line will yield an aperture, and so bear out
the name ascribed it: 'cooking pot' or 'well'.
In general, image seems to mean 'what is not word'.

Yet think how the earliest heat-scarred marks
scratched on the shoulder bones of oxen,
on turtle shells, were answers, and in the manner
of an answer would be read. Imagine
the diviner: grey-green as unearthed bronze,
blurred as the outline of some blistered glyph
which, when made out, would surely counsel war.

To unroll symbol and to weave connection,
the lines and trigrams, and the trigrams doubled,
must be yoked to words. Summon up the shadowy
Duke of Zhou working on his pronouncements,
one to a line. Much like a song sung just beyond
the outer reaches of my hearing are the 'Wings',
the commentaries and judgements, as captivating

as they are remote. If you proceed, they counsel,
you will 'tread on the tail of the tiger'. To step . . . unbitten?
The judgement says, 'There is no failure, but Bright Light
Instead.' To amplify, unearth a story from the Annals,
or cull from an old poem an allusion buried thigh-
deep in its rhyme. I see it now as once they saw it.
To surprise the tiger is, in this case, the right course to take.

In this case . . . ? You mean your case. Put aside your scruples;
it's time to master trepidation. So move from behind
whatever post it is that shields you — you know that divination
needs a supplicant. If you have questions (who does not have questions?)
you must bring in you. So far I've been content with
chance connection, coincidence breathtaking as the advent
after rain this morning of a snapping turtle —

nothing but serendipity when contemplating fire-cracks
on the undershell of turtles. Keep away — it will be laying —
they advise; and I avoid it as I would a call to war.
But now the turtle's image crouches in my path. Monolithic
as a rock, it has become the whole of Chinese culture,
dumped there saying chip away, why don't you?
You ought. You know you ought.

(from *Two or more islands*)

China, 'A Tired Old Country'? The Dangers of Group Thinking

MICHAEL POWLES

Newcomers to China thirst after the insights which 'old hands' are often able to provide. In the West, however, a kind of 'group thinking' has developed on some issues relating to China and the Chinese. Sometimes it misinforms more than it informs. These are some examples which I have encountered over my years of engagement with China.

When I first arrived and was preparing to go through the formalities of presenting credentials to the then president of China, General Yang Shangkun, I was warned that the ceremony would be rigidly formal: both sides would speak from well-prepared notes, more so even than usual because the ceremony was little more than six months after the Tiananmen Square bloodshed, and New Zealand would be expected to register its concerns.

But while, as instructed by Wellington, I spoke of the strength of New Zealanders' feelings about the bloodshed, and did so bluntly, President Yang Shangkun's reply was far from being rigidly formal, as I had been led to expect. His first remark was that he had been very friendly with Rewi Alley. He enlarged on that a little, and I wondered whether he was simply going to ignore my remarks about Tiananmen Square. But no, after quite a long pause, he said very deliberately that he didn't think many foreigners realised 'how close we came to losing Beijing'. Obviously this was not the time for a debate on the subject. I had stated the view of Aotearoa New Zealand and he had delivered a Chinese response. But I thought his comments were interesting both in themselves and in the fact that he had actually offered a kind of explanation.

I was told emphatically that middle-class Chinese had little empathy for the harder lives of the poor, either in cities or in the countryside. But following the disastrous Sichuan earthquake in 2008, a young woman in Shanghai working part-time as a Chinese-language tutor on top of her clearly well-paid business job, apologised that she would be missing sessions with our daughter. This was because she and her husband were going off in their SUV, stacked with food and other supplies, and with numbers of friends who also had SUVs, to drive into Sichuan to see what help they could give affected people there.

In 1990, I was invited with other ambassadors in Beijing to join an official tour of the Pudong area, then scruffy wasteland. Our host was a Shanghai vice mayor, who explained in detail the startlingly ambitious plans for the development of the area into one of Asia's key financial centres. When they could do so unheard, and sometimes even when they were heard, the visiting ambassadors laughed at the ridiculousness of what was proposed: the consensus of the group, including several serious China scholars, was that there was no way China could organise itself to create the financial centre described to us. But, a few years later, it had.

Soon after I had arrived in Beijing in 1990, as ignorant about China as anybody could be, colleagues did their best to get me better informed. I remember a freezing mid-winter picnic on the ice of a reservoir north of Beijing. They talked about their expectations for China's future, and most shared the scepticism I had heard on the tour of Pudong. I recall the view of one participant that China was a 'tired old country which would never develop into a modern state'. But, a few years later, it had, as the view of a really modern city from our Beijing apartment proves to us every day.

Similarly, it seemed a common Western view that the Chinese were not particularly competent technically. But visiting a geothermal power station in Tibet, not far from Lhasa, some of whose engineers had been trained in New Zealand, I noticed three generators in the power hall. I asked why only one was working, and was told that of the other two, one was Japanese and one was Italian. They both functioned only moderately well. But their own (New Zealand-trained) engineers had studied them and built a new machine incorporating the best of both foreign generators. It easily out-performed them. In addition, Chinese progress in a variety of technical fields, from rocketry to electric cars to the plethora of high-speed trains which now criss-cross the country, speaks for itself.

In social interaction, I was warned not to expect senior Chinese, even those who spoke good English, to engage in philosophical or even just serious discussions about Chinese or Western ways of life and values. But, only a few weeks after my arrival in China in 1990, a ministerial conference was hosted in Shanghai. I found myself on a tourist boat on the Huangpu River where dinner was being served: on the top deck to ministers, and on the second deck to lesser beings like me. I found myself sitting with a senior official from the foreign ministry, who had just returned from an ambassadorial posting overseas.

In the course of conversation he expressed some admiration for New Zealand, its form of government, and having what he called 'core values' which everyone accepted. I wondered how I could politely enquire about the situation in China, but the official opened up on that without prompting. He quite emotionally recounted how Confucianism had been trashed by Mao and replaced by the lightweight philosophy of the 'Little Red Book'. Then that in turn had been replaced by an almost unprincipled materialism. He maintained that New Zealanders, on the other hand, accepted the core values of Judaeo-Christian theology. I questioned that gently, but took advantage of his loquacious mood to ask how he saw China evolving in the years ahead. He said it would be a close-run thing whether tinkering with Confucian teaching (removing all the patriarchal and sexist stuff) might turn it into a body of core values which the population could accept. The alternative, which he thought equally likely, was that materialism would prevail and disaster and chaos would result.

***

I was told that there were taboo subjects, especially human rights, democracy, and the situation of Taiwan, which should not be raised publicly or socially. But sometimes these topics were raised by locals. A law professor in Shanghai wanted to talk about attitudes to human rights, about the differences between the legal systems in Hong Kong and on the mainland (he thought Chinese lawyers and judges could learn a lot) and that a next step would be to study Taiwan's political system.

Having been invited to talk on the subject of human rights to graduate law students at a large university, and conscious that I wasn't an altogether independent agent, I deliberately twisted the topic a little and spoke about regional, not national, human rights developments. As soon as I had finished, I was tackled by one outspoken young man who was very unhappy that I had avoided the topic in which he was most interested: human rights *within* China. I did my best to kick it into touch, but he came back again and said: 'Well, if you won't give us your impressions, can I give you mine?' I welcomed that escape route. The graduate student then gave a strong and bitter denunciation of the lack of progress on human rights domestically. When he finished, I was able (rather weakly) to say that there was one thing

New Zealand Ambassador Michael Powles and China's Foreign Minister Qian Qichen 钱其琛 toasting the twentieth anniversary of the normalisation of New Zealand-China relations in 1992. CARL WORKER

that I could be clear about: I doubted that when I had been in China almost a decade earlier anyone would have spoken as he had to a foreigner, and in front of his law faculty.

Discussions on potentially sensitive topics could sometimes have their light side. At one dinner for a visiting New Zealand minister, involving China's foreign minister and senior officials, one senior Chinese official was encouraged by his own minister to tell our minister about his fanciful scheme for funding the foreign ministry's pension fund. The scheme involved organising China's home-based diplomats to sneak out to the Great Wall in the dead of night and gradually dismantle parts of the treasured historic relic. These parts would then be shipped off overseas to be auctioned in New York and elsewhere by China's overseas-based diplomats. The Chinese officials had obviously heard the story before, but still found it hilarious. Many suggested possible improvements to the scheme. It was a while before normal conversation could resume.

Negative or disparaging Western group-think also extends to assumptions about the attitudes of Chinese to foreigners whom they encounter in daily life. But, once I had started regularly using the Beijing and Shanghai subway systems, I found that people were startlingly helpful — particularly when they saw me staring worriedly at timetables or route maps on platforms. Women (usually) would come up and ask, in English, if I needed help. This continued when the China–US rhetoric stepped up, even though, with few foreigners around, I could easily have been American. And in the countryside where I would sometimes be loitering around waiting for a walking party to return from a steep walk I had opted out of, locals were cheerful and welcoming.

In the city, the Covid restrictions have included the scanning of apps when entering buildings or even public parks. A very slow app on my phone would often result in my standing around a guard fiddling helplessly with the phone. Sometimes the guards would take the phone and help with the operation, more often they would just wave me through regardless. One particular guard, at Ritan Park near the New Zealand Embassy, clearly feels he now knows me well and is always warm in his welcome, usually with a cheerful mock salute.

An aspect of China group-think on the part of Westerners is a disparaging attitude regarding China's role internationally. Several years ago, a senior American official called on China to change its policies and become a 'responsible stakeholder' internationally. But currently, and in fact for several years, China has been a major supporter of the United Nations (UN), which, of course, is also high on New Zealand's own priority list. China is the second-largest contributor to the UN's regular budget (12 per cent), behind the United States (20 per cent) but ahead of major industrial powers like Japan (8 per cent) and Germany (6 per cent). It is also a strong supporter of UN peacekeeping, contributing more personnel than any other permanent member of the Security Council.

This is all positive, but very serious questions remain: when will the treatment of the Uyghur people in Xinjiang be improved? And, in foreign relations, when will 'wolf warrior diplomacy', experienced and felt in Australia and even in the South Pacific, be reined in?

Inside China
as an Outsider

JOHN MCKINNON

My wife Avenal and I first visited Beijing in September 1976. It was just a week since Mao had died, and two months since the Tangshan earthquake. Beijing was a city in mourning. But it was exciting, too. Mostly to discover that the language I had been struggling with for a year in Hong Kong was real, and that when I spoke it I could be understood, and I could understand what was being said to me.

Learning Chinese is difficult, and the older one is, the harder it is. The grammar is simple in comparison with English, but the complexity and variety of the tones, the characters, and the vocabulary more than compensate for that. I learned what in the West is known as 'Mandarin', but is better described as modern standard Chinese. 'Mandarin' is based on the educated speech of Beijing, and the Mandarin-speaking area encompasses a vast region, all of northern China, but also Sichuan and Yunnan.

The local dialects in these places can be incomprehensible to a second-language speaker of Chinese, but because they are deemed to be 'Mandarin' no interpretation is provided. So I once had the awkward experience of holding a conversation with a medical professor who was, I was assured, speaking Mandarin, but whom I could not understand at all (the technical nature or the subject probably did not help); I had to resort to 'open' questions to conceal how little I really comprehended of what he was saying.

South of the Yangtze, the dialects are so divergent that in any other country they would be regarded as separate languages. So in offices in Shanghai there are notices, in Chinese characters, exhorting all to speak Putonghua (the name Chinese in the People's Republic of China give to Mandarin). This is not because visitors may speak English or French, but to stop them speaking Shanghainese, to the discomfiture and confusion of non-Shanghai Chinese. Cantonese has a similar distinctiveness, added to which it is the official form of spoken Chinese in Hong Kong and Macao, and widely spoken in the diaspora, including (in a variety of forms) in this country.

We returned to Beijing for a visit in 1977, and for a two-year posting to the New Zealand Embassy in the middle of 1978. Beijing was a huge city in terms of its population, but it did not feel like it. Bicycles were the most common mode of transport. Cars were few and far between; camels were still in evidence, although mainly on the approaches into the city. This was our first experience living in a developing country and in one ruled by a communist party. Coming from First-World, democratic New Zealand, the contrasts were startling.

Even when reform and opening up began, it was difficult to get to know the people. My wife described it as living in black and white. When we travelled back to Hong Kong, where our first child was born, she said it was like moving into technicolour.

We had a pantry in our apartment, full of all the goods we could not buy easily in Beijing, from cuts of New Zealand meat, to Vegemite and Weet-Bix. I used to drive every day to the embassy, from our apartment in Sanlitun along Dong Da Qiao Lu. There were never any traffic jams. Later I was asked, why did I not take more photos? The predictable if disappointing answer is that at the time nothing seemed especially worthy of being photographed.

We left Beijing at the conclusion of my posting in the middle of 1980. I returned on a visit in 1996, again in 1999, and then as ambassador in February 2001. I had often said to my wife that we might be returning to Beijing in the course of my career. 'Has it changed?' she would ask. 'Of course,' I replied. 'Well, you would say that, wouldn't you?' was her response. But yes, Beijing had changed in the intervening 20 years, as had we. High-rises, traffic jams, stylishly dressed men and women, coffee shops, international-grade hotels. It was still recognisably China, but very different from the China we could only just remember from 1980.

In 1978, still in the aftermath of the Cultural Revolution, there were only two Christian churches functioning in the whole country, both in Beijing, and both for foreigners. There was a Catholic congregation which worshipped in Latin, and a Protestant one which worshipped in Chinese. We opted for the latter; it met in Dongdan, in what had been the YMCA. Come 2001, we joined another congregation, also Protestant and for foreigners only. We could have attended any one of a number of flourishing local congregations in the city, but we felt at home in one in which English was the language of worship.

It snowed for our first three days in Beijing in February 2001, a good omen we were told. Maybe, but coming from the New Zealand summer it just seemed cold. We visited the Temple of Heaven, a beautiful winter landscape, and then, eager to see what Beijing's new shopping centres were like, we went to the Lufthansa Centre. To us, comparing it with Beijing in the 1970s (the Friendship Store, and that only) it seemed like heaven.

To our mid-teens daughter, less so. She did come to China with us, but she had to start at a new school, meet new friends, and learn to live in a new city. We did arrange for her cat, Cinnamon, to be shipped to Beijing from

New Zealand. Cinnamon certainly made herself at home in the embassy, disturbing diplomatic and other events morning, noon and night with her pirouettes on the balcony rail, or her scrabbling to be allowed to enter the downstairs part of the residence when we were entertaining.

China had opened up in many ways between 1980 and 2001. One of the most important was that it was possible for foreigners, including diplomats, to travel to nearly all parts of the country, whereas in the late 1970s, travel in and around Beijing was very limited, and beyond Beijing was confined to major cities such as Xi'an, Guangzhou, and the like. We took full advantage of this, well, maybe I took more advantage of it than my family, to visit provinces such as Hubei, Henan, Hunan, Yunnan, Sichuan and many more, all out of bounds in the 'old days'.

Was it easier to get to know local people? Yes, officials were more engaging, and non-officials had lost the fear and curiosity which seemed to be the dominant reactions to foreigners before. Being an ambassador was both a help and a hindrance. A help because paths were smoothed, and assistance was always forthcoming. A hindrance because the Chinese, officials and non-officials alike, treat diplomats and ambassadors with a deference which seems strange to New Zealanders, and which can become limiting.

In the course of my first ambassadorial assignment I decided to track down a Māori cloak that had been presented to Chairman Mao by Ramai and Rudall Hayward, actress and film-maker, respectively, who visited China in 1957 at a time when there were no diplomatic relations between our two countries. The cloak had been categorised as coming from Sri Lanka, formerly known as Ceylon, and Xilan 锡兰 in Chinese. New Zealand is Xinxilan 新西兰, so the mistake was understandable. The museum authorities were generous in their recognition of the value of the cloak as a symbol of the relationship between New Zealand and China. Much later the cloak was loaned to Te Papa, and honoured there as a taonga, a treasure, for both our countries.

John and Avenal McKinnon (second and third from left) join members of the
Pūkorokoro Miranda Naturalists' Trust team, including Bruce Postill (left) and Wendy
Hare (right), to view bar-tailed godwits at Yalu River in April 2018, during John's third
and final posting to China. After a six-day flight from New Zealand, the birds stop
over on the river en route to their Arctic breeding grounds.

I am often asked about the difference between China in 2001–2004, my first term as ambassador, and China in 2015–2018, my second term as ambassador. My standard response is: yes, there are differences, but they are nothing compared with those which I could identify between 1980 and 2001. And that is so. There were differences, but it was more an intensification of changes which were already underway, rather than a change of direction. More high-rises, more traffic, more stylish people, more restaurants. And some of the landmarks from only 20 years before were no longer or had faded. In 2001 the Jianguo Hotel was the go-to place for the best Western meals in town. In 2015, it was quiet and tired.

For us as a family, the biggest change was that in the second term, as a result of embassy reconstruction, we no longer lived in the old compound in Ritan Dongerjie as we had in 2001, but in an apartment in the Sanlitun office building. And that building, and indeed that compound, had scarcely changed since the 1970s. When our elder son and his family visited us in March 2018, our daughter-in-law decided to place our two granddaughters, then aged four and two, in the Italian school principally because it was in our compound (the other reason was the excellence of the lunches). We discovered that the school was on the ground floor of the very same building in which we had lived with their father in the 1970s.

In my second term as ambassador I twice was able to visit sites where migratory birds from New Zealand rested before flying further north to breed. In May 2017 I went to the coast of Bo Hai, and in April 2018 to the Yalu River, on the border between China and the Democratic People's Republic of Korea (DPRK). Red knots were the predominant birds on the Bo Hai coast, godwits on the Yalu River. The fortitude of these birds — flying non-stop for six or more days from Aotearoa to China — is remarkable, only exceeded by their even longer non-stop return trips from their breeding grounds in Siberia or Alaska. These birds are also a symbol of the links between China and New Zealand, at home in both worlds. There was a serious purpose to these visits. China, like many countries, is faced with the tension between economic development and protection of the environment. My visits drew attention to the value we placed on wetlands, as essential to the health and journeying of these birds.

I twice visited Tibet: in 2001 with then Foreign Minister Phil Goff, and in 2003 on my own account. On the second visit we travelled out of Lhasa, including to Nagqu, reputedly the highest town in the world. I found it intriguing that seafood was seen as a delicacy, and priced accordingly, in this most inland of regions. In 2015 we went on a private visit to Xinjiang, and there visited one of the lowest towns in the world, Turfan. The cultural as well as the physical diversity of China was very evident on these visits. Many Tibetans and many Uyghurs are troubled by how their government is treating them. So are many outsiders.

I also visited a number of locations in Inner Mongolia. While the Inner Mongolian Autonomous Region is only 10 per cent Mongol, it still keeps the old Mongolian alphabet, whereas in Mongolia itself (I was also accredited to that country) it has been replaced by a Cyrillic script. Mongols are well known in history as horse riders, and I attended one race meeting in the region. But it was quite unlike race meetings in New Zealand as no betting is permitted, so handicapping is irrelevant.

What was the most interesting place I visited in China? An even more difficult question to answer. Easiest to say that I warmed to seaside cities, such as Dalian, Qingdao and Xiamen, I think because in New Zealand almost all our cities are coastal, and it is very hard for us to visualise urban development without a seascape. But every city has its attractions, and there are many which have populations far in excess of ours, but of which nobody outside China has ever heard. In many ways visiting a city where foreigners were few and far between was in itself remarkable. How could I forget Xiangfan, in Hubei (which I visited in 2004), on which occasion the fountains and boulevards were lit up for me I was told, but maybe I was mistaken.

That delusion was one sign that it was time for me to leave China. Another was when I quite took to liking *baijiu* (the fiery spirit and necessary ingredient of drinking games) at breakfast.

I was privileged to spend 10 years of my professional life in China. Such experience confounds generalities. China can be looked at through multiple lenses — commercial, geopolitical, human rights, and many, many more. But if we are to understand this vast society, we need to bring all of these different perspectives together.

Māori Business Relationships with China

MAVIS MULLINS

Interview with Jason Young, 27 January 2022

Mavis Mullins (MM):
> From my father, the Ruahine Range is my mountain
> The Manawatū River is my river
> I am of Rangitāne and Ngāti Ranginui descent
> From my mother, Koro Ruapehu is my mountain
> The Whanganui River is my sacred river
> I am Ngāpaerangi of Ātihau nui ā Pāparāngi descent
> I am Mavis Mullins Tihei mauri ora — these things give me breath.

Jason Young (JY): Thank you for agreeing to do this interview about Māori–Chinese business connections. First, could you talk a bit about your early years and how a daughter of a shearing family got into business?

MM: My whakapapa is very much based here in Dannevirke or Tamaki-nui-ā-Rua, but also up the Whanganui River where my mum was born and raised. We've been farmers on land that has been in our family since what we call mai rānō, 'forever'; I still farm the land that my parents, grandparents, great-grandparents and great-great-grandparents farmed. We can trace our family's history in this place back through more than 15 generations, so it's a special place.

What's particularly interesting, given what you've asked me to talk about today, is a kind of new journey for me and my family. In the early 1900s, a couple of Chinese brothers arrived in Dannevirke. One of them leased land owned by my family and set up a market garden. The other brother would come and collect the produce and go to the township to sell it. Well, people are people no matter where you come from, and my father was a product of a union with one of those men. We didn't find this out until many years later, but I'm sure it helps explain why I feel so comfortable working with Chinese. The fact that China is part of my DNA drives me to seek greater understanding, including an understanding of what Māori and Chinese share.

My upbringing was shaped by what is inherent in Māoridom: the connection with land. Our family life revolved around working and caring for the land, often for other people. You could say we were almost tenants on our own land; most members of the household looked for supplementary work, for example as farmworkers, shearers, scrub-cutters and fencers. My first qualification was as a wool classer. I spent time in Australia, studying at what was then the Melbourne College of Textiles, and developed a real passion for wool. That fabulous fibre has taken me on journeys that led to the restructuring of producer boards, finding novel uses for wool, and learning the science of wool.

JY: When did you first have business connections with China and with Chinese businesses?
MM: This came about through my role as the Chair of Poutama Trust. The trust is an entity that was set up [in 1988] with the remnants of a government fund used to support Māori economic development. What had been a $10 million fund had trebled by the time I left five years ago.

When we began to work closely with our people to enhance and develop their expertise, we discovered that their aspirations were centred on their families, not necessarily on the businesses they ran. The business was the means. They were more focused on educating their children and making their families secure than getting a foothold in the global business world. There are exceptions, of course. There are big Māori businesses such as Tohu Wines and Watson & Son, now owned by Ngāi Tahu; both have footholds in China. Overall, however, Māori SMEs (small and medium-sized enterprises) did not aim to build big enterprises. What we were doing in the Poutama Trust, therefore, was to connect small family businesses in the spheres of food, hospitality and education with what can be called tuakana–teina (big brother, little brother) models, small or medium-sized businesses based on extended families and Māori kinship relationships.

Following enquiries, we organised several exploratory trips to China. Taking some small business groups to China was probably the beginning of my efforts to understand China.

JY: Can you tell us about those trips, and how you and fellow travellers felt about venturing into the large and I imagine quite daunting Chinese market?

MM: I'll tell you about one that was a life-changing experience. In 2010, Tā Pita Sharples, Minister of Māori Affairs at the time, took a group of Māori business delegates to China. At a pre-tour meeting, he said: 'Look I'm not a businessperson, I'm an educationalist, and I aim to make a deep cultural footprint.' His belief was that if we could build a deep and sincere cultural relationship first, then anything could grow out of that. He said, 'I want us to build a cultural platform first.'

Many of us in that delegation were not as culturally committed as Tā Pita Sharples, and this meeting with him was a bit of an eye-rolling moment. We soon, however, got to understand and appreciate what he meant. He meant that, in making connections, each of us connects as a *person*, and we connect through what we have in common. We travelled to China as Māori, and we sought to create and strengthen linkages. We're always looking for linkages, for ways that we connect to one another as a person, not necessarily in a transactional manner. We looked to connect our waters, and our mountains; they are all part of who we are. There's also how we share kai together; food is a great connector. And we connect with song, with waiata. It was a matter of embedding some of this 'cultural normality' in our visit to China.

I tell you what, it worked amazingly! First, the Chinese are very connected to their whakapapa; they know their genealogies. Their history is as sacred to them as ours is sacred to us. The sharing of food and the manāki (hospitality) you offer to your guests are important in both cultures. And you know, of course, that Chinese love to sing! Any opportunity for both guests and hosts to sing was seized with enthusiasm. When, therefore, we waiataed to them, it went without saying that they would waiata back. We had some amazing moments when sharing like this.

A funny exchange related to connections occurring at a meeting with Chinese government officials: Pita Sharples gave a speech in which he declared that 'thousands of years back our people lived here'; our ancestors eventually moved to the Pacific Islands, and from there to New Zealand. Now, he said, 'we've come back to you as our older brother'. We listened to the interpreter translate this into Chinese and could see the very solemn nods of agreement among the Chinese participants. Then came Pita Sharples' cheeky conclusion: 'So I hope you guys have been looking after our place while we've been gone.' The gathering erupted into laughter. This is a great example of how our humour connected us with our Chinese hosts; it strengthened the connections we were forging.

One of the deep lessons of that trip for me, therefore, is that when you share your whole self with other people who cherish their own inherited cultural norms, you can find bridges and links between those norms and your own culture, you can acquire a learning that goes deeper than lessons learned from academic qualifications. This is not to disrespect academia; it is about *heart*. I am talking about connections that are made at 'heart and people' levels.

JY: What about connections between Māori businesses and Chinese companies seeking access to the New Zealand market?

MM: I've had a long involvement with Te Huarahi Tika Trust, Māori Spectrum Trust and Hautaki, our commercial arm. The trust had been set up in 2000 to bring about a third mobile participant, to break a monopoly in telecommunications here in New Zealand. To be frank, that was a vicious battle.

Through the international experts who worked with the trust we met Huawei. At that time, Huawei was not in the Australasia–Pacific region; it was very much a northern hemisphere and Asian company. By applying the cultural connections that we had with China, we formed a very deep connection with Huawei. As a contributor to that end, they supported and underwrote the building of our towers, and they became, and they still are for me, a trusted people. I know there have been other things that have happened relating to Huawei, but for me that changes nothing. When you connect on a very deep and personal cultural level, you can see beyond what is presented to you by others.

JY: This enabled the establishment of the successful 2degrees Mobile, didn't it? Did the partnership with Huawei, therefore, enable 2degrees to set up a 4G network for telecommunications?

MM: Yes, 3G, 4G and now 5G. 2degrees is now New Zealand's third mobile network, and it has driven prices down for all New Zealanders. We've put money back into the pockets of all New Zealanders, and this would not have happened unless Māori had committed to this project. Telecommunications is a very competitive market, and Te Huarahi Tika Trust was by no means the only telecommunications provider that aimed to become New Zealand's third mobile network. Because the execution timeframe was too long for these other providers, however, they were 'in' and quickly 'out'. For Māori, on the other hand, the venture wasn't primarily about the establishment of an economic platform, but about building a platform for our future, for our

He Pakiaka is a special welcoming space in the New Zealand embassy in Beijing and its rich representation of Māori culture and traditions resonates strongly with visitors. Martin Wikaira, head of the Ministry of Foreign Affairs and Trade's Māori Policy Unit, says He Pakiaka means the seed of a plant – a reminder that nurturing a relationship relies upon frequent, high-quality contact; the type of contact at the heart of Māori business relationships with China. MINISTRY OF FOREIGN AFFAIRS AND TRADE

children and our grandchildren. 2degrees has been a great story. It's been an *average* story for Māori, a learning experience. But it's been a *stunning* story for New Zealanders, for New Zealand Inc.

JY: You explain how shared cultural values and norms between Māori and Chinese can facilitate economic co-operation. Do you agree with those who suggest that a longer-term view of economic relations found in both cultures also contributes to successful Māori–Chinese business relationships?

MM: Absolutely. What matters are values. People from different places have common values, even though those values are given different names. Values relating to whakapapa and family and gifting, for example. Māori and Chinese people know that there's much more mana in giving than in receiving. When you go to China you're made to feel like you are the only person in the world; they're just so amazingly hospitable. That's a value that we also cherish. Values are deeply embedded in cultures. They have to be strong, and they have to be aligned. That's a key starting point.

A second point is that Māori think intergenerationally. We don't necessarily start with a 'five-year plan'; our plan is a 100-year plan; we plan for the next three, four or five generations. We make what we call mokopuna decisions, decisions for grandchildren, not decisions for ourselves. My generation won't get the benefit of our own good decisions, but we are benefitting from the mokopuna decisions made by our own parents and grandparents. Mokopuna is another key value embedded in Māori culture.

I also regard a sense of community, rather than individualism, as a shared kaupapa. When speaking of a 'sense of community', I guess I'm talking mainly about a 'communal sense of being' as opposed to the capitalistic attachment to private property and individual rights. I think that Māori also share with Chinese people a value that I'm going to call 'deep respect'. Even when things are not always right between negotiators, you start from a position of respect on both sides.

During the times that I have worked with Chinese people I have often been made aware of the values we share. The intergenerational focus is particularly pertinent at a time when climate change is forcing people everywhere to think about the kind of world that future generations will inherit from us. A growing concern for environmental protection is now evident in China, but rapid industrialisation during the past three decades has provided enormous environmental challenges.

JY: Would you say that in Māori culture we find strong environmental values, and do they influence the way in which Māori agribusinesses trade with Chinese businesses?

MM: Yes, environmental values are embedded in Māori culture. When you look at land you see the face of your children or the face of your grandmother. For Māori agribusinesses, the priority is not intensified farming that might increase profits, but rather the provision of kai for families; it's about ensuring that we have something that is good to pass on to the next generation and the next.

Are Māori businesses able to develop commercial enterprises in China, or work with Chinese partners, in ways that make possible the exporting of Māori environmental values and ideals? Before answering that question, we must note that Māori environmentalism has not very effectively constrained the unsustainable development of our own farmlands in Aotearoa. My work in biodiversity has confronted me with the size of the problem. Environmental stewardship has only recently been given space and a voice. In the past that voice has been a whisper — or ignored.

Some good things are happening, however. I chair the board of the Ātihau-Whanganui Incorporation, one of the biggest Māori multiple-owned land-blocks. We have a taiao strategy; that's a 'whole of place' strategy in which profits and productivity sit alongside elements such as the health of the people, the health of rivers, the health of the land and soil, and resilience to climate change. Having a deep connection with land and water makes Māori instinctive environmentalists, and that can influence and determine a lot of the ways we do business.

Does Māori environmentalism have anything to teach China? China does its environmental projects in a think-big way because that is what they can do. Down here in little 'God's own' we do things more modestly and quietly. We can say that it's good for us that China is so big and we're so little. We're just the size of a pin head, we are not a threat. So when we do get to talk, they are respectful but obviously non-committal. I do believe they respect that we are small but that we have strong opinions and big aspirations. Our smallness can certainly work against us, but it can also work in our favour. But I can't say that this goes as far as taking environmental advice from us, other than to say that we are aware of our shared values and long-term view.

JY: What about food exports to China? Do environmental concerns come into play? How are New Zealand food products and Māori business food products marketed in China?

MM: As I mentioned, I chair the Ātihau-Whanganui Incorporation. It's a significant red meat, honey and milk producer. We did a lot of work in China just learning and understanding that market. In the end, we chose not to go there. China is so big, so complex, and it is so far away. To be a successful foreign enterprise in China you really have to be a *big* business, a business along the lines of a Fonterra (which is 10 per cent Māori supplied) or the red meat entities (for whom we are significant suppliers) such as Silver Fern Farms. We looked at going to some of the third-tier cities with the idea of establishing just a single franchise or marketing a certain brand there, but even that didn't garner much enthusiasm. We're not ready for them, and I don't think they're ready for us. A point of difference between us and the Chinese is that we view our farm products as precious, as coming from Papatūānuku, coming from the gods; they are taonga and not commodities. We certainly know how to form business relationships with

90

Chinese partners, but it just doesn't feel like it's our time yet. Marketing under your own brand in China has proven to be very difficult for us.

That's when we came up with the food basket idea, a coalition of small New Zealand businesses that share the costs, risks and experiences of exporting food products to China. It could be supported by, for example, Tohu Wines and Watson & Son/Oha Honey, two very well-known Māori businesses. When they are in the basket, you can then pack in all the other little bits that reduce risks for new and small businesses. Also, being in the basket connects small businesses to supply lines set up by more established players. There are some that have become successful. Others not so much. I would have loved to have established a real footprint in China. However, now is not the right time for a lot of those small Māori businesses. Exceptions can be those that have continued to work collaboratively with other small businesses and, perhaps, to market a very specific brand in a specific place and with specific people.

JY: What about Chinese investment in New Zealand, particularly in whenua — in land and farming? I'm wondering if you have thoughts on that, and how to have the relationship structured in a way that works for both Māori and Chinese businesses?

MM: Yes. I can remember participating in a New Zealand China Council event in China at a time when our government's policy made things awkward for Chinese investors in New Zealand. A 'whole system' strategy needs to be developed. An important aim with China is to secure a safe and dependable food supply for their population. I say that they don't necessarily need to own the land to achieve that. If, however, a foreign investor has the opportunity and the resources and then the control that comes with ownership, why wouldn't they buy land?

It comes back, therefore, to our own policy settings, New Zealand's policy settings, and sometimes these don't serve us well. I become very anxious when I see land being sold to foreign investors. Māori people cannot, in fact, easily sell whenua. The Māori Land Act (Te Ture Whenua, 1993) makes it very difficult for us to sell our land, and thank goodness for that, because the globe now is the marketplace, not the next-door neighbour. Māori are now confidently relearning the science, both Western and our own ancient science, of sustainable land use. We must consider the long-term consequences of what we do with the land. There should be no place for short-term investors who seek to profit from rising land and house prices and have no interest in sustainable land practices.

Do China's food security needs require that we sell our land to Chinese investors? No, there are other options, so I don't know why we do it. Through stronger co-operative relationships with Chinese business partners, for example, we could work at establishing and securing supply chains for food products. Policies need to be structured for the long term, for the best long-term interests of New Zealand Inc. Māori are very clear about this: we are going to be here, owning our lands, in 100 years' time, and that gives a different perspective on how you do business, where you do it and with whom you do it.

JY: Our Foreign Minister Nanaia Mahuta has recently emphasised the importance of mutual respect and maintaining dialogue. She has also acknowledged the challenges in the New Zealand–China relationship. How do you see the relationship today?
MM: I think it's strained. Geopolitics, the Covid pandemic and several other global tensions are putting stresses on relationships, not just globally but nationally, and even within communities and families.

I was in Dubai with Minister Mahuta recently, and she noted how foreign trade agreements in the past have been built on hard power. The cut and thrust of confirming the transaction, the deal, is an exercise of hard power. She went on to say that 'I want us to balance that with soft power, the soft power that considers the impact and effect of trade deals on humanity.' Then she asked: Where does soft power fit within a free-trade agreement? She was addressing a group of high-level officials and people at the World Expo in Dubai. It was stunning! And what she said is relevant to our China relationship. First, we must be true to our values and purpose, and that will determine how we deal and negotiate with Chinese officials and businesspeople.

JY: What, in your view, does the Māori–China business relationship mean for the Māori economy here in New Zealand, and how would you like to see that develop over the medium to long term?

MM: Whether we go back to an 'old normality' or develop a 'new normality', I'd like to think that we have formed linkages and built a platform of cultural respect and cultural understanding that will see us move forward into the future in a positive way. We're not always going to like each other. But that's the case in all families. We need to make room for humanness in international relationships, an understanding that we're not all perfect, that we're all in different places and spaces. As for Māori and China, we have a connection that cannot be broken; we have a genealogical connection, we have a DNA connection. We recognise elements of ourselves in each other. That's what can transcend all the global disruption and anxiety that people all over the world are experiencing.

For me personally, I'm looking forward to the time when I can renew the relationships with colleagues based in China. I retain strong connections with Chinese New Zealanders, people who are still travelling between New Zealand and China either for business or family reasons. I look forward to us forever sharing a relationship of deep respect. And that's a foundation upon which commercial relationships can again be built in the future.

人People

A Haunted Taste

JACOB EDMOND

Sometimes you travel a long way only to discover something that was there all along in the place you left behind.

We normally think of travel as bringing new experiences, and indeed it does. I encountered many new things when I first visited China in 1997 to study Chinese at Wuhan University. If I made a list, it would include the sea-sized Yangtze, the brilliant Laotian student footballers who removed beer bottle lids with their teeth, a young man reciting a poem by heart in the twilight, and the earthy taste of lotus root.

Another thing on that list would be my first experience of being a racially marked minority. As a person of European descent, I encountered the kind of racialised othering that was in fact just as much a facet of life in Aotearoa New Zealand, but which, as a member of the privileged white colonial majority here, I had never experienced directly. Of course, my experience wasn't at all equivalent to the racism experienced by Māori and others here in Aotearoa. Whiteness continues to bring unfair privilege even when it is marked as other. Still, travelling to China brought home to me the racism of the place that I had left behind.

As a Māori poet, Hone Tuwhare (Ngā Puhi, Ngāti Korokoro, Ngāti Tautahi, Te Popoto, Te Uri-o-Hau; 1922–2008) was of course all too familiar not just with the racialised othering that I experienced in China, but also with white privilege and colonisation. He writes about this in his poetic tribute to his late friend and mentor R. A. K. Mason (1905–1971) in what is also, unexpectedly, a poem about China:

> Easy for you now, man. You've joined your literary
> ancestors, whilst I have problems still in finding
> mine, lost somewhere
>
> in the confusing swirl, now thick now thin,
> Victoriana-Missionary fog hiding legalized land-rape
> and gentlemen thugs . . .

Mason, Tuwhare suggests, had no trouble finding his 'literary ancestors'. British literature was taught in schools and universities and propagated through mainstream media. Mason could therefore begin his poem 'Song of Allegiance' with a confident identification of his predecessors: 'Shakespeare Milton Keats are dead'. Alluding to this poem, Tuwhare suggests that Mason has now joined this literary pantheon of dead white men, whom Tuwhare could not, in any simple way, follow.

Instead, Tuwhare worked hard to recover a tradition that was suppressed and disparaged for much of his lifetime. After moving as a child to Tāmaki Makaurau Auckland from his ancestral lands in Te Tai Tokerau in 1926, he partially lost his first language, Māori. He also witnessed the extension of this disenfranchisement from land, language and culture and the perpetuation of systematic racism during the 1950s, 1960s and 1970s, when many more Māori flocked to the cities and frequently found the doors to housing, education and opportunity shut. Tuwhare cites this 'legalized land-rape', racism and cultural theft in distinguishing his own experience from Mason's privilege, which is only partially the privilege of dying: 'Easy for you now, man.'

Through this informal address, the poem also affirms commonalities across the divide of racism and white privilege. As a Marxist atheist, Mason was also no lover of 'Missionary' zeal and class privilege ('gentlemen thugs'). The lines that follow offer the clearest statement of the two poets' commonalities, and this statement comes, surprisingly, through China:

> ... Never mind, you've taught me
>
> confidence and ease in dredging for my own bedraggled
> myths and you bet: weighing the China experience
> yours and mine. They balance.

Surprising, yes, that Tuwhare turns to 'the China experience', but perhaps it is less so when we consider that Mason had spent the last three decades of his life engaged with the country. In the year after his death, New Zealand established diplomatic relations with the People's Republic of China, realising Mason's long-held dream of greater friendship between the two countries. The following year, in September and October 1973, Tuwhare himself visited China for the first time.

I cannot definitively date the composition of Tuwhare's poem, but it seems almost certain that it was completed after that visit, particularly since Tuwhare added the China reference to an already typeset version of the poem, seemingly not long before it was published in the 1974 collection *Something Nothing*.

This was not the only late change that Tuwhare made to the collection to make room for his 'China experience'. He also added two new poems written during his trip, 'Kwantung Guest House: Canton' and 'Soochow'. Mason had himself visited China in 1957, and later published a chapbook, *China Dances*, that collected his China-related writings, including a short poem that he had written on that trip. It was surely only after completing his own visit in 1973 and adding his own China poems to his forthcoming collection that Tuwhare could say that his and Mason's China experience 'balance'.

There's another way in which it makes sense that Tuwhare would swerve to China to affirm connection after emphasising the two poets' differences. China, specifically the 'New China' inaugurated in 1949, was a symbol for them both of overcoming racism and inequality. Mason had seen in China 'our main hope for the salvation of the human race'. Tuwhare shared this vision.

Beyond the poem, too, Tuwhare's 'China experience' brought together his Marxist internationalism with his battle for his Māoritanga amid the 'confusing swirl' of racism and white supremacy, or what he termed the 'big pakeha-bourgeois chauvinism' that poisoned even the left-wing circles in which he moved. Tuwhare visited China as part of a 'Maori Workers' delegation' that included Tame Iti, as a representative of Ngā Tamatoa, Miriama Rauhihi (later Rauhihi-Ness) of the Polynesian Panthers (and also a member of Ngā Tamatoa), and two trade unionists, Timi Te Maipi and Willie Wilson. Hosted by the Chinese government, their tour took them to meet various so-called 'minority nationalities', with the goal of impressing on the visitors how much better China, as the self-proclaimed leader of the Third World, treated its diverse peoples.

From this perspective, the tour was a great success. In an interview with *Salient*, Wilson explained: 'Before I went to China I never had this hard-line attitude. I thought that this society was a bit racist but not totally . . . After being to China and seeing how the minorities are treated, how they are permitted to organise and run their own affairs, I was convinced . . . Minorities in China today enjoy a far more fortunate existence than Maoris in NZ.' Wilson might not have learned much about China, where Han chauvinism is just as pervasive and pernicious as Pākehā chauvinism, and where the Uyghur people today suffer its ugliest consequences. However, Wilson did learn something about New Zealand. Again, it sometimes takes a trip somewhere else to discover something about the place you left behind.

The racism of New Zealand society can hardly have been a discovery for the likes of Iti and Rauhihi, and yet for them, as for Tuwhare, the trip came at a crucial time, just after the Māori language petition of 1972, in which Iti and Ngā Tamatoa played an important role, and shortly before the 1975 Land March, to which Rauhihi, Iti and Tuwhare would all make major contributions. It also came just months after the inauguration of the Maori Artists and Writers Society at Te Kaha in June 1973, at a hui that Tuwhare organised and that Iti also attended. What Tuwhare calls 'the China experience' affirmed this battle for Māori rights, identity and independence, and perhaps helped galvanise further action.

Highlighting this connection, Tuwhare included another poem from his 'China experience' in his next and arguably most political collection, *Making a Fist of It*. Alongside poems commemorating the struggle against racism and colonialism in Aotearoa and South Africa, Tuwhare chose to include 'Song to a Herdsman's Son', which was 'written after a visit to Inner Mongolia'. This was, so far as I know, the only poem that Tuwhare wrote in response to his experience of visiting non-Han minorities, ostensibly the main purpose of the group's visit to China.

It's a small poem, but it is also big; it wants to encompass the whole world. The middle stanzas read:

> My fast horse: my strong horse,
> you're invincible.   Don't let the sun
> set.   Hurdle
> the Oceans, horse.   Encircle the
> Earth.   Let me embrace the World's
> People: follow the Sun.

The poem's ambition to 'Encircle the Earth' echoes the internationalism of the collection. It also echoes Chinese communist rhetoric depicting Mao as the sun. The poem is perhaps saved from the banality of propaganda by the final stanza, which deflates its previous excesses in favour of a domestic scene:

> But get me back in time
> to make my father, my mother,
> fragrant breakfast-cups of salted
> tea with millet — a glass of
> hot milk for my baby sister.

It's all very well to 'embrace the World's / People', but, the poem seems to ask, what about a particular people's way of life ('salted / tea with millet — a glass of / hot milk'), their land, culture and language? Given his knowledge of British colonialism, Tuwhare is understandably suspicious of how embracing 'the World's / People' can be a cover for the imposition of the language and culture of one people on another.

A similar worry about the disconnection between revolutionary rhetoric and reality troubles Tuwhare's two China poems in *Something Nothing*. These two poems reflect on the contradictions between the pleasures of luxury, art and other worldly indulgences, and the austere rhetoric of communist revolution. 'Kwantung Guest House: Canton' notes the luxuries that Tuwhare receives as a foreign guest: 'the roomy / air-conditioned train'; 'I'm overwhelmed by the size of my bedroom suite'. The poet is suspicious of such luxuries since they are 'built painfully' on the backs of 'heroic predecessors and revolutionary patriots'. Even so, he enjoys them: 'I lift the phone and ask for a beer'. The poem is built uneasily on this 'press of contrasts', on 'thought-shifts' that 'I try to sift'. In the end, though, 'my sifter breaks down', and Tuwhare remains lost in another kind of 'confusing swirl'.

'Soochow', too, warns against luxuries: 'Chairman Mao writes: "Revolution is not a dinner party".' Yet again, though, Tuwhare dwells on the contradictions, concluding with his own supper: 'But for dinner tonight, I will savour a slice or two / of the lotus root, crisp and white.'

We are back again in 'the confusing swirl', and in more ways than one. The turn to the bodily pleasures and cultural specificity of food once more undermines the propagandistic rhetoric, recalling Tuwhare's similar struggle to find his own culture and ancestors amid the confusing swirl of Pākehā colonialism. But it also leads Tuwhare home in another more personal way.

In tasting the lotus root, Tuwhare becomes 'A small child again / dribbling a haunted taste.' Like Proust's madeleine, the lotus root sends Tuwhare back in time, hurdling oceans, to that part of his childhood spent in Chinese market gardens in Auckland, where his father worked, and where he perhaps first experienced that now 'haunted taste'.

To be haunted by childhood was also, perhaps, to be haunted by the experience of racism, which impeded Tuwhare's search for his literary ancestors, and drove but also complicated his Marxist internationalism. In the 1990s, Tuwhare would return again to his childhood, researching the appalling racism encountered by Chinese market gardeners in 1920s and 1930s Auckland and by the Māori who worked with them.

***

This essay, too, is haunted by travel, memory and traumatic histories. At a twilight gathering at Wuhan University, I recall a local student reciting Gu Cheng's 顾城 (1956–1993) best-known poem, 'A Generation (一代人)'. By then, Gu Cheng was remembered not only as a poet who gave voice to a new individual sensibility after the enforced collectivity and violence of the Cultural Revolution, but also as the poet who had gone mad on Waiheke Island and had murdered his wife before taking his own life.

But I had a more personal memory of Gu Cheng as the eccentrically dressed 'famous Chinese poet' who came for dinner during my last year of primary school and talked intensely with my father (a poet of a homegrown and less famous kind).

It was only on hearing Gu Cheng's words recited that evening in Wuhan that I realised that my 'China experience', too, had begun long before I set foot in the country.

Tuwhare also visited our house in Auckland during those years. (My maternal grandparents published his first book, and he was a good friend of the family.) Only in writing this essay have I realised that my childhood memories of the visits of these two poets intersect in what Tuwhare calls 'the China experience'.

Tuwhare's 'haunted taste', then, suggests to me the need to find a way through the confusing swirl of international relations, racism, colonialism and nationalist chauvinism, be it Pākehā or Han Chinese, to other, more complex kinds of collective and individual history.

The lotus root takes me back first to Wuhan in 1997, then to Auckland in the 1980s, and, finally, reminds me that Tuwhare's China experience began not when he crossed the border from Hong Kong in 1973 but in a market garden in Avondale, Auckland, almost half a century earlier.

Sometimes you travel a long way only to discover something that was there all along in the place you thought you had left behind.

Finding Dr Li Lairong: Pioneer of New Zealand–China Science Co-operation

TONY BROWNE

Dr Li Lairong 李來榮, an eminent horticulturist from Fujian, epitomised early New Zealand–China scientific co-operation. Dr Li had reached Hawai'i in December 1941, en route home from doctoral studies at Penn State University, when the Japanese attacked Pearl Harbor. Unable to continue to China, Li's ship headed south, ending up in Wellington. Li offered his services to the Ministry of Agriculture in Wellington, then to the Plant Diseases Division of the Department of Scientific and Industrial Research (DSIR) at Mount Albert in Auckland. He was, it seems, the first scientist from China to work in the DSIR. His efforts to increase Chinese market gardeners' vegetable production built his reputation here. In 1944 he set out to return to China via India and the Burma Road. His ship was torpedoed. He spent the rest of the war in a Japanese POW camp in Java, finally getting home to Xiamen in 1947.

Dr Li's career progressed smoothly in the early days of the People's Republic of China, with him becoming president of the Fujian Institute of Subtropical Botany and, in 1956, president of the Fujian Agriculture College, now the Fujian Agriculture and Forestry University. He published three books and close to 100 scientific papers. His correspondence with his New Zealand colleagues continued until it became difficult during the Great Leap Forward, and was stopped entirely by the Cultural Revolution.

He was denounced, removed from any professional role, and detained for a decade.

———————————

My first visit to Beijing, in May 1974, coincided with that of the first Royal Society of New Zealand delegation. The delegation included Dr Ted Bollard, the then Director of Dr Li's old DSIR team. Ted went with the aim of getting back in touch with Dr Li, but could make no progress with his hosts at the Academy of Sciences. Two years later, as I was preparing to take up my first posting in Beijing, Ted charged me with taking up the effort to make contact. Dr Li himself had been in touch with the embassy, including sending a small box containing *Actinidia* (kiwifruit) seeds in 1975. But non-official contact between diplomats and Chinese citizens was severely constrained, and Dr Li was not able to continue the correspondence. All that was known in New Zealand horticultural circles was that Dr Li was in Xiamen. But Xiamen was 'closed' to foreigners and there was no way that we in the embassy could go there.

In Beijing from 1976 to 1978 I was coming to grips with the intricacies of dealing with Chinese officialdom. In 1977 Ted Bollard asked me to arrange a visit by an apple scientist, Dr Don McKenzie. This became the opportunity to ratchet up the pressure to contact Dr Li. As the official in the embassy responsible for science contacts (although as an historian I was scientifically illiterate), I went to the International Department of the Academy of Sciences to discuss the visit, and in the course of this discussion to say that we in the embassy, and the DSIR in New Zealand, hoped that we would then have the chance to meet Dr Li Lairong.

This request was met with a confused response. Those I was speaking to did not know him, and were extremely suspicious in the xenophobic atmosphere of the time that a Chinese citizen might be maintaining contact with foreign scientists and officials outside formal channels. I had to spend a good deal of time making it clear that the initiative to make the contact was ours, that Dr Li was not aware of our approach, that his connections with New Zealand were long-standing, and from long ago. I explained that we were going through the Academy to make the connection, not trying to establish it without their knowledge or support. And so on. In contact with Chinese officials at the time anything difficult or out of the ordinary invariably met the response, 'Sorry, it is not convenient.' I arranged a second meeting to go over Don McKenzie's programme. Again I went through the history of Dr Li's links with New Zealand and the value we would place on the chance to meet him. The response was ratcheted up. They didn't know him and hadn't heard of him. 'It may be difficult,' I was told.

The late Sir Brian Talboys, then deputy prime minister, visited China in October 1977. One of my responsibilities was to organise his programme. This included organising a dinner for Foreign Minister Huang Hua in the Great Hall of the People to reciprocate the hospitality that Huang Hua would extend to Talboys. I sent a message to Ted Bollard asking him to fly up a couple of trays of Chinese gooseberries, as kiwifruit was then commonly known in New Zealand, so that we could have them on the tables. They were, as far as I have been able to establish, the first shipment of kiwifruit from New Zealand to China, the forerunner of the millions of trays that Zespri now sends there each year.

I included on the guest list the director-general of the Academy, who had given me the 'not convenient' and 'difficult' responses, and arranged for him to be seated next to me. This meant that for two hours he had to listen to me without the chance to terminate the discussion. He heard the story once again, probably twice again, of how Dr Li had come to

New Zealand, the work he had done for New Zealand, the friends he had made there, the respect in which he was held, the contribution we believed he could make to the development of scientific relations between the two countries. I pointed to the size, taste and quality of the fruit that had come from New Zealand to highlight our expertise in horticultural research. (Huang Hua's wife, He Liliang, had been so impressed that she filled her handbag with kiwifruit to take home and show her friends!)

By the time the dinner was over, or perhaps just to shut me up, the response had moved from 'It may be difficult' to 'I'll see what I can do'. I heard no more, and assumed that nothing would happen. Don McKenzie arrived, and I took him out to the Institute of Botany. About 80 were in the audience as Don went through his research into the most effective techniques of apple cultivation, the work done on apple breeding, and so on. His interpreter got hopelessly out of his depth, and the discussion was headed for mutual bemusement when an elderly man at the back of the room quietly intervened, saying 'Dr McKenzie, I think that what the young man is trying to say is . . .' Don and I looked up in surprise, for this person hadn't been introduced to us, and we hadn't been given any indication of who was to be present. From then on, he took over the interpretation. When the lecture finished, he quietly introduced himself as Dr Li Lairong. He had, he told us, received a summons out of the blue from Beijing, ordering him to come to a meeting in the capital. He hadn't been there for about 15 years.

A few weeks later I met the director-general again. He had a message for me: 'We want to thank you for introducing us to Dr Li.' Within a very short time Dr Li was back in Beijing, this time as a delegate to the Chinese People's Political Consultative Conference. The many years of anonymous obscurity were over. Dr Li himself sent us a message when he got to Beijing to tell us of the change in his status, but we weren't able, in the environment of the time, to meet again there. Even so, the link quickly began to pay dividends. Very soon afterwards the Institute of Botany called me to come

Dr Li Lairong (second from right) with Prime Minister Robert Muldoon in Xiamen,
1980. NEW ZEALAND FOREIGN AFFAIRS REVIEW, JULY–SEPTEMBER 1980

and see them. They took me to a room with a series of specimen cupboards from which they brought out many different varieties of *Actinidia* seeds. They shook a dozen or more onto pieces of paper, folded them up, and asked me to send them to the Plant Diseases Division in Auckland. DSIR scientists methodically worked through them over the next few years.

I was back in New Zealand for six months on the China desk in Foreign Affairs when in early 1979 we received a message from Beijing that the Academy of Sciences was proposing to send a delegation to New Zealand. The message had dates and names. It was to be led by Dr Li Lairong. I recall the visit well, and the pleasure it gave Ted Bollard and others — particularly his wartime colleagues at Mount Albert — to have him back in New Zealand.

The media took up the story. David Young wrote a good profile in the *New Zealand Listener*. I received phone calls from around New Zealand from people who had known Dr Li during the war. People flew to Wellington to see him. He was great company, reliving the memories and experiences of his time in New Zealand 35 years earlier. I attended the Royal Society meeting with the delegation. Dr Li's formal statement was, inevitably, full of the correct political content that his minders from Beijing had written for him. We saw past that, however, and simply took pleasure from the occasion at a personal level. The Royal Society elected him an Honorary Fellow of the Society.

In 1980 Robert Muldoon made his second visit to China. The embassy asked the Chinese authorities to let him visit Xiamen, becoming the first foreign head of government to do so after the Cultural Revolution. Dr Li was part of the reason the embassy wanted him to go there. There is a photo of Dr Li walking along the waterfront with the prime minister like a couple of long-time buddies.

Stories get exaggerated and develop a life of their own. When I got back to Beijing as New Zealand Ambassador 25 years later, I told the story of Dr Li's rehabilitation and both his historical and his renewed New Zealand connection. It wasn't long before I had it played back to me, with embellishment. Foreign Minister Li Zhaoxing, in particular, would make a point of telling New Zealand visitors how grateful we should be that one of his relatives was responsible for introducing the kiwifruit into New Zealand. I tried to correct him one day, suggesting that, as he knew the story because I had told it to him, he may as well get it right. But he knew he was on to a good thing, and when he told his version to Premier Wen Jiabao and Prime Minister Helen Clark at dinner at Premier House in Wellington, I knew better than to cast doubt on the pleasure he got from his 'family' link.

Plant & Food Research (the successor to the old DSIR Division) now has a Li Lairong Research Fellowship for emerging Chinese horticultural scientists to come to New Zealand. Dr Li died in 1992.

Madame
Sun Yat-sen's
Apple Pie for
Pudding

MARY ROBERTS-SCHIRATO

In the late 1970s, as a New Zealand–China exchange student in Beijing and as a relative of Rewi Alley's, I used to go into central Beijing every Sunday for lunch and an after-lunch walk with Rewi and various other family members. Sometimes a visitor would also join us, a New Zealander working in Beijing, or someone like Han Suyin visiting briefly from overseas. These lunches were resumed when I returned to teach in Beijing in the mid-1980s.

Lunch was always delicious, and nearly always completely Chinese in style, but sometimes, for pudding, there would be apple pie sent as a token of a friendship dating back to 1930s Shanghai. The apple pie came from Madame Sun Yat-sen (Song Qingling), a friend of Rewi's from those Shanghai days.

Being taken under Rewi's wing enriched my experience of living and studying in China in so many ways. It gave me an opportunity to learn about aspects of recent Chinese history in a way not available to most of my fellow students. It also offered me a comfortable family space in which to relax and take a break from dormitory life (which none of the Antipodean students had, because it was too expensive for us to fly home for a visit during the length of our scholarships, whereas some of the European students would go home in the summer). And it brought me into contact with a man who applied a thoughtful, sensitive intelligence, as well as a strong sense of self and the strength of his own capabilities, as he looked back on a long and varied life, most of it lived in China.

Rewi's older sister, Gwen, was like a grandmother to me in Wellington (my 'real', wonderful grandmother, cousin of Gwen and Rewi, lived in Nelson), and his younger brother Geoff owned a magical house and garden out in Upper Hutt, which was always exciting to explore. Being well acquainted with two of Rewi's five surviving siblings meant that I was already very familiar with the distinctive Alley style when I went to Beijing. I had met him on his previous visits to New Zealand, we had even all gone to the beach at Rabbit Island in Nelson, but from those early contacts I had really only retained a general impression of him as 'an Alley'.

It was because of Rewi that I wanted to study in China. Gwen's house was full of his books and things he had sent back from China. As a child (my family lived with Gwen at one point) I read the books, played with and asked about the history of the objects. I knew I wanted to go to China, so I started learning Chinese (although it was Cantonese) at the Chinese Anglican Mission in Wellington when I was about 10 years old.

When my dream really did come true and I was accepted for the exchange programme, Gwen wrote to Rewi to tell him 'Kay's daughter' was coming to study in China and that he was to keep an eye on me. Which he duly did.

Rewi turned 80 the year I arrived in Beijing, and, to the great excitement of the Foreign Students Office at the Peking Languages Institute and my Chinese fellow students, I was invited to his birthday party at the Great

Hall of the People, hosted by the newly rehabilitated Deng Xiaoping. My only smart shoes had three-and-a-half-inch heels (I am over six foot tall) and my Chinese fellow students laughed immoderately when they heard that I had met Deng and shaken his hand wearing those shoes. The thought of the contrast between my height and his was irresistibly funny. I'm sure Deng Xiaoping barely noticed, though he did crack a joke, in his speech at the banquet, about his height being stunted by his time spent working in a Renault factory in 1920s France.

My Sundays with Rewi followed a fairly set pattern. I would catch the two or three buses necessary to get into town, and arrive about a half-hour or so before lunch. Usually Rewi's adopted son Mike, his wife and daughter and sometimes his son would be there, and sometimes also one of the sons of Rewi's other adopted son, Alan. At times there would be other visitors or family members. On occasion Alan's work would bring him (and maybe his wife, too) from Gansu to Beijing. There would be general chit-chat and discussion of the week's events.

After lunch we would sit and chat some more, and then a car and driver from Rewi's unit would arrive outside the door and we would drive to some park for a stroll. My favourite regular venues were the Summer Palace and the Bell Temple, but over my first two years in Beijing we must have visited virtually every public park at least once, and sometimes we went to seasonal destinations such as the annual chrysanthemum displays at a former Buddhist temple. It was always a toss-up what kind of car we would get. Very occasionally it would be a Red Flag limousine, which always attracted curious glances, as 'Red Flags' were thought to be used only by high-ranking officials, and people would wonder who was seated behind the discreetly drawn curtains.

On these walks Rewi would chat and reminisce. He didn't talk much about his childhood, although like all his siblings he loved and admired his mother and thought nostalgically of the much-loved family home. He would talk a little about the war (the First World War), though not

113

often. He talked a lot about the farm at Moeawatea, in Taranaki, which he farmed with another man after the war, and quite a lot about his early days as a factory inspector in Shanghai and his later work with the Chinese Industrial Cooperatives (Indusco), which he helped found, and the Shandan Bailie School.

The stories included tales about working with Madame. 'Madame' was not Madame Sun Yat-sen, but her sister Madame Chiang Kai-shek (Song Meiling): nearly always referred to as 'Madame' by Rewi in tones of disdain. Rewi was responsible for the overall management of Indusco, which entailed far more liaison with 'Madame' than he cared for. His stories of wartime Chongqing were always fascinating, even though they often revolved around the stress of dealing with 'Madame' and the general level of KMT (Kuomintang) corruption.

Knowing Rewi, and listening to his stories of the China he had known before 1949, a China that was as ancient to me as the China of the Tang dynasty, watching and listening to his interactions with Chinese friends, and, from time to time, eating Madame Sun Yat-sen's apple pie enabled me to see another way for foreigners and Chinese to interact. The changes in the 40 years between 1937 and 1977 had created a completely different socio-political context for foreigner–Chinese interactions.

When I arrived in Beijing in September 1977, it was very difficult (although not impossible) for a foreign student and a Chinese student to be friends in more than a superficial way. Foreigners were rare and regarded with a certain degree of wariness. There was a general tendency to try to give foreigners special treatment; push them to the head of the queue, stand up and give them a seat on the bus, provide them with special food. We spent quite a lot of time trying to fend off such treatment.

Peking University women's swim team, summer 1979. Mary, the only foreign student in the team, is in the back row, fourth from right. MARY ROBERTS-SCHIRATO

There was also a certain level of suspicion of foreigners. I didn't have a camera, but sometimes when I was out with fellow foreign students who were taking photographs we would be told by members of the public that it was 'forbidden', even at tourist spots where Chinese tourists were happily taking photos.

When I was on the swim team at Peking University (Beida, for short), the team always found it hard to find a venue for winter training. Beida had no indoor swimming pool at that time; rumour said it had been filled in during the Cultural Revolution. One winter, we got permission to train at a pool on an army base. All went well until some officer happened to notice I wasn't Chinese. I was banned, and another pool had to be found so that I would be able to train with the team.

This combined attitude — that foreigners required special, fancy treatment and that they weren't entirely to be trusted — made it difficult to form close friendships with people. Even the one teacher at the Peking Languages Institute who did become something of a friend did not dare invite me to his apartment to meet his wife and daughter until I went back to Beijing in the mid-1980s when these attitudes were easing.

As well as the general socio-political atmosphere that made it hard to form close friendships, there was also the difference in background and experience. Even the least well-travelled and least worldly-wise of the New Zealand students had, through the medium of films, books, TV, radio and the press generally, a wider-ranging and more informed view of the world than our Chinese counterparts. They, on the other hand, had gone through the famine of the late 1950s and early 1960s as toddlers, the Cultural Revolution as children, and the rise and fall of the Gang of Four as teenagers. In some ways they knew much less than us; in others, much more.

I remember my Gansu-born roommate at Beida, born in the same year as me in the mid-1950s, telling me that during the famine when her mother was breastfeeding her younger sister, she was sent to stay with her grandmother in the countryside because her parents did not have enough food for her — just enough to keep her mother's milk flowing for the baby sister. Her story concluded, quite matter-of-factly: 'there were no boys in the family, so I survived'.

Shanghai in the 1920s, when Rewi arrived, was, of course, a stratified society in which most foreigners occupied a very different complex of spaces than those of most Chinese people. However, it was unregulated enough that foreigners and Chinese who were so minded could interact within the same spaces and form friendships that were less encumbered or even unaffected by the status of 'foreigner' or 'Chinese'. Rewi's stories of his days in Shanghai, and then his time travelling the country for Gung Ho,[1] gave me a view into that world where Chinese and foreigners had a wider range of overlapping experiences and knowledges of the world, and could form closer ties on a more equal footing than seemed to be possible in the late 1970s.

Since I first lived in China in the 1970s, I have been back several times, and also lived in Macau for some years in the 2010s. By this time, the constraint of a low-level suspicion of foreigners and a lack of shared knowledge and experience of the world had largely evaporated, and I found myself forming close friendships with some Chinese people in a way that reminded me of Rewi's ties with his friends from the Shanghai days. They also made me recall that apple pie that seemed to symbolise the more cross-cultural Chinese sensibilities of Rewi's China of the 1930s, which had vanished by the 1970s but were echoed in my China of this century.

---

1 'Gung Ho' refers to Chinese Industrial Cooperatives (*Gongye hezuoshe* 工业合作社), a movement Rewi Alley established to promote grassroots development.

Vic Wilcox, the People's Republic of China and the New Zealand Communist Movement

KERRY TAYLOR

In early May 1989, 'The Internationale', anthem of the world communist movement, echoed across the foothills of Auckland's Waitākere Ranges. It was being played at the funeral of Victor Wilcox, a 77-year-old immigrant from the United Kingdom. Wilcox, a lifelong communist radicalised on the gum-fields of the Far North during the 1930s, had been a paid official of the tiny Communist Party of New Zealand (CPNZ) since 1939. Indeed, during his nearly 30 years as general secretary of the party, a post he assumed in 1951, having deposed incumbent Sid Scott, he was the public face, the very personification, of New Zealand communism.

During this period, Wilcox was part of a strain of communist thinking that believed that the greatest internal risk to the CPNZ, and to world revolution, came from those like Scott, who were accused of diluting the radicalism of communism by flirting with social democracy and accepting the notion of peaceful co-existence between socialism and capitalism.

In the late 1950s, this same fissure was at the heart of the bitter struggles of the Sino–Soviet dispute. The CPNZ had been increasingly in touch with Beijing through the 1950s, and, as the decade advanced, the party was courted aggressively by both of the communist superpowers, which were now in a state of serious ideological conflict. But the acute concern within the CPNZ leadership about the perils of social democracy made them ripe for the picking by the more insurgent Chinese Communist Party (CCP). Profitable, but secret, financial arrangements and active person-to-person lobbying saw the CPNZ increasingly side with China, initially privately, but then openly.

The 1960 CPNZ conference was attended by a Chinese delegation, and by 1963 Wilcox and most senior party officials were won over to the China side of the dispute. At their annual conference in May 1963, in front of a large cluster of international delegates from fraternal communist parties, Wilcox declared that the CPNZ would take a 'firm stand against revisionism', a clear signal they had taken sides. The CPNZ was in fact the only Western communist party where the majority of the leadership, and rank-and-file membership, took the China road.

For a period, Vic Wilcox rivalled Rewi Alley as the most well-known New Zealander in the People's Republic, although few in New Zealand would recognise his face or name. His first trip to China had been in September 1959, when he had led a New Zealand delegation to attend the commemoration of the tenth anniversary of the founding of the People's Republic. The courting and hospitality on the Chinese side was very intense; aside from 1969, Wilcox was invited to visit Beijing every year between 1959 and 1971. The flight log for each trip was recorded for posterity by the New Zealand Security Intelligence Service (NZSIS) and by its equivalent across the Tasman, the Australian Security Intelligence Organisation (ASIO), as all travel to China from New Zealand was then routed though Australia.

Wilcox usually met the top party leadership on his visits, including Mao Zedong, Zhou Enlai and Deng Xiaoping. In the mid-1960s, the CPNZ, as a Western party on-message with Beijing, assumed great symbolic importance for the CCP. Thus, Wilcox, and his many colleagues who also frequently visited the People's Republic, were received as if they were global statesmen. Indeed, it has been suggested that the CPNZ in effect performed a consular role for the CCP prior to the establishment of formal diplomatic relations between New Zealand and the PRC.

An NZSIS profile from the late 1960s suggested, however, that Wilcox had let things go to his head: 'in recent years [he has] seen himself as the Mao Tse Tung [Mao Zedong] of New Zealand'. This egoism, and his increasingly acute health issues, including periodic depression, heart problems and a reliance on alcohol, saw Wilcox's star diminish over time, although this was for many years an inner-party secret. By the early 1970s, the NZSIS noted that the relationship with the CCP 'lacked the fervour and warmth of the mid 1960s'. The CPNZ's 'star was in the eclipse' as China repositioned itself internationally and the leadership of the CCP became increasingly divided.

Ideological fracturing within New Zealand Maoism saw further erosion of Wilcox's influence and leadership role. From 1968 this was manifest in an increasingly bitter conflict between the Wellington District and the Auckland-based national party leadership. In part, this was over differences in the implementation of a 'united front' policy in relation to the mobilisation against the Vietnam War and support for the emerging anti-apartheid movement, but it was also due to the perception that Wilcox and his senior colleagues were aloof and out of touch with the party on the ground.

In 1970, the whole of the Wellington District was expelled from the CPNZ. The Wellington Maoists, led by official China News Agency Xinhua correspondent Rona Bailey, and watersider Jack Manson, established themselves as an effective alternative to the CPNZ, who derided them as the 'Manson–Bailey gang'. The new group was formalised in 1976 as the Wellington Marxist–Leninist Organisation, and reframed in 1980 with the establishment of the Workers' Communist League.

Wilcox was concerned about the role played by the CCP in sustaining this breakaway group. He was also concerned that Bailey was in direct contact with Beijing through her own networks. This posed the threat of alternative views being communicated to the CCP about the situation on the ground in New Zealand. Wilcox, as the 'great leader' in New Zealand, had tried to monopolise and manage the CPNZ–CCP relationship personally.

For the first time since the late 1950s, 1972 saw no official delegation from the CPNZ visit Beijing. According to the NZSIS, this gap coincided with China's restructuring of financial support for the CPNZ, ultimately reducing the overall financial flow to it. In 1973 Wilcox, and fellow secretariat member Dick Wolf, once again made the long journey to Beijing, discussing there a wide range of issues, including foreign policy in general, and financial support for the party in particular. Wilcox also expressed at that time his frustration about the perceived lack of Chinese support in stamping out the dissident group in Wellington.

Countering the image of back-channel tensions, in September and October 1973 a group of Māori activists, led by party members Hone Tuwhare and Willie Wilson, visited China. Organised under the auspices of the CPNZ, the group also included Tame Iti, Miriama Rauhihi and Timi Te Maipi. Not for the first time, the objective was to give the impression to international partners that the CPNZ had more influence among Māori than it did in reality.

In that same year, the opening of the PRC Embassy in Wellington proved somewhat contradictory for Wilcox and the CPNZ leadership. Clearly, a trip to Wellington would be easier on all concerned than the long multi-flight journey to Beijing, and the CPNZ probably anticipated an enhancing of the relationship between the two fraternal communist parties.

In practice, it would seem it led to a further cooling of relations. NZSIS sources suggest the embassy quickly became aware that Wilcox had a tendency to 'exaggerate' both the importance and the success of the CPNZ on the ground. Further, relations between the party and the embassy were not run directly, party leader to ambassador, but rather through a designated liaison person, a process that Wilcox felt diminished his mana. The cooling can be overstated; Wilcox and the ambassador did meet in Auckland for an official 'bilateral' in 1973, and Wilcox was a frequent visitor to the embassy when in Wellington on party business. At the same time, however, a sign that the context had changed from the mid-1960s came in 1974 when Wilcox again visited Beijing, but for the first time since 1959 none of the top CCP leaders met with him.

From the mid-1970s the CPNZ was increasingly riven with personal and ideological disputes. On the table for dissection in minutiae were the relative merits of CCP policy, in its increasingly complex and contested variants, and that of the Albanian Party of Labour, increasingly seen by influential leaders in the CPNZ, such as Dick Wolf and Ron Taylor, as the true standard-bearer of the Maoist tradition. Since the late 1960s, Wilcox had been less enamoured of the Albanian path than his colleagues, which ultimately left him on the back foot within the leadership group. He had always sought to manage conflict within the party by staying at arm's length from the hurly burly of the ideological duelling. This had earlier seen him criticised by the Wellington District as being out of touch. This critique, progressively reframed as laziness, alcoholism and occasionally 'big headism', was increasingly adopted by his own colleagues on the central committee, the leader of that criticism being Dick Wolf.

Wilcox was formally censured by the secretariat in 1974 over the political work he undertook on his trip to China in 1974, a visit that was supposed to be for medical purposes only. In 1975, another storm surrounded his dealings with Ted Hill of the Communist Party of Australia (Marxist–Leninist) or CPA (M–L), the main Maoist group across the Tasman. The accusation was that Wilcox was acting individualistically, and against the wishes of the collective. Ironically, his isolation from his own colleagues brought him much closer to the Chinese Embassy in Wellington, and he was now accused by his critics of conspiring with the embassy to interfere with the internal affairs of the party. (A well-documented archive of the internal debates within the party leadership is held at the Alexander Turnbull Library.)

In March 1977 Wilcox took the step that had been inevitable for nearly a decade, standing down as the general secretary of the CPNZ. While his resignation was accepted, it was not at the time revealed to the party's own rank-and-file, although by early 1978 rumours of his departure were circulating widely. Wilcox used his international contacts in both China and Australia to bolster support, circulating articles from *Peking Review*, as well as the *Vanguard*, the paper of the CPA (M–L), the latter being highly critical of the CPNZ for its treatment of Wilcox. This brought him further censure for international factionalism.

The damaging civil war was publicly exposed in June 1978 when the CPNZ newspaper, *People's Voice*, announced with some relief, and a lot of political bile, that Wilcox was no longer a member of the CPNZ. He was criticised as a drunkard, and for being lazy, unscrupulous and unworthy of the tradition the party stood for. In short, he was, in the minds of the CPNZ leadership, an opportunist, justly exposed. Others, including Wilcox himself, saw his removal as a purge by a hard-line pro-Albania group, members of which were themselves considered by their ideological opponents as revisionists of Maoist orthodoxy.

Wilcox aligned himself with a new pre-party formation that supported the Chinese line in international debates. He became chairman of the Preparatory Committee for the Formation of the CPNZ (M–L). The

Preparatory Committee, as it was known, never became more than a small ginger group, most influential in the New Zealand China Friendship Society. Wilcox and his old comrades, Jack and Joyce Ewen and Don Ross, maintained close relations with the Chinese Embassy, and he was invited on several occasions to visit China, which he declined on the basis of his failing health.

Years of struggle took a great personal and political toll. For most of the 1980s, Wilcox was essentially inactive and literally a greying figurehead, a nod to former glory. The Preparatory Committee had by 1989 reframed itself as the Organisation for Marxist Unity, but it remained tiny. The man who had once rubbed shoulders with Mao Zedong, Zhou Enlai, Deng Xiaoping and other global figures slipped into obscurity, locally and internationally. In his last years he was more content running a small mail-order geranium business from his home in the Waitākere Ranges. Victor Wilcox died on 29 April 1989.

Learning from Dai Qing

PAULINE KEATING

Dai Qing 戴晴 was a visiting fellow at the Australian National University (ANU) in Canberra when I first met her. This was in early 1995 when she was working on her study of leftist opposition within the Chinese Communist Party. She had been imprisoned for almost a year after the crushing of the 1989 democracy movement, and was a key actor in that story. That is what most of us wanted to talk with her about.

It is fair to say that in 1989 hardly anyone in New Zealand had heard of Dai Qing. By the mid-1990s, however, most China specialists knew of her as a courageous critic of China's Party-government, and also of the dissident intellectuals (including student leaders) whom she judges had been strategically inept in April–May 1989. Geremie Barmé noted in 1992 that since beginning her career as a journalist in the early 1980s, Dai had become 'one of the most incisive critics of the rule of the Communist Party' in mainland China.

I took up a lectureship in history at Victoria University of Wellington in early 1989, and immediately began developing an honours course that was eventually titled 'China and Democracy'. I had been working as an English teacher in Beijing in 1978 when the 'April Fifth' poets of 1976 were coming in from the cold. Many of them helped to give impetus to the 'Democracy Wall' movement that had its brief moment in the sun in late 1978. The experience of living in China in the late 1970s and early 1980s,

125

when de-Maoification was in its 'liberal' and liberating phase, has had a big influence on my teaching. It shaped the approach I brought to the study of 'China and Democracy', as did the June Fourth massacre and its aftermath. The violent crackdown and cruel punishments of democracy activists rocked my naive optimism, an optimism that had survived four years of living in the PRC and is not yet burned out. Now it is a bruised and tempered optimism.

In a CCN interview with Dai Qing, screened on New Zealand television in 1992, the interviewer marvelled at the freedom Dai Qing seemed to have. Dai, in response, compared her situation in 1992 with that of 1966 when, she said, she had been a 'tool of the Party'. She insisted that 'China is changing; Chinese people are changing'. In some of the scholarship on the events of 1989, a similar optimism is found among authors who saw the massive 'people's movement' as evidence of a 'nascent civil society' in China.

Dai Qing also saw evidence in 1989 of the capacity of Chinese citizens to self-organise, but advised caution. She points out the Beijing government's strong resistance to the convening of a Women's NGO Forum in 1995; the forum was supposed to be adjunct to the United Nations' Fourth World Conference on Women in Beijing that year. Because the United Nations (UN) authorities refused to buckle, and because China had almost no legal non-governmental organisations (NGOs) at the time, the Beijing government hurriedly mandated the immediate establishment of women's NGOs all over the country. Dai Qing scornfully declared them nothing more than GONGOS (government-organised NGOs) and the UN conference 'nothing but a big show'. Hillary Clinton, a participant in the mainstream UN conference, asked to meet with Dai Qing while she was in Beijing. Dai was happy enough to co-operate with her minders in an arrangement that kept her out of the capital for the duration of the conference and away from Hillary Clinton.

As a journalist with *Guangming Ribao* 光明日报 since 1982, Dai had been gathering scientific opinion in opposition to the building of a 'mega-dam' on the Yangtze River near Yichang. While scientific opposition to the Three Gorges Dam failed to stop its construction, the anti-dam movement began Dai Qing's close collaboration with China's environmental scientists (she herself has an engineering degree). Her book *Changjiang! Changjiang!* 长江! 长江! (*Yangtze! Yangtze!*), published in Chinese in 1989, was the first of a string of books and articles about the folly of the Three Gorges project and the damage done by dam-building in general, and made calls for open and free discussion of China's deep and deepening environmental problems. In the aftermath of 1989's June Fourth tragedy, and her deep disappointment with the failure of a popular movement, Dai Qing dared to find the possibility of effective 'people power' in the environmental movement that was beginning to emerge.

The 1989 crisis had made the Beijing government more than ever nervous of 'social organisations' and their potential as seedbeds of organised opposition. In the view of many commentators, however, environmental NGOs have a better chance of retaining some autonomy because their goals so obviously align with state goals. China's environmental degradation was dire by the late twentieth century. The damage done by human exploitation of the natural world over thousands of years, combined with the accelerated industrialisation of the reform era, had pushed the country's environmental problem to a tipping point. An environmental catastrophe could undermine the 'Chinese miracle' and, therefore, the Party-government's hold on power.

China's leaders have come to recognise this, but back in the 1990s economic growth was unassailably their top priority. The severity of environmental breakdown and the lack of concerted government action resulted in local people taking matters into their own hands and organising collective action to prevent and repair environmental damage. This helps explain the emergence and survival of the relatively large number of environmental NGOs in the two decades following the 1989 crisis.

Friends of Nature 自然之友, founded in 1994 by Liang Congjie 梁从诫, is said to be the first legal environmental NGO in China. Liang, a professor of history at Peking University, was the grandson of Liang Qichao 梁启超, one of China's most important reformers at the turn of the century. Liang Congjie, therefore, brought great respectability and kudos to China's infant environmental movement. I am sure that Dai Qing understood this when she joined other green activists in persuading Liang to organise and lead Friends of Nature. Dai had probably begun her environmental activism before Liang Congjie. After her arrest and imprisonment in 1989, however, she knew very well that any attempt she made to establish an NGO would give it the kiss of death. She has never attempted to organise or join an NGO in China. She has, however, myriad friends, supporters and followers in China's environmental NGO movement throughout China. She provides great moral support to the movement, and is generous with the advice and networking that she does.

Dai Qing made several visits to New Zealand and Australia during the 1990s and 2000s, and readily accepted invitations to speak at public meetings. She was interviewed by Kim Hill on Radio New Zealand in 1997, was a keynote speaker at the NZASIA Conference at Massey University in 2001, and at Chinese Studies Association of Australia conferences in Sydney and Melbourne. In Canberra in 2007, she delivered the sixty-eighth annual Morrison Lecture on a topic related to her 'historical investigations' (specifically, on the philosopher and activist Zhang Dongxun 张东荪).

Usually her speaking topics related to the Three Gorges Dam, China's environmental crises, and the brave people who were trying to do something about the crises. I think it was during her first visit to Wellington, in 1997, that she spoke to a packed audience in Victoria University's Memorial Theatre about the damage that the damming of the Yangtze River was doing, and the continuing opposition to the dam during and after its construction (it was completed in 1998). At the end of the lecture, a member of the audience grabbed a bucket and tried to run up and down the aisles calling for donations to support China's anti-dam activists. Dai had to earnestly insist that she could not accept money.

I usually spent time with Dai Qing during my visits to Beijing, and was impressed with the intense purposefulness of her life there. She has not had regular paid employment since she lost her job at *Guangming Ribao* in 1989, but she has never stopped being busy and productive. She sees her primary occupation as an investigative journalist who is committed to democratic openness and human rights. Like most good writers, she has a love of writing, and her best chance of unbroken writing time was at the Little Mountain Hut for Interrogating History (问史小山房) she and her husband Wang Dejia had built in the Western Hills, at Guanjiantai (观涧台), to accommodate fellow conservationists and other lovers of nature.

Dai has not been able to publish in China since 1989, but that has helped ensure an even larger international readership than she might otherwise have had. Since the 1980s, Probe International, a Canadian 'environmental advocacy group', has published English translations of Dai's major books, and its website carries or provides links to articles, commentaries and transcripts of oral history interviews that have been penned by Dai over the past 20 years and more. It has dedicated a web page to Dai's latest publication, a booklet in Penguin's 'Green Ideas' series: *The Most Dammed Country in the World* (2021).

The house in the Western Hills was built on a hillside in a district zoned for reforestation and for eventual development as a tourist site. A requirement that residents plant trees on the hillsides was tied to the lease. I got to do some tree-planting with a group of American college students in 2004. Their professor was a good friend of Dai Qing's, and Dai had arranged with local authorities for bundles of saplings to be made available to the foreign friends for planting. It was a lovely early-spring day, and we tackled our task with gusto. When the planting was finished, we walked down the hill to a reception room where we met the district's Party secretary, had tea and biscuits and were all given certificates. Each had our names, the number of saplings we had planted, and a thank-you for our contribution to making the Western Hills green again. Dai wrote to me a few months later to tell me that a farmer at the bottom of the hill had let his goats roam up the hill, and they had eaten most of our saplings.

During a 2008 visit to Beijing, Dai Qing arranged for me to attend a weekend 'environmental fair' held at the Green Cow Organic Farm in outer Beijing. The farm is now linked with the CSA (Community Sustained Agriculture) movement, but that connection probably did not exist in 2008. On the day of my visit to the farm, local environmental NGOs had set up stalls inside and outside what looked like a local meeting room; pictoral displays explained who they were and what they did. The variety of initiatives on display was remarkable, particularly because China's environmental NGO movement was barely 10 years old at the time.

I was startled and delighted by the stall set up by a cycling NGO. I was startled because my bike had been as necessary to me as food and shelter when I had lived in Beijing in the 1970s, not part of an 'alternative lifestyle' but very much the norm at the time. I was delighted because I had spent enough time in smog-bound, car-jammed Beijing to appreciate the urgent need to develop alternatives to the city's millions of fossil-fuel-burning cars.

Dai Qing introduced me to a new 'people's movement' in post-1989 China. From the very beginning, this movement has been hamstrung

Dai Qing and Pauline Keating in a reforestation zone of the Western Hills, 2004.
PAULINE KEATING

by the multiple rules and regulations designed to stifle the autonomy of NGOs. International NGOs (INGOs), in particular, are closely watched and tightly constrained, even more so today. But the point that Dai Qing made in the early 1990s remains valid. The Beijing government urgently needs not just the obedient co-operation of citizens in environmental repair and reconstruction, but also the environmental activism that is a consequence of the freedom to speak out and to self-organise. The building of an 'ecological-civilisation' (a goal written into the PRC Constitution in 2018) cannot be achieved without the vision and commitment of people like Dai Qing and the environmental activists I met in Beijing. Their patriotism is not the plastic patriotism prescribed by the Party, but a patriotism rooted in a cherishing of the 'good earth' that has nourished and sustained one of the world's great civilisations for thousands of years.

I used this argument to frame a third-year environmental history of China course that I introduced into the history programme at Victoria in 2009. I called the course 'Wild China, People's China: An Environmental History of China from the 1000s BCE to the Present'. I've learned such a lot from Dai Qing, and a lot of what I've learned helped to shape and inform that course. I have always hoped that it would be a worthy contribution to Dai's legacy.

Poets in Exile: Yang Lian and Gu Cheng in Auckland

HILARY CHUNG

For a number of years from the late 1980s to the early 1990s, Auckland was home to two noted young Chinese poets, Yang Lian 楊煉 (b. 1955) and Gu Cheng 顧城 (1956–1993), both of whom were to become New Zealand citizens. Important members of the 'Misty' (*menglong* 朦朧) or *Today* (*Jintian* 今天) group of poets, they took exile in New Zealand after the June 1989 Massacre. Yang Lian lived in a ramshackle house on Grafton Road, and Gu Cheng on Waiheke Island, where he was later to take his own life, having murdered his wife, the poet Xie Ye 謝燁 (1958–1993). The extracts below are from Hilary Chung's essays about these poets, 'Wintering in Auckland: Yang Lian's Winter Garden and Sea of Dead Lambs' and 'Ghosts in the City: The Auckland Exile of Yang Lian and Gu Cheng,' in *ka mate ka ora: a new zealand journal of poetry and poetics*, Issue 2 (July 2006) and Issue 11 (March 2012), respectively.

New Zealand was both the place of multiple dislocations in Yang Lian's life and the central point of orientation within that dislocation. His New Zealand poetry is at once specifically located in Auckland or other New Zealand landscapes and abstractly dislocated from them. In his exploration of the complexities of location and identity, he reformulates and updates the paradise/slaughterhouse dichotomy which Patrick Evans traces in New Zealand fiction in his article 'Paradise or Slaughterhouse: Some aspects of New Zealand proletarian fiction', *Islands*, 8(1) (1980), 71–85, whereby the colonial vision of New Zealand as a garden paradise (rearticulated today as '100% Pure' or Middle Earth) is variously transformed and disfigured. For Evans, the slaughterhouse (or meat works in its modern manifestation), which is the other side of the pastoral idyll, symbolises the repressed violence in New Zealand society in the work of writers from George Chamier to Ronald Hugh Morrieson or David Ballantyne. Yang's evocation of agricultural carnage and his transmogrified gardens extend these explorations of cultural dislocation, which are figured by class and the effects of colonisation, to the defamiliarising impasse of exile. In each case the subversion of the impossible idyll arises from observations of the normative realities of New Zealand life which contradict a specific set of cultural expectations, be they Chinese or (post)colonial. As such, Yang Lian's poems offer a complex of mutually informing resonances and perhaps ironically find for themselves a place within an enduring New Zealand tradition of displacement.

The ghost motif is deeply embedded in both the poetry and the prose written by Yang Lian during his exile in Auckland. As a central facet of his exilic poetics it is predicated on the contemplation of the trauma of exile as a version of death, where existence can only continue in a state of utter alienation. In this state every aspect of the unfamiliar exile environment not only has to be confronted, but this external confrontation also becomes the catalyst for the most intense interior confrontation of every aspect of his function and existence as a poet. By contrast, Gu Cheng's poetic contemplation of ghosts relates to a state of mind and existence which kept the world at a distance both before and after physical exile in New Zealand. Indeed, in its benign incarnation, removed from almost all worldly intercourse on Waiheke Island, exile meant rebirth and fulfilment in an embrace of the natural environment of the island. While in Auckland Yang Lian wrote 'everywhere is a foreign land / in death there is no home to go back to', in Berlin, doubly exiled, Gu Cheng wrote of Waiheke Island 'That is my home, where my life belongs, the place I love.' Unlike Yang Lian's motif which relies on the total alienation of the ghostly from the mortal world, Gu Cheng's tragedy lay in the necessary mingling of these worlds whereby ghosts enter the city. His poem 'Ghosts enter the city' presents the desperate hope that even if the ghost does 'slip and fall' he might continue to swim in an intermediate state between life and death. Tragically, in the end, the ghosts of his psychosis took possession of the city of his inner self, making Yang Lian's poetic vision an epitaph for his friend's exile.

Hong Kong Revisited

JOHN NEEDHAM

The bus stops at the university's original centre, and the setting for one of PK's poems, 'An Old Colonial Building'.[1] On its steep, cramped slope, the university, like the city at large, is in a state of continual demolition and construction, and the poem opens with scaffolding, noise and dust. But as I get off the bus it's already Saturday afternoon; the rock-drills are silent, the dust has settled, and the place feels quite deserted.

A handsome three-storeyed structure of red brick and cream stucco, its tiled and lofty corridors are separated only by balustrades from the inner courtyard with its palm-trees and fishpond. The pond is the poem's main image. Its surface reflects the building's tower so clearly that the goldfish, 'swirling orange and white, their gills opening and leeching', seem to be swimming in and out of a round window in the cupola. And PK sees this water 'riddled with patterns of moving signs' as a symbol of ambivalence.

I walk around the first-floor corridor, peering over the balustrade, until I can see the same image. It's just as the poem says. But my own impression is one of density rather than uncertainty. The reflected cupola simply adds to the visual interest, as I wonder whether to report my impression to PK.

---

1 PK is the Hong Kong poet and essayist Leung Ping-kwan (梁秉鈞 1949–2013), who sometimes wrote under the name Ye Si 也斯.

As I continue my way up flights of steps, across courtyards, and through further buildings, towards my hostel at the top of the campus, I stop for a moment outside the library, where a student is standing guard over a cardboard architectural model. This, I assume, is connected with a poster on the library door advertising a lecture-series called 'Hong Kong: City of Vision'. But in fact, he tells me, it's a plan for the development of Chang'an Avenue, the main thoroughfare of Beijing. He's evidently just taking the model somewhere and has paused to rest.

I look at his space-age construct, all white and gleaming, with its dynamic unity of flowing and soaring lines; and I think of Chang'an as it actually is, the long, dusty straggle of old and new and half-finished buildings, in every style from Ming to post-modern. The discrepancy between the actuality and the student's idea is very gross, but what strikes me now is that PK's *City at the End of Time* is built on a simple reversal of it. 'An Old Colonial Building', for instance, rejects the city centre's 'tall buildings of chrome and glass' in favour of the ambiguous, marginal pond. A variant of the metaphor occurs in 'The Leaf at the Edge', where the 'beauties at the centre' of the pond, the lilies, are rejected in favour of the 'under water', where 'roots grow together, new leaves furl in the heart'. And this contrast between a showy but sterile centre and obscure but fruitful margins, the real 'heart', pervades the whole book.

The steps end in a courtyard next to the dining room, and I see that I'm in time for the lag-end of lunch. The place is almost empty, and I take a seat by the window, for the view. The hillside, dropping all the way down to the waterfront, is studded with tall, slender apartment blocks. The constraints of terrain and population have given them all a certain regularity of height, mass and distribution, and they have an oddly natural look, like great groves of buildings. Beyond them the sea carries its usual traffic, a string of long black barges behind a tug; two slim grey warships, like toys; cargo-boats moored on the open water, each with its attendant cluster of junks and sampans. Beyond that again, the blue hills of Lantau stretch away across the Pearl River estuary towards Macau. But the big downtown office-blocks are obscured by a building just below the hostel; the view seems without a centre. And how naturally the eye seeks one.

The traveller, as the plane descends, looks down past the quivering wing-tip, towards the assembly of gleaming cubes that signifies 'city'. If you approach at night, of course, the whole place seems like a centre, a glittering field of light in the void; but soon you're homing in on a brighter core; and after the plane has run the gauntlet of the Kai Tak tenement blocks, great honeycombs of light so close to the plane that you can see people cooking in their kitchens, it's disappointing to be taxi-ing back along the dark nowhere of the runway, with its dim lights and dark shapes of hangars. But of course you quickly look towards your next centre, the concourse, the hotel, the people you'll be meeting.

Fortyish, of compact build, wearing an open-necked shirt and grey slacks, and carrying a supermarket bag, he isn't at all the sort of *outré* figure I'm half-expecting, but his air of looking for someone he doesn't know suggests that it's the poet; and when he sees me in turn, his affable, unremarkable face reflects a similar sequence of thoughts. In a moment we've met, and this abrupt resolution of our slight uncertainties gets us off to a friendly start. He soon suggests that we go downtown to a bar called (it really is) The Fringe Club.

Despite the name it's in the central district, and as we enter I am vaguely prepared for 'bohemian' manifestations, but my expectations are met in an unexpected way. The place is oddly shaped and on several levels, as though randomly formed by the edges of other structures, an impression strengthened by the raw concrete walls, exposed wiring, and by the tables and chairs, which, though uniformly bleak and unlovely, come evidently from a variety of sources. But the suggestion of a bare and improvised existence is rather negated by the well-appointed bar, with its prompt, polite bartender, and by the clientele, who are mostly male, sitting talking in pairs and small groups, and looking as comfortably conventional as PK and myself.

All this soon prompts me, when we're settled over our beer, to raise directly the question of centres and margins. Surely, I say, after reporting my impression of the fishpond, we all of us belong to a number of centres, or 'circles', to use the more common word. A home circle, a work circle, a sporting circle, and so on. And we're outsiders with respect to many others.

PK readily agrees, but remarks that in China, for instance, there is a sense of a national centre, which Hong Kong lacks. In part he's clearly thinking of the 'takeover', but I suspect he has literature in mind as well as politics. To the mainland Chinese literati, 'Hong Kong poetry' is a phrase with the same oxymoronic resonance that 'Australian poetry' still has in some English ears. As things stand now, Hong Kong is a distinct entity, with a unique post-colonial profile and its own niche in the international news. Its poetic pond is very small, but, as the book in my pocket confirms, PK at least gets enough oxygen of public attention to keep him swimming. He is bound to feel nervous of being swamped when Hong Kong goes back into the great sea of China.

The relations between PK and his society are evidently various. He has a job at the university, his poems get published; and at six o'clock (he tells me) he has to go to visit his mother; the plastic supermarket bag, laid carefully on the table beside his beer, contains his gift of food for her, I'm sure. Described like this, his social profile suddenly reminds me of Philip Larkin, though he shows no signs of Larkin's morbid, maudlin propensity to blame his parents for 'fucking him up'. The Chinese family system, of course, does have its darker side; in the 1960s many of my students were anxious to escape and become 'Western individualists', but PK seems rather a witness to its virtues. A Chinese 'clan' includes not only female and male, old and young, clever and dull, nice and nasty, but also, as a rule, both rich and poor. And this keeps them all aware of both human variety and identity (for they are all undeniably 'family'), of the individual and the universal, the two vital human elements ignored by the sociologising cultural critics.

But I'm still not quite happy with the gap between PK and myself. It seems one of those odd Forsterian junctures, when everything feels propitious to a moment of real human contact, but nothing happens; some element is lacking; 'the universe doesn't want it', Forster would have said, which here may simply mean that beer in the afternoon sits uneasily on my stomach. PK himself looks content enough, and perhaps he is. Forster, I recall, was also wont to feel that 'the East' tends to mistake social form for authentic meeting — the quotidian reality for the rare ideal. But his own conception of the authentic as something rare and evanescent seems in turn peculiarly Western, a product of the urge to nail reality to an instant. The Chinese are more inclined to see the truly human as a formal creation, and one that takes a good deal of time.

I must try to be more Chinese; I start talking to PK about Hong Kong in the 1960s, when Repulse Bay, now a mini-city, was just a quiet hotel and an avenue of flame-trees running down to a beach, and when Giancarlo and his band played 'The Twist' every night in the Blue Heaven, which must, I remark, have been virtually on the spot where we're sitting now. PK was still a schoolboy then, but he recalls the period with enthusiasm, endowing it with the mythic quality that we give to the era of our childhood. He dwells with particular affection on the old Lee Theatre, where he evidently spent far too much of his time, and acquired his passion for the cinema. One of my wife's maternal uncles, I tell him triumphantly, used to own it; and I'm pleased to sense that this gives me a touch of mythic status in his eyes. He is, in short, being very gracious, and we both know of course that this is all a nostalgia game; no communication of souls, but nonetheless an enjoyable enough encounter of self and other.

And a casual encounter; it's not likely that we'll meet again. But still we are busy weaving each other into the patterns of our experience. PK is now connected with my memories of Hong Kong, the Blue Heaven, Repulse Bay, the Lee Theatre. And our meeting in the first place isn't entirely random. I have a long interest both in poetry and in this particular city; and that a British scholarship boy of the 1950s should go to work in Hong Kong, marry a local scholarship girl, and revisit the place from time to time, falls into a number of quite obvious larger patterns, including some of the humble kind beloved by Samuel Smiles. There are, of course, chance elements. The last time I saw my old student, it happened that *City at the End of Time* had just come out, so he gave me a copy. Had I visited him at another time, I might never have seen the book nor, consequently, PK himself.

At length we say our farewells, and PK makes for a taxi rank across the road, where a huge office block, designed with a slight bulge in the concrete at every floor, seems to be muscling its way up into the smoky light of the zenith. Down here in the streets the neon and the traffic are growing more insistent. Night-town awakens. But for my wife and myself, it's home to mother. And tomorrow we return to New Zealand. Our son and daughter are flying in from China and we're travelling on together.

A New Kiwi Chinese Celebrates 50 Years of Relations

BO LI

Time passes by as days roll one into another. I've been living in New Zealand for 25 years. New Zealand is without a doubt my home. When I recall the past as I talk to my schoolmates, friends and relatives in China, no one believes I have been living in this country down under for so long.

I'm from Beijing. There, I had my own business. Although it was small, it was running well, and my wife was working in a stable job for the local government, receiving a good income. I had a three-bedroom apartment without a mortgage. I was living a comfortable life. Every immigrant has their reasons to migrate to a new country. I'm the same. My excuse is that New Zealand was a better place for my daughter's education, with less pressure. But actually, I just wanted to change my lifestyle to a new environment and to start over again by facing a new challenge.

The very first day we arrived in Auckland, we stayed in a motel. The next day, I tried to find a house to rent. I'd been told it's $270 per week. That was a shock. We pay rent in China as a monthly payment, and I had never heard of rent on a weekly basis. There was insufficient information in those days, and we knew nobody in New Zealand. You can imagine what it was like. I still remember the embarrassing situation. The three of us finally settled in with three suitcases of luggage. We soon found a school nearby, and my wife and I walked to school with our daughter and our new life began.

Before I found a job, I studied English in a class held in a church. Kiwis are friendly. People offered all sorts of help that we needed as new arrivals. I remember a particular conversation that I had one day. A man came and asked me where I came from. When he learned I'm from China, he surprisingly said, 'Are you starving there? China is a Third-World country, right?' I could see he was serious, but I didn't know how to answer him. I asked if he had ever been to China, but he hadn't. I looked around, and it seemed that others expected me to answer. I felt they might have similar questions. I said nothing because some places in China may be very poor, but I didn't know.

Finding a job took me nearly 12 months, simply because I didn't have work experience in New Zealand. I tried to start my own business, but my poor English didn't leave me a chance. After great effort, the advantage of my work and business experience in China was finally considered, and I was employed by a Kiwi branding company as its production manager. Those years were a great time for my family. I didn't feel any pressure and we decided to settle in New Zealand long-term.

One day, an English language school moved into our company building. Many young Chinese students turned up and were speaking Chinese. I noticed more and more Asian faces walking on Queen Street and I realised something was happening. The new international-student era had come. Then in 2001 a new business direction emerged for me. In 2002 I joined a graphic design company as its partner and executive director. I had travelled full circle and come back to running my own business again. This business worked on behalf of New Zealand businesses to target

Bo Li with the New Zealand postage stamps that he designed for the Chinese Lunar New Year in 2019. BO LI

the Asian market in New Zealand and promote products and services. The Asian population was growing fast, and every business wanted a share of this market.

I was also deeply involved in politics, becoming the first mainland Chinese immigrant candidate to stand for the general election (in 2002). This was a significant event and a landmark for the local Chinese community and mainstream politics. Since then, Chinese have been an important part of the New Zealand political scene. In 2008, I was invited as a member of the New Zealand Free Trade delegation to witness the signing ceremony of the New Zealand–China Free Trade Agreement in Beijing. This was a highlight of the trade negotiations between these two countries. I got to see China rising at full speed. Beijing had changed so dramatically that even I, someone from that city, would easily get lost.

Asiaworks Ltd was established in 2010. As the managing director, I focused the business on the New Zealand Asian community and invested in a joint-venture Chinese business in New Zealand. There is a need for China businesses to step into the New Zealand market as China is getting stronger in business. I also joined the New Zealand China Trade Association (NZCTA) as a committee member and as the chair of the subcommittee on Chinese business (members), to help improve communication on trade business issues and on consulting to New Zealand small businesses on how to trade with China.

As a Chinese person living in New Zealand, I actively promote the Chinese culture. With my graphic design ability, I have worked with New Zealand Post over the past 10 years as the art director designing the Chinese Lunar New Year stamps. I was the first person to release Chinese films in New Zealand cinemas as a commercial operation. I joined the Auckland

Chinese Community Centre as a committee member, and I have linked new Chinese migrants with local Chinese to run the annual Chinese New Year Festival Market Day in Auckland and the Lantern Festival.

The journey of joining the New Zealand community has not been without the occasional bumps in the road, however. For example, Asiaworks had a business car, but as 'Asiaworks' can't fit on a personalised plate, we instead had the plate 'Asia01'. A few years ago, when I visited an open home house viewing and parked my car on the road, I heard other visitors whisper 'Rich Chinese' and walk away. I'm not rich. I struggled to help my daughter buy her house when she got married. I'm an ordinary person like other Kiwis. I can't fly just as Kiwis don't. But as time has gone by, people have changed their view of Chinese in New Zealand. This is in part a reflection of the fact that as China is becoming stronger, the Chinese are getting richer. Perhaps that is seen as more of a threat than the earlier stereotype of the impoverished Chinese. Perhaps it also indicates a need for communities to get to know each other better.

This year New Zealand and China celebrate the fiftieth anniversary of their diplomatic relationship. As a New Zealand Chinese, I hope the two countries keep the good relationship and keep moving forward. New Zealand needs a large market, and China needs a friendly Western country.

Where Shi Le
Used to Hunt

MICHAEL RADICH

For a moment, the thought of mortality was atypically present, but the moment was banal, even sordid, limned with no light of epiphany. We were on a motorway somewhere between Beijing and Xiangyang city in Hubei. As I remember it, we were hemmed in on all sides by fabulously long double-decker car transporters, each carrying a couple of dozen cars. Nobody was going slow. Our Merc was supposed to take about eight hours at legal speeds to get to our destination, but in the end we made the trip in less than six. The car transporters were making the same cracking pace, and their laden, extended tails flicked and whipped with the strain. As part of the blithe and carefree conversation that one naturally conducts under such circumstances, my companions, a monk and his borrowed driver, told me that such trucks were so dangerous that they were about to be outlawed.

It was March 2017. I was back in the PRC for the second time since three life-changing years, as a New Zealand exchange student and then teaching, had come to an end in 1992. But the brief trip back in 1999 hardly counted, so it was more or less 20 years, going on 30. Small wonder that I barely knew the place. I found myself living a weird, mild echo of the much more profound shock of encounter with so-called 'reality' that I'd experienced when I'd first arrived, six months after Tiananmen, in December 1989: *This is China?*

I was in that Merc because my travel arrangements had been stuffed up. Someone had changed the dates for the conference I was heading to, and hadn't told me until it was too late to change my flights. Once I arrived at the conference in Xiangyang, I would have to, very awkwardly, park my suitcase off to the side of the podium, give my presentation, and then scurry away, jumping back in the car without even hearing my co-panellists, to repeat that hair-raising ride in reverse back to Beijing.

It was initially a silver lining to spend time with my white-knight monk. I had wanted to meet him since 2004, in the run-up to my PhD dissertation, when he was one of a handful of people worldwide working on the same topic as me. In the end, though, I was left with a sour taste in my mouth. Shortly after I met him a storm broke in the teacup of our field: one of my idols, a senior Japanese scholar, included a note in his new book to the effect that the monk had plagiarised his work. The Japanese doyen had wrestled with the question of what to do. But word went around that the monk's plagiarism was habitual, and his victims were more typically younger scholars in China, with next to no recourse. The Japanese man I call *sensei* was persuaded that he had a duty to expose the malpractice on behalf of others, because his position made it safe for him to do so. The cheating monk, however, was high up, and I doubt the episode made any dent in his career trajectory.

On our way to the conference, we pulled in off the motorway to a rest stop. (My idiotic inner scriptwriter, for all that I knew better, was stuck in the China of 1992 and could not stop exclaiming at the changes wrought in the intervening years: A motorway! A rest area!) The place was cavernous, and clean and tidy, if rather plain and functional. The food was surprisingly good (although who knows what was the benchmark for my surprise).

Unless my memory tricks me, the rest stop was actually called Dazhai 大寨. This village was the much-promoted Maoist model for agricultural development in the 1960s and 1970s. In any case, in the middle distance, across the motorway or perhaps a vast carpark, part of the erstwhile model village could be seen, straggling unglamorously down a hillside. The sight of it was anticlimactic, another misfired epiphany, perhaps. Later, after I got back to New Zealand, Duncan Campbell told me the tale of his own visit as a New Zealand exchange student, in the twilight of both Mao and Dazhai's glory. Ironically, as Duncan told it, that visit was one of the key moments when the Potemkin façade began to slip.

A few days before, I had made a pilgrimage of my own, my first visit to Fangshan 房山 in the mountainous outskirts of Beijing. There was no disillusion to match Duncan's Dazhai visit, but disappointment for me all the same. The point of the visit was to see the astonishing corpus of Buddhist *sūtras* there, at Cloud-Dwelling Cloister 雲居寺: a good crack at a complete canon carved in stone, mostly between the seventh and thirteenth centuries, then buried in the ground, and disinterred the 1950s.

Since leaving China at the end of 1992, I had become a scholar of medieval Chinese Buddhism ('medieval' is a fighting word in some quarters, so I'll specify: mainly third to sixth centuries). I had an introduction from a well-connected and well-meaning friend, the same man whose organisational acumen later had me scuttling away from my own presentation. The main effect achieved by this entrée, though, was that I spent some of my precious time on-site sitting in a gleaming reception room, taking a polite tea with a director, and contemplating a vase of flowers on a glass tabletop. My host's line of conversation clearly assumed I didn't know the first thing.

I was then released to wander the site alone. Like any other tourist, I saw the actual stones, and the texts they bear, through glass so thick it could well have been bulletproof. (This modern engineer's vision of a bunker for the apocalypse is fitting enough: the founder of the site, Jingwan 靜琬 (d. 639), is thought to have feared the coming endtimes 末法, and started the project to preserve the Dharma against its foretold destruction.) Another big letdown was not being able to see the centrepiece of the site, Thunderclap Cave

雷音洞, the initial cave in Jingwan's design, featuring central pillars and stone slabs with engraved texts set into the walls. It remained closed to me, as to everyone else, and I have not seen it to this day.

At another point on our hell-for-leather drive to Hubei, the monk and I hurtled past a turnoff to Handan 邯鄲. My mind returned the standard association, the sarcastic four-character phrase (*chengyu*) 'aping the Handan gait' 邯鄲學步, from my Classical Chinese lessons at Fudan University in Shanghai years before; the people of Handan have the trendiest way of walking. Some hapless fool tries to mimic their style and fails, and the upshot is, he cannot do the Handan walk, but forgets how to walk properly like himself.

I toyed with the idea that these moments were trying to rise to symbolic status. Perhaps Handan is the story of my life. Perhaps it is the fate of Western Sinology as a whole, or at least a danger it is heir to. Perhaps, equally, it is a figure for the path trodden by China in the modern world. But then, it might just be the way all cultures go, forever between one thing and another, so that authenticity or essence is all Dazhai: theatre and masks.

My deep and meaningful musings foundered fast on the facts. After all, I wasn't walking, I was sitting in a Merc racing juggernauts southwards. And we never made it to Handan at all. The subject of our conference was the fourth-century Buddhist monk Faxian 法顯 (?–418/423?), and was held in his birthplace, Xiangyang 襄陽, though we might be forgiven for thinking that Faxian himself couldn't get fast enough or far enough out of the place (like me out of Dargaville, perhaps). Faxian is famous — outside China, still insufficiently so — for one of the most remarkable journeys that history has recorded. He left China around 399 or 400 and travelled west through the Tarim Basin to Gandhāra, through 'India' (mainly the Gangetic plain), and on to Sri Lanka and home via a Southeast Asian maritime route. He finally arrived back in China a dozen years later, the first person we know of who made it from China to India and back.

Sixteen hundred years later, Faxian is still one of Xiangyang's main claims to fame. Given that Faxian was a local point of pride, it crossed my mind that my message might be unwelcome: I was arguing that one of 'his' texts is not really his. But I might as well not have worried. The mayor, for instance, came at one point to press the flesh, and have a photo-op with the international scholarly crowd. However, he did not try to conceal his lack of interest in us or what we were doing in his city.

Shortly beforehand, it transpired, a bursting property bubble had left Xiangyang high and dry. This city was full of windowless concrete husks of abandoned high-rises, like coral exposed by a freak low tide. I was looking out on that bleak prospect, from a swanky lounge in our spookily flash hotel, when a fellow conference-goer remarked that Shi Le 石勒 (274–333) had liked to hunt in the hills on the horizon. Shi Le and his son Shi Hu 石虎 (295–349), the rulers of the Later Zhao 後趙, are most famous for spectacular cruelty. According to a dodgy factoid that stuck with me from class, they may have had red hair and blue eyes. In my world, their main significance is that they patronised a miracle-working monk from the Western Regions, Fotudeng 佛圖澄 (d. 348), and also his disciple, the great bibliographer and commentator Dao'an 道安 (312–385). This short chain brings us back to the time of Faxian himself.

For some reason I couldn't quite put my finger on, I found strangely meaningful the idea that that bloodthirsty 'barbarian' hunted in those hills. It was the only moment on that trip when I felt much connection with the pasts I study. In the present, all I could see was that dystopian forest of dead buildings. They looked like an outsized parody of the stone slabs of Fangshan: steles of an unlettered colossus.

At the time, I interpreted most of that trip flippantly, in the key of farce.

Looking back now, I think it can be viewed as a small prism, refracting larger patterns. My adult life — since Duncan changed its course by suggesting that I apply for a China scholarship — has been dominated by one thing or another called 'China', and trying to figure out what that might mean. That 2017 refresher dose of culture shock on the way to Xiangyang, small enough to be aesthetic rather than traumatic, captured in miniature many old themes: the fascination not only with things 'Chinese', but what closer scrutiny shows not to be 'Chinese' at all; truth and deception, ideals and disillusionment; politics and the quest for knowledge; the struggle between past and present; feats and failures of communication; the looming doom of the apocalypse as an ironic fixture through long sweeps of history; and the quest for something remote and other, and the subsequent quest to see yourself in what you find. I have long been unsure that I believe in anything called 'China', but I am grateful, all the same, for a life spent grappling with many things travelling under that name.

Lost in Shanghai

ALISON WONG

We haven't had a chance to unpack our bags when Jervey announces that he's going to the house where Mao Zedong and comrades founded the Communist Party. It's now a museum. Any takers?

Do you know how to get there? I ask. I haven't had time to consult any Shanghai city guides or English–Chinese dictionaries. I don't have a map or smartphone. And I was so busy before leaving home that I didn't manage to brush up on my Mandarin.

Jervey is the only other native English speaker on the Shanghai International Writers' Program. It's 2014 and I'm the inaugural New Zealand writer, here in Shanghai for the full calendar months of September and October. I rather like the irony of the two of us representing the English-speaking world. I'm a fourth-generation Cantonese New Zealander now living in Australia. I grew up speaking only English, but learned some Mandarin 20, 30 years ago. Not very well. Jervey is African-American. He's been to China before. Not long ago. His wife back in the United States is China-born-and-raised, a graduate of Shanghai's Fudan University.

No problem, Jervey tells me. His wife has told him the metro lines to take, where to get off; he has the confidence of an old China hand.

We all follow Jervey.

Except when we get off the train at the recommended stop there are no arrows pointing to the exit for the famous birthplace of the Party, and when we get out onto the street there are no blue signs with white lettering telling us where to go. We are in the middle of . . . somewhere. It is suspiciously undeveloped. More like the Shanghai I remember from 20 years ago than the area near Zhongshan Park where we are staying.

Jervey gets out his iPhone but Google Maps isn't working. And then I realise Jervey doesn't know any Chinese. Nothing. Except perhaps *ni hao* ('hello') and *xiexie* ('thank you'). He shrugs. He's never needed to bother; he's always followed his wife.

Have I told you I can lose myself anywhere? The day before, my first morning in Shanghai, I woke hungry, and, with no food in the apartment, somehow managed to find my way around the corner to the Cloud Nine shopping mall where we'd had dinner upon arrival. Too low in blood sugar to search nine floors for a good breakfast or to find and read a Chinese mall directory let alone a menu, I walked into KFC, looked at the colour photos and ordered a combo of rice congee and pan-fried turnip cake, the most I'd spend on breakfast the whole of the residency.

But then I had a problem. Which entry/exit in this huge complex had I come through? Onto which street? Where did I cross the road? What did my apartment block look like among the myriad high-rise apartment blocks? The building had a memorable name, Modern Universe International Business Building (literal translation: New Time-Space International Business Building), though at the time I hadn't managed to read and memorise the Chinese characters. Even having a business card with the address didn't seem to help. People looked at me blankly, pointed vaguely, told me it was somewhere around here, over there, they didn't know. I knew the apartment was only a few minutes' walk. But where? It must have taken me three-quarters of an hour going back and forth, around and around.

Okay, so I raise my blood pressure trying to find my way even in a small city like Geelong, where I've lived for years. A minor hiccup. Now, as the only person in this ragtag group of writers who once upon a time knew some rudimentary Chinese, it's all down to me.

I know this museum has a name, but haven't a clue what it is. I know I used to know how to say 'Communist Party' in Chinese, but I haven't had much use for the words, for any Chinese words, in 20 years. When I was last in Shanghai. Now, I feel like Pooh Bear tapping his slow brain.

Think think think.

The only vaguely relevant words I can dredge from the sludge at the bottom of my brain are: *Mao Zhuxi wansui* ('Chairman Mao ten thousand years' — usually translated as 'Long live Chairman Mao').

Think think think.

With the others following, with plenty of gesticulation, I approach a bemused passer-by. *Mao Zhuxi kaishi?* ('Chairman Mao began?') I ask with a mix of hopefulness and desperation. Every few hundred metres I ask; the man sitting on the tricycle seat of his empty wooden cart, the woman selling fruit at a roadside stall, the man walking towards us along the dusty street. Apart from one passer-by who doesn't know what this lunatic is on about, every person points the way.

We turn into a long, wide, tree-lined avenue. Behind fencing we see the rubble of neighbourhoods being demolished. We walk past high, rendered walls.

Eventually we come to another metro stop and blue signs with white lettering and arrows. *To the Museum of the First National Congress.* And now here it is. (Jervey recognises it; I didn't know what we were looking for.) The famous charcoal-brick house with its red curved pediments decorated with flowers and leaves, its red curled ornamental mouldings, one of the few original (rather than reconstructed) *shikumen* 石库门 houses left in upmarket Xintiandi 新天地. It sits impressively on a corner, preserved because of its political significance, pedestrian crossings on both streets leading towards it.

In 1983 when I first came to China, to Xiamen University on a New Zealand–China Student Exchange Scholarship, Deng Xiaoping had just declared the city a Special Economic Zone and opened it to foreigners. Twenty of us were the first foreign students at the university, and bit by bit others joined us. In Xiamen I could have gone up to every foreigner I met and introduced myself. But now in Shanghai, there are plenty of Indian or Japanese businesspeople or other foreigners of indeterminate nationality to share the lift in our Modern Universe. As I walk across the road towards Cloud Nine, I hear French, multiple languages I do not recognise. As I travel alone on the metro one evening, I count nine obvious foreigners in the same carriage. I say *obvious* because I am not counting anyone who, like me, could be mistaken for a local.

I hear that Shanghai has 250,000 foreigners who have lived here for at least three months. This does not count tourists or those like us on the residency, who are here for only two months. It does not count the millions who come from other parts of China as tourists, students, professionals, businesspeople, or migrant workers from the countryside. Later, when I ask directions to an address on busy Nanjing Road — should I exit left or right from the metro? — the first three Chinese people tell me they are not from here. They do not know.

My perplexity with language has always been with Chinese, Cantonese, Mandarin, Shanghainese. But now I find Mandarin a huge improvement on Spanish or Hungarian. We use Skype to message each other in our rooms. 'What's that?' I ask Jaime about the link he's posted in Spanish. A warning about worms from the raw-fish sushi we pick up half-price at night across the road by the metro. After a while I realise that Enrique's typed 'jajaja' is pronounced 'yayaya'. 'Hola!' says Victoria. I learn to give and receive shy cheek-to-cheek air kisses. 'I think you can understand me,' Imre says. 'Just try.' But all I hear of Hungarian is 'vah vah vah'.

I ask a woman in the park which way to enter the Shanghai Museum. It's a huge building, the size of a city block, and with my propensity for fainting in hot weather I don't want to walk one way only to find the entrance is on the other side. 'I'm sorry,' the woman says in an American accent, 'I don't speak Chinese.' Somehow I am dumbfounded. Before I can make the mental shift, switch to English, say anything at all, tell her I know what it's like, she's gone.

I am waiting in the metro when a woman rushes up and asks which train to take. I don't recognise where she wants to go. I don't know which line she should take, which direction, the stop where she should get off. But so much is communicated beyond mere language, by context, gesture, expression. *Duibuqi wo bu zhidao* ('Sorry, I don't know'), I say to her. A woman standing nearby joins in, takes over, asks where she wants to go. They staccato-talk: question, question, clarification, answer. I understand little of what they are saying. Does this bystander actually know what she's talking about? Is that the answer the woman sought?

The bystander waves the woman to the opposite platform, then turns to me shaking her head. What a stupid woman, she's saying. How does she come out without knowing where she is going?

地 Place

The Temples of Xi'an

MARGARET T. SOUTH

The temples I know best are those located in or within a day's journey of the city of Xi'an (the former Tang dynasty capital Chang'an) in the Wei river valley, Shaanxi Province. With two exceptions — the Great Mosque which serves Xi'an's Muslims, and the Louguantai, which houses a Daoist community — these are all Buddhist.

Some of the foundations date as far back as the Eastern Han dynasty (25–221 AD), but most were established during the Tang (618–907). Their initial splendour has long since faded. Wars and revolutions, religious persecutions and natural disasters have all taken their toll. The more durable monuments have been the pagodas and dagobas, which, being masonry, have tended to survive longer than other temple structures, many of which have been destroyed and rebuilt several times. In recent years a considerable amount of restoration work has been undertaken, some with the financial assistance of Japanese Buddhists whose own patriarchs learned their doctrine in Chinese institutions. Even so, the original vast complexes no longer exist.

The restored temples, in particular, have a great many visitors, especially at festival times, but in the major centres they are crowded at any time of the year. As a result, the monks often find themselves in an invidious position. Without the visitors there would be no money for maintenance or restoration. With the visitors there is little opportunity for the practice of quietude and meditation. Without the practice of quietude and meditation how can those cravings and desires — which, the Buddha teaches, bring about all the sorrows of the world — be overcome?

Coming as I do from a country with a small population where religious institutions are not regarded as great tourist attractions or even attended very regularly by their own adherents, I find these crowds especially distracting. A poet once wrote: 'When the heart is still, the place itself becomes so.' In visiting a Chinese temple, or any other crowded place for that matter, how often have I longed for this 'still heart'!

Yet for the Chinese people this is not a new problem. From all accounts the great Chang'an temples in their heyday were also crowded, as was the capital itself. Moreover, scholar-officials in their poems expressed their longing to escape from 'this world's noise and dust'. This was not just a figure of speech, and their great delight was to go wandering in the mountains south of the city, sheltering for the night under the pines and refreshing themselves with early-morning dew. There were temples there, too, 'among the clouds', but as these are not easily accessible to foreigners, especially those advanced in years and rather short of breath, I do not know what remains of them.

The visits recorded in the following poems were made in the autumn of 1984, the winter of 1984/85, and the spring of 1989, while I was first a teacher and then a visitor at the Xi'an Foreign Languages Institute. I am deeply indebted to the officials of that Institute for a great many kindnesses and for their assistance in making these visits possible.

The Temple Bell

Records show that there were numerous Buddhist temples in the Tang dynasty capital of Chang'an (modern Xi'an) and several quite close to where I am now living. Today most of these temples no longer exist and, with all the new construction work being carried on in the city, it is difficult for even a monk to find a quiet place in which to meditate.

Rammers pounding, thudding, thumping,
Concrete mixers turning, churning.
All day power saws screaming, screeching,
All night hammers tapping, banging.
Retreating within I contemplate the past.
As the present fades so too does the noise.
A mossy path, a monk's secluded cell,
At times, half heard, the echo of a bell.

The Greater Wild Goose Pagoda

On a sunny morning in early autumn, I climb the Greater Wild Goose Pagoda (Da Yanta). Built during the Tang dynasty in the grounds of the Ci'en temple, it is one of only two structures in Xi'an to have survived since that time.

Standing alone it dominates the earth,
Soaring up its top is in the clouds.
From directly below it seems much taller still,
Its ancient steps ascend beyond the stars.
Tier after tier, view after view,
Higher and higher, I sample each in turn.
On the seventh tier the best one of them all,
Spread out like a map the whole of Guanzhong.
Sunshine and shadow, valleys and hills,
Mists and miasmas, rivers and streams.
A solitary mound, and emperor's tomb,
A plume of smoke, a peasant's home.
Down in the city nearly everything is new,
But out in the countryside little seems to have changed.
I see now what men saw then,
Tree lined roads and fields of wavering grain.

On the southern horizon the famous Zhongnan range,
I share its blueness with the poets of the Tang.
Spring and autumn they too climbed this tower,
As poets will a thousand years from now.

The Great Mosque

On the twenty-fourth day of the tenth month, I go with a friend to visit Xi'an's great mosque built by the Hui people, one of China's national minorities.

In Huajue lane the Hui have built a mosque,
Behind high walls away from the city's dust.
A succession of courtyards paved with mossy stone,
A series of archways capped with turquoise tile.
Ascending the terrace, I admire the minaret,
Summoned to prayer leaves gather on the roof.
The Iman delays but while the faithful wait,
An ancient ginkgo sheds a pool of light.

Tripitaka

On the sixth day of the first month, I visit the burial place of the Tang dynasty monk Xuan Zang, known as *Tripitaka* (Three baskets), in the grounds of the Temple of Flourishing Teaching (Xingjiao) in Chang'an county, south of Xi'an.

In search of the Law you travelled to the west,
Across tall mountains braving frost and ice;
Deserts too, long stages without food,
Where shrieking demons guard the sandy wastes.
The sacred texts so difficult to find,
Against all odds three baskets you obtained.

The holy script not easy to translate,
Returning to the capital you laboured many years.
But here among the pines at last you lie at rest,
Soothed by the sound of the river at your feet.
Released for a while from this world's noise and dust,
I bow three times and offer my respects.

The Temple of the Town God

Each city in China has a town god and a temple in his honour, but when I went to visit the one in Xi'an I could not find it.

The town god had a temple somewhere here,
In vain I sought it down a dusty lane.
I thought I saw its roof above a wall,
But the gate was barred, and I came away again.

'The Earl of Zheng Overcame Duan in Yan': China's Past in Our Futures

DUNCAN CAMPBELL

Enrolling with the History Department of Nanking University in early September 1977, after having studied Chinese language at the Peking Languages Institute for a year under the auspices of a New Zealand–China Student Exchange Scholarship, we were asked what we might like to study. Although my reasons for being in the People's Republic of China, to the extent that I was fully conscious of them, were decidedly contemporary and largely political, I nonetheless suggested that it might be a good idea to learn some Classical Chinese or *wenyan* 文言, the language that for thousands of years had underpinned the development of Chinese civilisation and its expansion of empire. It proved a fateful suggestion; almost 50 years later, I find myself still engaged in this task.

Several days after the question had been posed us, then, a small group of the some 15 foreign students allocated to the university that year turned to the first lesson in Volume One of (the only recently rehabilitated Peking University-based linguist) Wang Li's 王力 (1900–1986) *Classical Chinese* (*Gudai hanyu* 古代漢語), first published in 1962. The following year, when I acquired a copy of the first post-Cultural Revolution reprinting of the 1695 anthology of prose compiled by the Shaoxing school teacher Wu Chucai

吳楚材 (1655–1719) and his younger nephew Wu Diaohou 吳調侯, *The Finest of Ancient Prose* (*Guwen guanzhi* 古文觀止), I discovered that this traditional primer, too, commences its work with this text. The passage is a lengthy one, taken from the *Zuo Commentary* (*Zuozhuan* 左傳) to the *Spring and Autumn Annals* (*Chunqiu* 春秋) traditionally attributed to Confucius.

It is dated to the first year of the reign of Duke Yin of the State of Lu 魯隱公 (r. 721–711 BCE), the duke 'Sorrowfully swept away, unsuccessful' (隱拂不成), as the great nineteenth-century Scottish translator James Legge (1815–1897) explains his posthumous name, and cued to a line in the annals that reads: 'Summer, the fifth month; the Earl of Zheng overcame Duan in Yan' (鄭伯克段于鄢).

It tells the story of the two sons of the ruler of the powerful and wealthy vassal state of Zheng, Zhuang and Duan, and their mother's partiality for the younger son at the expense of the elder one whose breech birth (*wusheng* 寤生) had alarmed her. When in time their father dies and the elder son inherits the title of Duke, the mother conspires with Duan to have him replace Zhuang. Warned by his advisors about what was about to happen, Zhuang however refuses to act against his mother, both because she is, after all, his mother, and because he believes that in any case unrighteousness inevitably reaps its own just result.

When finally he is forced to act, overcoming Duan in Yan, the area to which Duan had fled, Zhuang has his mother incarcerated, vowing that 'We will not see each other before we reach the Yellow Springs' (不及黃泉無相見也). Regretting his actions soon thereafter, the duke's dilemma is resolved by a loyal border official called Ying Kaoshu, who suggests to him that he have a tunnel dug deep enough to reach the subterranean springs where he could arrange to meet up again with his mother. When the two eventually do so, they burst into song. And the passage ends with an appropriate couplet from another of the Confucian canon, the *Book of Odes* (*Shijing* 詩經), in praise of filial sons.

Problems of succession, the intricate balance in the relationship between power and knowledge (Ying Kaoshu reminds Zhuang of his filial obligations to his mother by refusing to eat the meat broth offered him by the duke, on the pretext that he intended to take it home for his own mother to eat), the play of modes of word magic (in the line from the classic that occasioned this commentary, for instance, the Duke is demoted to Earl for his failure to properly educate Duan, and Duan is not referred to as the younger brother because he did not behave in the manner required of a younger brother), the eternal clash between high-faluting normative values and altogether more sordid political realities — the passage seemed a fitting introduction both to the classical language and to the abiding characteristics of Chinese political culture, contemporary as much as ancient.

During the mid-1970s, such issues were playing out along the plane-tree-lined streets of Nanking, as they were also within the walls of the university. Sun Shuqi 孫述圻, for example, the man given the task of being our preceptor, had not been allowed into a classroom for almost 20 years.

Others among his colleagues had suffered more grievously at the hands of the Red Guards unleashed on them by the Great Helmsman, Chairman Mao. Kuang Yaming 匡亞明, a great scholar of Confucianism and one of the first major victims of the Cultural Revolution, restored to the vice-chancellorship of the university soon after we arrived, had had his kneecaps smashed. Many of the recently returned books proudly displayed in the home of Cai Shaoqing 蔡少卿 had been defaced with large but painstakingly inscribed crosses over the names of their authors. (These books I caught sight of when this wonderful historian of secret societies, ignoring explicit university instructions to the contrary, invited us to join his family for a meal. Many years later, he in turn visited us in Wellington.)

The enraptured glint in Sun's eyes as he now recited a text, the dart of his small, delicate hands as he sought to illustrate some point to us, revealed his joy at once again being in front of a class and allowed to read the books of old. In doing so, he lent us, if only briefly, the fond illusion that China's past, in all its enthralling complexity, was once again to be allowed to inform its present and future in a manner unfettered by arid Marxist frameworks. 'Practice', after all, was now to be 'the sole criterion for testing truth' (實踐是檢驗真理的唯一標準), the Nanking University philosopher Hu Fuming 胡福明 had argued in his influential article of that title, which was published in the pages of the *Enlightenment Daily* (*Guangming ribao* 光明日報) in May 1978.

Tragically, however, if the massacre of June Fourth, in 1989, revealed the iron-cast political limits of the Reform and Opening Up (改革開放) era, the beginnings of which I had been witness to, more recent decades have disclosed the extent to which China's renewed and emotionally-charged engagement with its various pasts (historical, cultural, social and religious) has been hijacked by the Party-State. Once consigned to the dustbin of history as an obstacle to modernity and then stigmatised as the explicit target for violence, labelled the Four Olds (四舊) of old ideas, old culture, old customs and old habits, China's past is now increasingly deployed in bombastic and vainglorious claims to exceptionality.

The past has been reduced to a singular master narrative that valorises unity above all else, and which relies on an ahistorical notion of 'Chineseness'. The centrality of these notions to the legitimacy of the Party-State and its various territorial claims finds easy evidence. Xi Jinping's 習近平 first public act upon assuming presidency of the People's Republic of China in 2012 was to pay a visit to the *Road to Revival*

Above: Sun Shuqi reciting the poem 'To the Tune Wavewashed Sand' by Li Yu 李煜 (937–978), the last ruler of the Southern Tang, written shortly before his execution and containing the line 'And in my dreams I forgot that I was a guest in another land' (夢裏不知身是客). Southern Tang Tombs, Nanking suburbs, 1993. ROBYN HAMILTON

Right: Nanking University, 1977. DUNCAN CAMPBELL

(復興之路) exhibition at the newly-opened National Museum of China, an occasion on which he first spoke about 'The China Dream' (中國夢).

More recently, in Xi's speech marking the hundredth anniversary of the founding of the Chinese Communist Party, 'history' is mentioned more than 20 times, the second half of what he had to say on this occasion punctuated by the phrase: 'Taking history as our mirror, and creating our future, we must ...' (以史為鑒開創未來必須). And yet a central consideration about that past is that this idea of 'Chineseness' was established at the expense of the brutal eradication of a multiplicity of alternative political and cultural entities. This ideal of a unified China only remained both viable and desirable to the minds of the élite, if only fitfully realised, to the extent to which it required (and continues to require) increasing levels of autocracy, particularly as the extent of empire grew rapidly during the late imperial period. Further, in terms of China's abiding contributions to global civilisation, these have been predominantly the products of periods of disorder and disunity, the Warring States period, for instance, or the Six Dynasties era.

I was reminded of the tyranny of this sanitised straitjacket of a past acceptable to party authorities recently when I was compiling a glossary to accompany a set of short stories by a contemporary Chinese author that I had translated for a publisher in the People's Republic. My draft was returned to me, with some degree of embarrassment on the part of the editor with whom I was dealing, marked with the annotations of the internal censor. I had, it seems, perpetrated three categories of error. I had mentioned unmentionable names. I had failed to employ the Party-State authorised formulations (or *tifa* 提法) to refer to particular historical events. And I had made mistakes, it was claimed, with the dating of, for instance, both the Yuan and the Qing dynasties, both of which 'alien' dynasties have now been given extended reigns, the better to be understood as part of Chinese history, the founding of the latter dynasty no longer dated to 1644 and the fall of Peking to the Manchus, for instance, or to 1636 when they name themselves the Qing, but rather to 1616 when they declared themselves to be the 'Later Jin' 後金 dynasty. According to Document Number Nine, any deviation from authorised interpretations of China's history represents 'historical nihilism' (歷史虛無主義).

I remember once asking teacher Sun Shuqi what it was that he read in bed each night before falling asleep. His reply was that presently he was working his way through Fan Ye's 范曄 (398–445) *History of the Later Han* (*Hou Han shu* 後漢書), a work that is commonly regarded as the most difficult of the Standard Histories. He was later to publish *An Intellectual History of the Six Dynasties* (*Liu chao sixiang shi* 六朝思想史). Both the Six Dynasties and the Later Han periods were notoriously chaotic periods, the first creatively so, the latter having descended into bloody tanistry. I often wondered if, as a victim of the Cultural Revolution, his knowledge of these earlier and unsettled periods of China's history lent him a sense of comfort or induced one of despair.

It is often suggested that what fuels contemporary Sinological disenchantment with the People's Republic of China is the extent to which that nation has failed to become 'more like us'. In my case, I think that the opposite is perhaps closer to the truth. Only a China more comfortable with the complications of its own unruly past might best contribute to our collective search for a sustainable future. For now, a fragile and thin-skinned superpower, seemingly incapable of any authentic dialogue with either its own past or its present and future responsibilities, domestically the People's Republic of China seems to have become a society characterised by a catastrophic collapse in trust, while externally, it increasingly acts with the swagger of the playground bully. Might China, as the repository of such a rich civilisation, still have important contributions to make to the wellbeing of humankind? Or will it continue to be simply another authoritarian one-party nation-state? If the former, then one suspects that that alternative future might be found somewhere among the many alternative pasts that characterise the grand arc of its historical trajectory.

Stages of Enlightenment

AMANDA JACK

Nanjing, spring, 1992. Bored with my language classes at Nanjing Normal University, I thought I might try my luck at studying some traditional Chinese theatre. I had a smiley conversation with the Foreign Students Office, they pulled a few strings, and introduced me to Chen Zhengwei 陳正薇 (1933–) from the Jiangsu School of Performing Arts. Chen Zhengwei, herself a successful Peking opera performer, claimed to be the last student disciple of renowned Peking opera performer Mei Lanfang 梅蘭芳 (1894–1961). Several years before she had successfully trained a young German ballerina named Wute 烏特 (Ute), and she was keen to repeat the experience. She offered to teach me the Peking opera excerpt *Tiannü sanhua* 天女散花 ('Goddess Scattering Flowers') once made famous by Mei Lanfang.

Devotion, refinement and virtue, qualities that Tiannü 天女 had come to symbolise, were not really familiar qualities to me. A goat farmer's daughter from Kaukapakapa, I had focused more on creative solutions and making do. Nonetheless, I thought I would give it a go. With a boldness rooted in naivety I gave myself over completely to Chen Laoshi's (Teacher Chen's) programme of instruction, a simplified and speeded-up version of the training she and Mei Lanfang himself had undergone from the ages of 11 and eight.

Starting in early March, I biked the 5-kilometre ride from the student dormitory along plane tree-lined streets to the Jiangsu Performing Arts

School. I arrived at each lesson breathless but ready for the bizarre range of warm-up exercises: *yatui* (壓腿); *titui* (踢腿); *xietui* (斜腿); *pantui* (盤腿); *piantui* (片腿); *gaitui* (盖腿). Leg stretches, leg kicks, high kicks, splits and backbends. I, the clumsy beginner that I was, worked at her pace; first learning basic exercises, then dance moves, and then singing, and eventually the whole lot with musical accompaniment.

Poking around the Performing Arts School one day, I happened across a hall full of children contorting their bodies into inhuman shapes. Their heads were folded forward and pressed on knees so tightly that the whole flattened body could fit through a hollow tube. The splits, so wide that their legs stretched past 180 degrees. Their backbends folded as though they had a hinge inserted in their spine. I turned from that hall fascinated and nauseated. I was relieved that my body would never be pushed to such limits. But I was defeated already; it was only confirmation that I would never be a proper Peking opera performer. The only time when I wasn't out of my depth was on the bike ride home.

I persevered, but my mind was split in two. I spent my time outside of class complaining about my training and cursing Wute. And my time in class sweating and straining, and doggedly focused on perfecting these ridiculous exercises.

One 'me' chastised myself for my lack of humility and gratitude. Chen Laoshi was offering me a whole tradition. I was learning one of the most perfect forms of theatre in the world. I was clearly not refined enough to learn or fully appreciate the richness on offer. What's more, certain signs had pointed to success. Auspiciously, two characters in Mei Lanfang's name were directly associated with me. My Cantonese given name is Fong (in Mandarin, Fang) 芳, and lan 蘭 features in the Chinese name for New Zealand 新西蘭. I was fated to line up behind these great performers.

The other 'me' shrank from this idea. Every move that I was to make on stage, every sound, had already been perfected by Mei Lanfang, and there was nothing left for me to do but mimic. If, earlier in life, I had received any theatrical training at all, it was to exercise and enjoy my originality, exert my personal right to choose, and to invent. My previous amateur acting had focused on leading with emotion to bring what was inside me out and into the performance. I guess there were smatterings of Stanislavski's Method Acting and other popular Western acting techniques in my training, which focused on 'naturalistic' performances. A sulky voice inside me said, 'This was a gymnastics class, not acting.'

I fought with myself, but an equally intense, intimate and fraught relationship with my teacher developed. Expectations clashed. So did backgrounds and cultures. The dance moves became more elaborate. I spent weeks on my entrance alone, with Chen Laoshi 'singing' the rhythm in the same way that one might sing the tabla. I went through the motions, but inwardly gave up on mastering the *woyu* 臥魚, a moving one-legged twist which ends up in an elegant seated position.

Chen Laoshi didn't keep her thoughts inside. She tried to motivate me by frequent references to Wute. But my attempts were often *bumei* 不美 ('not beautiful') or *sha* 傻 ('stupid'). She told me I was regressing, I told her she was pushing me too hard, and there were days when she attended lessons but didn't speak a word to me.

Suddenly alone and without instruction, I chose to interpret her criticisms of me in the language of my beloved theatre director Ros Gardner from Auckland. Chen Laoshi wasn't referring to beauty and stupidity in the normal sense, but rather saying that my internal focus wasn't pure and sharp. I inserted her words into a system that I understood, and ascribed them a meaning that I could accept. What she really meant, I told myself, was that I wasn't *centred*. I was concentrating solely on form and style, with no sense of the emotions and character I was portraying. Chen Laoshi was encouraging me to act, and it was my duty to bring to the stage my own interpretation of Tiannü. I kept telling myself that.

What I didn't know was that as far as the great European dramatists were concerned, this very struggle between acting from within and stylised form had been fought and won. As early as the mid-1930s, it was already decided that the style and tradition that Mei Lanfang brought to the stage were to be admired and emulated. Stanislavski himself watched Mei Lanfang perform in the USSR and declared him a great realistic actor. A whole new theory of acting developed in Russia after Mei Lanfang's performances. Bertolt Brecht said that realistic performance certainly occurred in Peking opera, but it was not the main point. What he admired was the exquisite control that Mei Lanfang commanded of his body. Body was both his instrument and his source of expression.

The opera *Tiannü sanhua* is based upon a chapter from the Buddhist *Vimalakīrti-nirdeśa*. Tiannü is a goddess living (hidden to ordinary mortal eyes) in the house of Vimalakīrti, an eminent *bodhisattva* disguised as a dissolute layman. Vimalakīrti performs magic tricks to prove a couple of important doctrinal points: transcendence of dualism (i.e., non-discrimination), and the superiority of Mahāyāna over other perspectives. Tiannü, meanwhile, scatters magic flowers over the *bodhisattvas* and great disciples who have come to visit. Then she uses her magical powers to exchange bodies with the Buddha's leading monk, Śāriputra. She becomes him, and he becomes her.

The correct meaning of non-dualism, as it's called in clumsy Buddha-speak, is precisely what the *bodhisattvas* were debating when Tiannü performed her magic. If even they had trouble, my chances of getting it are surely slim. But as the *sūtra* has it, Vimalakīrti conveys the correct understanding in action, in any case, rather than in wordy explanations. Let's see then, if I can make more sense of it by the time I reach the end of my story.

Representations of this scene in the history of the visual arts began with narrative depictions of the whole *Vimalakīrti-nirdeśa*, usually with the Buddha and Vimalakīrti taking centre stage. But as artistic, religious and social trends changed, so too did depictions of the *sūtra*. In the early Tang dynasty, *Tiannü sanhua*, although a minor scene, was often included. Sometime in the Song dynasty, images began to appear of the beautiful Tiannü alone. The Peking opera version of this story was created by Mei Lanfang and his collaborators in the early 1900s. It also had its own agenda, far removed from the original Dharma teaching. This new opera was all about reinventing Chinese artistic tradition in a modern era, and in particular, about conveying the beauty and grace of the *dan* character 旦角 (a woman played by a man) to Chinese and international audiences.

Back in rehearsals, I moved on to learning how to scatter the flowers, which are symbolised by long silk cloth. I found an unused room on the top floor of the student dormitory and flung my silk around. Dusty, lacklustre petals.

I don't recall advancing to singing. I have a brittle Gestetnered copy of some music as evidence. It doesn't look at all like a Western music score. I can no longer read it.

One day, Wang Laoshi, the old guy who accompanied me with the *jinghu* (a stringed instrument like an *erhu*), had been replaced with a new accompanist. Chen Laoshi told me that Wang Laoshi had lacked verve.

I have a body, but it is not my body. I am dressed in makeup and a costume. Under thick layers of powder and cream my face becomes a mask. The skin at my temples is pulled and held back with little 'clips'. These are bound in place with a tight headband, which is in turn covered with a heavy headdress, my costume. As I wait in the wings to make that entrance, I lose my senses. I can no longer smell anything except for the makeup. The clips on the skin of my temples prevent me from blinking.

I can't hear my voice above the loud clash of the *qi* and the *kan* and the bright vibrations of the *jinghu*. I have a splitting headache.

I am hidden under all this makeup, costuming and music accompaniment; my own efforts are overshadowed. Any shame about my incompetence will be lost to the gong and the cymbals. I ought to have abandoned this project long ago, when I stumbled across the room full of child acrobats. My sole focus now is to get the performance over and done with.

Transformation. Mei Lanfang's version of *Tiannü sanhua* focuses on the pretty bits: Tiannü's graceful entrance, her beautiful voice, the scattering of the magical flowers. But remember, in the *sūtra* Tiannü does more than this; she transforms her body into the body of Śāriputra, and she also demonstrates profound understanding. And on that hot, early summer day, Tiannü transformed into me.

Was Śāriputra's transformation into a goddess as fussy and uncomfortable as my own? Did he end up with a headache? The goddess mocked him as she mocked me. But did he immediately shake off his arrogance and pride to become contrite and humble? Did he understand immediately what Tiannü had set out to teach him?

Whatever Śāriputra learned didn't get passed on to me. It turns out I do have a self, and I am not willing to let go of it. I have a body that refuses to fully bend into the elegant shape of Tiannü. I have ungraceful thoughts, unbecoming for Tiannü. I let the tradition down. I let Mei Lanfang and Chen Laoshi down. I let Wute show me up. I was unable and unwilling to give up my individualism to become an instrument of the art of Peking opera. I sure didn't turn into Tiannü, at least not so far as I knew at the time.

I was still discriminating between her and me, my way and Chen Laoshi's way, grace and awkwardness, emotion and style, content and form. Tiannü came out of nowhere and scattered her flowers all over me. Like the *bodhisattvas* and devotees of the Buddha all that time ago. I am still trying to shake them off.

Song Dynasty Dragon Kiln Revival

PETER HOLMES

Chinese culture can be extraordinarily pervasive, even sometimes invasive in its manner of presentation. Take ceramics as an example. In its sheer Oriental complexity and technological diversity through time, Chinese ceramics became a veritable treasure trove that, although it could be studied from a distance, would eventually require a journey to the source as a prerequisite of full understanding.

For me, such a journey began in 1965 when I discovered the world of clay during sculpture studies at art school. An apprenticeship soon followed at an Australian ceramics workshop to develop professional skills and traditional ceramic techniques. Further work with a Japanese master potter cast an additional influential force over my own development. A traditional Oriental black-iron glaze known as *Tenmoku* 天目 ('Eye of Heaven') attracted my interest and soon began to characterise my work. Special qualities of this glaze were known in recent European literature and through stories of tea, ancient kilns, and historical provenance deep in Chinese history. So, in retrospect, my journey had already begun. Black-iron glazes have their origin in Fujian Province during the late Tang dynasty (618–906), before reaching a peak of production of tea bowls at Jian identified by industrial-scale kilns in the Song dynasty (960–1279).

My formal Chinese culture studies began at Auckland University in 1989, including history, language and archaeology. (My MA thesis, entitled 'The systems of ceramic production and distribution in South-Eastern China during the Tang and Song dynasty', was completed in 1998.) 'Chinese Traditional Culture' with Professor John Minford was an obvious choice of course to background traditional culture, but rather suddenly that year the traditional past was dramatically displaced one day in June by the scale of political events unfolding rapidly in Tiananmen Square. Professor Minford arrived for class to deliver the most memorable impromptu exposé of the perilous state of contemporary Chinese culture.

I completed the year with a research paper on the ancient cultural traditions of 'Jian Ware Tea Bowls of Fujian' and a deep awareness of the past and the confrontation of contemporary cultural issues. Chinese language studies were very intensive, so I quickly took advantage of an opportunity for a small group of students to attend a residential language school at Shanghai University in the summer of 1991–92.

The Chinese cultural milieu surrounding student life at the time was very inclusive, and friendships developed easily despite language issues. I had met the artist Weiming Chen 陈维明 and family, recently arrived from Hangzhou and busy adapting to local culture. We discovered we had much in common. My intention to attend the summer school in Shanghai was discussed, and it raised a distinct possibility of meeting with the Chen family still in Hangzhou, even the possibility of their hosting a group visit one weekend. Needless to say, Fujian ceramics were never far from my thoughts.

Our group of six quickly acclimatised to Chinese university life, dormitory food, accommodation, new class routines, the local market. During the first week, we contacted the Chen family and arranged to visit them once classes had concluded, but promptly received an invitation for a weekend visit. Our plans for tours of Suzhou and Nanjing were quickly altered to include Hangzhou, just two and half hours by train south of Shanghai. We enjoyed such a very memorable weekend, sightseeing around the West Lake, eating wonderful food, that I made arrangements to return before travelling south to the Fujian kiln sites. In the European literature, the Jianyao zhan 建窯盞 site at Shuiji 水吉 was relatively unknown, apart from articles by Malcolm Farley, who arrived in 1922 to teach at Fuzhou University, and James Plumer, who documented the Shuiji kiln site in 1935.

The Shanghai experience had involved us in many journeys, incidents and encounters as well as the classroom, but sadly all too soon it was time to choose new directions. My attention was now drawn to another rail journey back to Hangzhou and the prospect of Fujian and the ancient kilns further south. The winter landscape of snow and ice in Hangzhou was spectacular, scraping snow and ice off the balcony for tea, icy footpaths and a tricycle cab driven to a standstill in snowy wind. Then the journey south to Fujian began by late-night train with Suzi Chen 陈素子 as my guide, thankfully, to negotiate a very crowded railway station, and find the train and my crowded three-tiered bunk cabin.

After another memorable rail journey to Shaowu in Fujian Province, we were met by our driver with a jeep for the hour-and-a-half trip to the Wuyi Mountain Villa hotel. The hotel sheltered under the shadow of the famous Dawangfeng 大王峰 (Great King Peak) in the foothills of the Wuyi mountain range near the Nine Twists Stream. The rugged hinterland of Fujian is dominated by the Wuyi mountains, the source of camphor and much of China's tea, not to mention an ancient ceramic industry.

Shuiji felt very close; suddenly it was much more than literary study and reflection, for I would soon be physically immersed in the industrial detritus of centuries. Suzi had thoughtfully arranged a trip for us to

Traditional Jian Zhan Hare's Fur (*Tenmoku*) from Jian kilns, Fujian. PETER HOLMES

acclimatise ourselves, down the Nine Twists Stream, drifting for a couple of hours on a bamboo raft to muse on journeys and times past in this ancient mountain landscape, with the occasional teahouse and calligraphic graffiti visible from the river. The relationship between tea production and the industrial complex of Jianyao zhan in Fujian is complicated, but may in some way explain its eventual demise. Extant surface remnants of this industry are still highly visible at two sites, one at Shuiji and a second site 19 kilometres south-west of Shuiji at Yulingting 遇林亭.

By late afternoon after walking 2 kilometres through a remote, sparsely populated, forested valley we came across a stele that identified the 'Mountain boundary (*shanjie* 山界) upon which Yulinting or the Pavilion Marking One's Encounter with the Forest stands'. A considerable quantity of shards and saggars (ceramic containers used to protect pottery during firing) visible in the undergrowth clearly identified the site on a slope above the access track, but there was no evidence of a kiln.

We encountered a local farmer with several bowls for sale who talked about the site, which, we soon discovered, provided him with a valued source of seasonal income. The highly variable quality of tea bowls recovered from shard heaps necessarily creates some difference of opinion on actual value, so after some hard bargaining under the dim light of a single bulb, the auction was passed in at ¥400 on the advice of my companions. By this time, it became a dark, wet trudge back to find the jeep, to recover at the hotel with a traditional steamboat dinner for all. In 1999, Yulinting was to become a significant feature of the UNESCO cultural and natural heritage listing of the Wuyi Mountain Reserve.

After an early start on another cold, wet day, we drove south to Jianyang for hot noodles. Shuiji and the Jianyao site are located about another hour to the west. In fact, the kiln site is located just beyond Shuiji at Houjing 后井, via a farm track alongside the hills and rice paddies filling the valley floor. The firebox at the roadside defined the front of the kiln, with brick-wall remnants clearly visible, rising up to the crest of the hill and beyond as we later discovered. Local farmers also arrived almost simultaneously with a selection of Jianyao zhan (bowls) from the vast shard heap visible alongside the kiln, but there was barely time to take photos and examine a ceramic shard or two that looked interesting before, with bargaining just getting underway, we suddenly had to depart. Apparently the intention was to return officially at a later date.

While driving to the site we had passed an isolated traditional-style covered bridge along with a collection of older-style wooden buildings on the way to Houjing. However, the covered-bridge image, albeit compromised by the weather, did reveal a traditional 'corridor bridge' or *langqiao* 廊桥 close to Shuiji. It was built in the 'combined beam arch' style; although once a common feature of the rural landscape and enmeshed in local folk culture, many have not survived and they are now relatively rare, although Fujian remains one of seven major concentrations of 'corridor bridges' in China.

A special highlight of the day was a visit to the new Fujian Wuyishan Nature Museum, displaying incidentally the first English sign I had seen in the area. Local walks in the park negotiated traditional mountain paths, and we explored by jeep more-remote areas of extensive bamboo forest that supported the local chopstick industry. At one remote village deep in the hills, the only visible inhabitants were some very shy children who ran for cover when we appeared and pretended to hide in the school nearby.

Our expedition back to the kiln site the next day in three vehicles included an interpreter and the Jianyang museum people, who I believe had arranged lunch at Jianyang on our way to the site. However, the arrival of vehicles this time surprised several locals excavating the site to recover saleable bowls, who, not wishing to be apprehended for site disturbance, hurriedly departed into the hills pursued by museum staff. Suzi and I therefore had time for photos and to walk the entire 130 metres of the kiln, as well as to survey discarded shards and kiln fragments for items of archaeological interest. The place was identified as a key heritage site in 2001, and has now moved from local jurisdiction to state protection.

Our expedition returned to the Jianyang museum to examine some unusual bowls recently discovered, but technical language, even with an interpreter, presented some difficulties. So, together with some shards and discarded kiln furniture, we made our way back to the Wuyi hotel. After an eventful day, I was very surprised to find a local mountain festival celebration underway, accompanied by a special dinner of local 'yu tou' eel 鳝鱼头, baked and served in a long split-bamboo lidded dish, along with a plethora of other wonderful dishes to celebrate and toast.

I discovered later that permission for foreigners to access the Jianyao site was necessary and strictly limited by the local government in Jianyang, a circumstance that served to explain some of the incidents of the previous two days. A dramatic revival of traditional Jianyao zhan production at Shuiji is now well underway, with a number of re-created traditional-style dragon kilns (*longyao* 龙窑) among other modern gas and electric kilns.

Our train tickets to neighbouring Jiangxi Province and the Imperial Kilns at Jingdezhen 景德镇 were delayed until the next day, so there was time to explore the ancient cliff tracks above the Nine Twists Stream with two young teachers who appeared as guides, offering an interesting opportunity to exchange our language skills.

***

After another adventurous night-train journey, two days in Jingdezhen satisfied a potter's eye and offered lessons to be learned in moving from the ancient past to large-scale porcelain production still underway. Some quick adjustments were necessary, but I did see the timeless skill of potters still highly visible against a skyline of smoking kiln chimneys and streets lined with porcelain markets.

Getting back to Hangzhou via Anhui Province was another adventurous 12-hour journey, by bus this time, through sparsely inhabited scenic mountain landscapes. Nonetheless, the sight of Hangzhou and the West Lake was a very welcome one. I had just six days left to explore the local environs, so Suzi presented me with a bicycle to negotiate both the perimeter of the West Lake and the notorious local 'bicycle jams'.

The most visible and important feature on these cultivated hills are the tea plantations and their teahouses that surround the West Lake. So it was decided that I would host Suzi, Chen, and interpreter Jian Ying for a plantation walk, a climb up Mount Wu to view the West Lake, before walking down to the Longjing teahouse for lotus tea. Chen's thoughts and reflections on this memorable occasion are expressed beautifully in a traditional brushed handscroll presented to me as not only a 'memento', but also a treasured *memento vivere*, and I hope that this essay may express something of my gratitude to the Chen family for making my journey into the past possible.

Return to Liangzhu

WEN CHIN POWLES

I.

I had the good fortune some years ago of getting to know Liangzhu Museum 良渚博物院 in Zhejiang. The museum sits on the vast (290-hectare) archaeological site of one of China's cluster of prehistoric civilisations that had drawn sustenance from one or the other of the two great rivers, the Yangtze and the Yellow rivers. Liangzhu culture 良渚文化 (3300–2300 BCE) is considered unique among these Neolithic civilisations for having nurtured the most highly developed jade culture in the ancient Chinese heartland. Its abundant, high-quality jade creations display elaborate carving styles and unique sacred images. They were put to sophisticated use in ritual and decoration, and are ultimately extremely mysterious in their antiquity.

An attractive low-slung modern building, Liangzhu Museum sits serenely by ponds of lotus, the iconic watery landscape of a Chinese summer. Under rolling fields lie the remnants of an ancient city that UNESCO has designated an outstanding example of an early regional centre of power and belief. When I first saw it in the summer of 2012, the stone-white museum shimmered under the blazing sun, while inside its cool corridors and galleries gleamed with the unusual jade artefacts uncovered from the Liangzhu tombs. It was a real joy to visit Liangzhu again last spring and renew a friendship with its director, archaeologist Jiang Weidong.

Liangzhu culture rose in what is now Hangzhou. The fertile delta area was already supporting rice cultivation, with an early canal and reservoir system developed by the Liangzhu people, who numbered some thousands. Their society was hierarchical and bound by a belief system of deity worship. One recurring elaborate image, *shenhui* 神徽, a half-human, half-animal motif, is incised into the ritual jades found in the tombs.

Notably, *shenhui* are seen on the tactile surfaces of the mysterious *cong* 琮, tubular jade objects of varying height, square on the outside and circular on the inside, an object that was not a vessel (being open-ended) but, scholars surmise, a channel which the Liangzhu elite might have believed could connect them to the godly realm. The lustrous, perfectly round Liangzhu jade discs, *bi* 璧, some as large as dinner plates, are similarly stunning. *Bi* are holed in the centre, some carved, some completely smooth, all perplexing as to their original significance in the social structures, ceremonies and burial of the Liangzhu leaders. In addition, jade axes, sceptres, beads, and bird and animal sculptures depict a thriving society of 5000 years ago.

The aesthetics of Chinese jade also tend to catch the eye of New Zealanders, for they bear a resemblance to Aotearoa's pounamu. Ten years ago, a Te Papa team organised a major exhibition of taonga pounamu at the National Museum of China in Beijing, a project marking the fortieth anniversary of diplomatic relations between New Zealand and China. I was privileged to be part of that team, which was how I got to know Liangzhu Museum.

Te Papa's project centred on the rare treasures in *Kura Pounamu*, the largest exhibition of pounamu ever shown at Te Papa, in 2009–2011, developed with Ngāi Tahu. Curated by pounamu expert Dougal Austin (Kāti Māmoe, Kāi Tahu, Waitaha), Te Papa's senior curator, mātauranga Māori, the exhibition showcased over 200 taonga that spanned a thousand years of history, culture and creativity, and their significance for Māori. With Dougal, the Te Papa team organised a specially curated touring version of

Kura Pounamu for Beijing in the northern hemisphere autumn of 2012, at the same time paving the way for reciprocal exhibitions from the National Museum of China to Te Papa. Later, these became two jointly curated acclaimed exhibitions shown in Wellington in 2014 on Chinese history and art: *China: Throne of Emperors* and *Shi Lu: A Revolution in Paint.*

There was an ambitious tail to the Beijing exhibition of *Kura Pounamu.* Te Papa aimed to show this taonga to other Chinese audiences outside the capital city. Thus we worked on a touring plan that, post-Beijing, would start at the Liangzhu Museum in Hangzhou in 2013, move to Guangdong Museum in Guangzhou, then on to the Three Gorges Museum in Chongqing in 2014, and finish at the magnificent Shaanxi History Museum in Xi'an (which has a long-standing relationship with Te Papa) that summer.

Alongside negotiations with the recipient museums, the navigation of local conditions and complex logistics (all of which could be the subject of a separate essay!), each venue was chosen for some of its special characteristics that spoke to Aotearoa: Liangzhu, the most important site of early Chinese jade culture; Guangdong, 'the tūrangawaewae of the ancestors of the first Chinese New Zealand families in Aotearoa' (see below); ethnically diverse Chongqing; and Xi'an, the historical Qin imperial capital and, a thousand years later, the cosmopolitan Tang Dynasty centre of the famed Silk Road. With the support of both the New Zealand and the Chinese governments, Te Papa's first touring venture in China was highly successful, bringing taonga pounamu and their stories, plus the mana and significance of pounamu in contemporary Aotearoa, to new audiences.

II.

Dougal Austin has written of his impressions of *Kura Pounamu* on Chinese audiences during the exhibition's tour. Below, I quote extensively from his blog (see Te Papa blog, 25 July 2013: https://blog.tepapa.govt. nz/2013/07/25/kura-pounamu-he-aha-o-ratou-whakaro):

The *Kura Pounamu* exhibition has just opened at Guangdong

Museum in the southern city of Guangzhou. Formerly known as Canton, Guangzhou is the tūrangawaewae of the ancestors of the first Chinese New Zealand families in Aotearoa. This follows successful showings firstly at the huge National Museum of China in Beijing and at Liangzhu Museum which is located in the heartland of China's over 5,000 year old jade culture on the outskirts of the city of Hangzhou. I have been fortunate to travel to China three times with the *Kura Pounamu* exhibition to fulfil a range of professional and cultural responsibilities associated with the tour. And I have been very interested to also get a feeling for what Chinese think about it.

Like most New Zealanders, Māori and Pākehā alike, but perhaps not the growing Asian demographic, I have had little prior exposure to Chinese culture. So for me this has been both a physical and a cultural journey into previously unknown territory. I was initially uncertain about whether our cultural differences would be so great and unaccustomed to one another that the Chinese people would view the exhibition mainly through the eyes of their own culture. Māori and Chinese have something special in common. They are both jade cultures. But would Chinese experience our *pounamu* primarily according to long held Chinese understandings of jade? If so the *kaupapa* or 'mission' of the exhibition might fall short of the true cultural exchange aimed for.

It had been explained to me that jade is a sacred stone to Chinese people because of their ancient belief that it brings good luck. At one time every Chinese person would carry at least a little jade on themselves for that purpose. I have observed that jade is still worn today by Chinese people, particularly by women. A pale coloured jade appears to be favoured. I have viewed the impressive exhibitions of Chinese jade at the National Museum

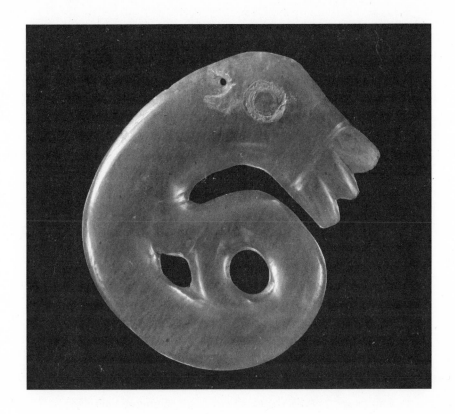

This koropepe (spiral-shaped manaia pendant taking inspiration from a mythical eel or fish) showed in various places in China as part of the *Kura Pounamu* exhibition. It is made from the tangiwai (bowenite) variety of pounamu and has an eye inlay of red sealing wax. Its iwi origins are unknown. MUSEUM OF NEW ZEALAND TE PAPA TONGAREWA, ME000065

of China and at Liangzhu Museum. I have seen a wide range of jade tools, fearsome weapons, beautiful adornments, and ceremonial treasures on display. Clearly there is some convergence between our cultures in our mutual appreciation of the qualities of strength and beauty inherent within this exceptional stone, and the means to which jade could be put.

The opening events for *Kura Pounamu* have been high profile occasions attracting a great amount of interest from many including all manner of Chinese officialdom, VIPs and throngs of media. Tribal representatives Shane Te Ruki, Archdeacon Richard Wallace, Professor Piri Sciascia, Lisa Tumahai and Susan Wallace have officiated with the opening blessings, speeches, and other duties, giving effect to the concept of *mana pounamu*. And returning to the exhibition afterwards to quietly observe people making their way through, I have been at once pleased and relieved to see the obvious interest, esteem and respect accorded to our stone and to the ancestral treasures made from it. Chinese visitors are drawn to the four large touchstones positioned within the exhibition and young children are lifted up so that they too can touch and rub them. Earlier on I had questioned fellow Chinese museum colleagues about how the Chinese public might relate to our exhibition and to our pounamu which is generally much greener than the pale coloured jade favoured by Chinese. The reply indicated that this wouldn't be a problem; Chinese would understand that this is a different jade from theirs and that the Māori treasures are from a different culture which they will also be interested to learn about. Such appears to be true.

A significant gesture by both the National Museum of China and Guangdong museums has been the Māori waiata learnt to proficiency by staff to sing at the opening events. In terms of visitor behaviour according to my unofficial survey I would place the Chinese a little to the Māori side of Pākehā; they read labels as well as spend a fair amount of time studying the taonga and enjoying the aesthetics and tactile experiences. No reira, kua marama rātou: 'they get it' or they get it sufficiently. As it tours throughout the great middle land of *Zhong Guo*, or 'China', *Kura Pounamu* is connecting with Chinese visitors who are taking from it a very favourable first impression of Māori culture and of our treasured stone. It is an encounter where *Poutini, the pounamu taniwha*, meets the famous Chinese dragon.

To Dougal's thoughts I would add that the mihi whakatau at Guangdong Museum was particularly moving. Jade is especially loved by the southern Chinese, including the old diaspora families outside China like my own. Traditions include the gifting of jade jewellery to mark births and weddings, and the handing on of jade pendants, bracelets, rings and earrings to later generations. When guests in Guangdong were invited to place their hands on the pounamu kōhatu (touchstones), more than one were visibly moved.

III.

As I returned to Liangzhu that day in April, I thanked the heavens again that the early enthusiasm of Director Jiang Weidong had made *Kura Pounamu*'s onward journey possible. His instant interest in taonga pounamu mirrors the common affinity between Māori and Chinese for the inherent strength and resilience, and sheer beauty, of the stone.

Coming from a perspective of several thousand years of Chinese jade culture, Jiang, now deputy head of Liangzhu Archaeological Site's management committee, continues to express his awe and respect that Māori created taonga pounamu with artistic genius and consummate skill over a much shorter period of historical time, and that the mana of pounamu has continued to flourish. We enjoyed reminiscing about the exhibition. 'There are only very few jade cultures in the world,' he reminded me, 'and China's and New Zealand's are two of them.' He admires the diversity and beauty of pounamu, seen in the toki, mere, hei tiki and hei matau that formed much of the 2013 exhibition. The natural variety of pounamu, from kawakawa to inanga, was evident in the ever-popular kōhatu, especially the 170-kilogram *Te Hurika* ('Snowflake'), which delighted and was touched by young and old alike.

I recall the opening ceremony graced by the mihi whakatau, the first, and only, Māori ceremony Liangzhu has ever witnessed. Mellifluous Jiangnan music had followed, and the first Jiangnan dance to open a Te Papa taonga exhibition. In the 25 May 2013 edition of *Te Panui Runaka*, a photograph shows Director Jiang cradling the pounamu kōhatu that Ngāi Tahu rangatira Lisa Tumahai and the late Professor Piri Sciascia gifted to Liangzhu to celebrate *Kura Pounamu's* opening. To this day, it is the only exhibition from outside China that has ever been shown at Liangzhu Museum.

At this, the fiftieth anniversary of New Zealand–China diplomatic relations, polarising geopolitics may interfere with our values of manākitanga (kindness, care, the spirit of reciprocity and our common humanity) and whanaungatanga (connectedness) when it comes to exchanges with China. But I hope not. Sharing the best of our cultural treasures may be one of the most effective means to ensure that these values remain strong. And there is a lot yet to be learned from human history, regardless of place and irrespective of politics.

Reflections on Being a Foreign Student in Shanghai in the 1980s

REBECCA NEEDHAM

Although my status in China has always been that of a foreigner, the idea of China was never completely foreign to me. My mother was originally from Hong Kong, where she and my father, originally from Yorkshire, met and married before immigrating to New Zealand in the 1960s. Having set up the Palmerston North branch of the New Zealand China Friendship Society in the 1970s, their interest in China grew to the point of organising a joint teaching assignment as 'foreign experts' at the No 1 Foreign Languages Institute in Beijing. And so it came to pass that in January 1978 my family moved to China for six months, making the Friendship Hotel in Beijing our temporary home, and marking the first of a lifelong series of interactions with China that have profoundly shaped my personal and professional life.

If the 1970s constituted my first contact with China, then the 1980s marked my student years there, and the 1990s my first posting to Beijing as a New Zealand diplomat, followed by assignments in Shanghai (2000s) and Guangzhou (2010s). There have been some incredible highlights for me along the way, especially as a diplomat in China where the elevated status accorded to senior government officials served up some unforgettable moments. However, it was my experiences as a young foreign student in Shanghai in 1986 and 1988 that were probably the most formative in terms of my own personal development, and to some extent my view of the world.

The foreign student scene in China has expanded exponentially since the 1980s, when studying Chinese was still a novelty, and China was still definitely considered as off the beaten track. Fast-forward to 2018, there were almost half a million foreign students enrolled in Chinese universities, putting China behind only the United States and the United Kingdom as one of the top three global destinations for international students. China's now sophisticated foreign student ecosystem includes an array of university exchange agreements, Confucius Institutes, private language schools, digital learning tools and online platforms, and even a popular Chinese TV reality show. I'm not sure whether all of these new bells and whistles have improved individual language-learning outcomes, but there is certainly much greater choice in modes of learning and access to it, infinitely more variety in learning materials, and, one would hope, a more enjoyable experience to be had along the way.

In the 1980s, foreign students occupied a particular space in China. They (along with overseas Chinese, which I half-counted myself as) were a subgroup of the genus *Foreigner*; they lived in a world largely separate from the local Chinese, not necessarily of their own choice but because it was hardwired into the system. *Foreigners* lived in separate residential areas or in international hotels, and were encouraged to shop at 'Friendship Stores', all of which were mostly off-limits to ordinary Chinese. A two-tier currency system also operated from 1980 to 1994, limiting foreigners to buying and using Foreign Exchange Certificates (FECs), and restricting the use of local renminbi (RMB) to Chinese nationals only. A lively black market quickly sprang up for FECs (valuable because they could be converted back into foreign currency or used to buy imported goods), and any foreigner visiting China at the time would have been familiar with furtive unsolicited invitations to 'change FECs' around foreigner hangouts.

Foreign students lived in mini international enclaves on campus, with separate dormitories and canteens, in every way more generous than the local student options — including, for example, twin-share dorm rooms for foreigners compared with the same-sized rooms for six Chinese students. Within this subgroup were broadly two types of foreign student: those from rich, mainly Western countries, who were primarily there for the China experience with a focus on language learning; and a second group, mainly from China-friendly developing countries (think Africa, developing Asia, etc.) who were there on bilateral scholarship programmes. For this second group, mastering the language was simply a means to an end; they were there first and foremost to acquire a university degree.

This diverse mix made for a cultural and geopolitical melting pot at foreign student dormitories. At the two universities I attended, the Chinese language programmes were dominated by French and Japanese university exchanges, which by dint of their size tended to form into broadly self-contained country groups who socialised and travelled together. The rest of us were an assortment of countries of origin and Chinese language levels that made for culturally and linguistically diverse classrooms, if not always harmonious social relations.

Perhaps unsurprisingly, the most extreme outliers even back then were the North Korean students, who were in separate classes and kept very much to themselves. Back then my knowledge of the DPRK was limited to the occasional world headlines, for example the blowing up of the Korean Air passenger plane in 1987, and the bizarre mythology surrounding Supreme Leader Kim Il-Sung, passed on to me by my Japanese classmates. I had just a single interaction with the North Koreans over the entire year in 1988, when two of them snuck into my Japanese classmate's dorm room to watch the opening ceremony of the Seoul Olympics on his small black-and-white TV. They were very quiet and left early. I heard afterwards that not only did they get into trouble for joining our party, but they were also in a state of shock after seeing the modern South Korean economy that was showcased during the broadcast. Much later I came to understand that as much as the 1988 Olympics was South Korea's 'coming-out party' on the global stage, it was also a huge blow to DPRK illusions that there was any realistic comparison between the North and South.

A lesser divide existed between the students from West and East Germany, just an aloofness which was obviously mutually felt, despite German unification being just around the corner. What they did have in common was a commitment to their studies, the Heidelberg group in particular adding welcome intellectual weight to the foreign-student discourse on China.

Another interesting group were the six Soviet engineers who livened up our dormitory for several months in 1988 with their free-wheeling discussions about everything that was wrong with their country, very much in the spirit of Gorbachev's *glasnost*. Memorably, they wore a lot of denim and drank a lot of beer. Speaking of beer, the famous Shanghai REEB brand was in those days very attractively priced for the foreign-student market at less than 20 cents a bottle, and fuelled a number of intercultural breakthroughs, including validation that in the global drinking stakes the Kiwis trailed the Russians and the Germans by some distance.

It wasn't all fun and games though, especially for the African scholarship students, sizeable cohorts of whom were spread across several universities in Shanghai (and elsewhere), and who were at times the targets of quite shocking verbal racial abuse from local Chinese students. However, I came to understand that this hostility was also tangled up with resentment over the more generous government scholarships and overall better conditions for African students compared with locals. This was exacerbated by contact between African students and Chinese women sometimes falling foul of different cultural expectations around dating. These tensions came to a head at the end of 1988 with a series of unfortunate events, leading to Chinese student protests against African students at a university in Nanjing, which then spread to campuses in Shanghai and Beijing.

But what of the language-learning experience? Appearances sometimes to the contrary, learning Chinese in fact remained the primary goal for the majority of foreign students. Most language programmes ran Monday to Friday, with three to four hours of class time each morning, and afternoons left for review and preparation. There was little variety in learning materials back then, and our lessons were dominated by the ubiquitous *Practical Chinese Reader* textbook series, which chronicled the everyday lives of two foreign students in China. For many Chinese language students, the names *Palanka* and *Gubo* (or 'Gubbo' as an Australian classmate insisted on calling him) will be as familiar as old best friends — or worst enemies. Recently looking through the revamped *New Practical Chinese Reader*, I noted the homage paid to the original series with the introduction of a new character, *Libo*, evidently the offspring of 'Gubbo' and his then Chinese girlfriend *Ding Yun*. (Although presumably they were married before *Libo* arrived on the scene.)

Another language learning rite of passage was the sometimes awkward transition from speaking Chinese in the classroom to using it in real life, which in Shanghai was exacerbated by the locals' heavily accented Mandarin. Like many foreign students, including those who had already completed entire Chinese language courses at their home-country universities, I arrived in China with limited oral fluency, and in the early days had to overcome considerable self-consciousness before managing to gradually extend my verbal skills beyond those of a small child.

Even as my language ability improved, the additional effort required to articulate myself in Chinese was a regular reminder of the language power imbalance that exists for a non-native speaker in a predominantly monolingual environment. The lived experience of always being on the back foot when using Chinese forced a much deeper acknowledgement of the default privilege I had of being a native speaker of English, the universal lingua franca. On the flip side, I also came to see the downsides of native English-speakers remaining monolingual, including the tendency towards more-fixed perspectives; on that score alone the revitalisation of te reo underway today is an enormously positive shift in New Zealand's national identity.

As everyone will tell you, the surest way to improving your Chinese is by making Chinese friends. However, it did take time, and a few unsuccessful 'language buddy' experiments at my own university, for me to realise that more initiative would be required to find people whose company I genuinely enjoyed. It was with this in mind that I co-opted a fellow student to help me 'infiltrate' the Shanghai Theatre Academy (one of the top film schools in China), which led to us gate-crashing their in-house screening of *The Last Emperor* one Saturday night. As it turned out, after the screening we somehow managed to strike up a conversation with three graduate students at the Academy, and they were to become good friends for the remainder of my time in Shanghai.

Two of them, Yutao and Dehui, were acting graduates with the sort of good looks that today would not be out of place in an Asian boy band. Dasheng, the least-good-looking but the one with the best sense of humour, was studying to be a director. All three were bursting with talent and confidence, and, as they were already getting work in local productions, they projected a worldliness about the emerging Chinese TV and film industry that felt glamorous and exciting. Being honest, our initial appeal to them would have simply been the novelty value of having foreign student friends, but at some point I like to think we all moved beyond the stereotypes and developed a genuine friendship. In a remarkable gesture of friendship for that time, Yutao invited me to visit his family home over the summer vacation. Although this meant a major adjustment to my original summer travel itinerary and a minor breach of foreigner accommodation regulations, my three-day homestay with the Jiang family in Harbin that summer remains one of my most enduring 'people memories' of China.

This fragmented picture of life as a foreign student in China in the 1980s might read in parts like an historical account. However, on reflection, perhaps the fundamentals of the experience haven't changed that much. That is to say, the foreign student experience was, and probably still is, as much about the international exchanges as experiencing and learning about China. When our respective borders reopen, I certainly hope to see the resumption of young New Zealanders taking up foreign student opportunities in China. If they get even half as much out of the experience as I did, then it will be time well spent.

1989:
Beijing Under
Martial Law

BRIAN MOLOUGHNEY

When I arrived back in Beijing in late August of 1989, I knew I was returning to a city under martial law, but I had little idea of what that meant. At first things seemed normal, with people going about their lives as usual. It was only later on that first evening that I began to get an idea of what life under martial law entailed.

A friend invited me to join his family for dinner, and after our meal generously offered me the use of one of the family's bicycles for the rest of my stay. By the time I rode out of their compound it was dark, and instead of the normal city nightlife I found myself alone, riding along eerily quiet, deserted streets. Every intersection was manned by police and soldiers, with the military presence increasing as I got closer to the university district. Tanks and armoured vehicles were lined up near every junction, with units of soldiers exercising along the streets. While it was scary, I wasn't stopped or questioned about why I was breaking the curfew, not on that first evening nor at any other time during my stay.

This was the second time the Chinese government had imposed martial law in 1989. The first time had been in March, in response to protests in Lhasa that marked the thirtieth anniversary of the turmoil that had led to the Dalai Lama's flight into exile. Those protests received little attention from the outside world. But when a new wave of protests erupted in the Chinese capital just a short time later, everyone paid attention. Like many others, I had watched as the chaotic enthusiasm of the early days of the movement gradually coalesced and gathered momentum. What began as a student protest soon mushroomed into a popular uprising that involved people from all walks of life. Friends in Beijing and Hong Kong became involved, excited at the possibility of being part of a movement for change, but wary also of how the government would react. The longer the occupation of Tiananmen Square continued, the more concerned they became.

I had been living in Nanjing during an earlier phase of protests in 1986, which had started at the University of Science and Technology in Hefei and then spread to a number of campuses across the country. The spark for these protests had been the students' frustration over their inability to select candidates for public office, but the protests soon became a vehicle to express a broader level of dissatisfaction with the restrictions the Communist Party placed on them. As the protests in various cities gathered momentum, the government stepped up its media campaign, stressing the general public's concern at the disruptions the protests caused, as well as the fear that this might be the start of a return to the chaos of the Cultural Revolution. In Nanjing, university authorities and city officials worked together to contain the protests, and after a few nights the movement petered out.

Over several evenings I had gone out onto the streets of Nanjing to observe the protests, which were mostly orderly and only ever involved a few hundred people. A French friend who was watching with me was dismissive of the students' efforts, suggesting that they needed to 'come to Paris to find out what a real protest was'. While my friend had a point, and the Chinese protests were nothing like what we had seen on New Zealand streets with the anti-Springbok Tour protests in 1981, in both France and New Zealand we enjoyed a level of protection from the arbitrary power of the state, which people in China did not.

The significance of that became all too obvious in late May and early June of 1989. On 20 May, the State Council imposed martial law in Beijing, signalling the government's intention to bring the protest movement to an end. Even with this declaration, few imagined the brutal way in which the government would 'restore order'. Just as had been the case in Lhasa earlier in the year, the Party-State deployed the full force available to it in order to ensure compliance from its citizens. The result was a massacre, with thousands of ordinary Chinese people killed or injured.

In the wake of the crackdown, the official media blamed the protests on a small handful of malcontents, who were supposedly working in conjunction with foreigners to overthrow the government. Under such circumstances it would have been no surprise if people viewed me with suspicion. Instead, I was received with the same openness and generosity that I had become accustomed to from ordinary Chinese people. Over the next few weeks I was able to get on with my work, while I gradually became used to living under martial law.

Few people I met wanted to talk about what had happened in their city, but those who did were united in expressing anger at the government. The most memorable exchange occurred on the underground, when I was drawn into a conversation with people who were still in disbelief that their own government had responded in such a brutal way. I was surprised that these people were so willing to express their anger in public, but not one of them seemed concerned about telling a complete stranger that they could not understand why their government had turned on its own citizens in the way it had. That was the general feeling I took away with me when I left: the sense of incomprehension, anger and sadness conveyed by the people I met.

你們已無言，而石頭有了呼聲
THIS STONE STANDS AS
WITNESS FOR THOSE
WHO CAN NO LONGER SPEAK

紀念一九八九年六月四日被中國政府血腥屠殺的北京天安門
民主烈士，及一切為中國人民的自由理想而獻身的先驅們．

In memory of the victims of the Peking Massacre of 4 June, 1989,
and all those who have given their lives for the ideal of freedom in China.

一九八九年九月十七日立
17 September, 1989

The Tiananmen Square memorial boulder, St Andrew's Presbyterian Church, on the corner of Alten Road and Symonds Street, Auckland. TREVOR HARDY

Soon after this I moved to Dunedin to take up a position teaching Chinese history at the University of Otago, and virtually every year since then I have been engaging students in discussions about the events of 1989. At first this was easy. Everyone had seen television coverage of the protests, the government's crackdown and the repression that followed, and most knew something about the flight of people from China as they sought safe haven elsewhere. Our classroom discussions were soon enhanced as academic analysis emerged about the complex issues that had arisen as the Party-State tried to shift China from the rigidity and constraints of the early years of the People's Republic to a more flexible and open society during the 1980s. In addition, the documentary film *The Gate of Heavenly Peace* was a great asset for classroom teaching, especially the short excerpts from the film available on the project's website.

But while it was possible to reach some understanding of what had led to the protest movement, it was much harder for a New Zealand audience to comprehend how a government could respond in such a brutal way to what most considered to be the legitimate concerns of its citizens. That required getting inside the ethos of a Party-State, something that is difficult for those of us enculturated to life in a democratic society.

Over the years a number of mainland Chinese students have joined my classes, and it has been interesting to observe how they respond to the sessions devoted to the events of 1989. Some have simply avoided these classes, preferring not to be implicated in discussions that they know are not permitted in China. But the majority have been keen to find out more. They know something important happened, but little more than that. For most Chinese students taking my courses, it is the sessions devoted to the events of 1989 that they find most interesting, and they seem to appreciate the opportunity to talk openly about them with New Zealand students. We hear much today about the aggressive nationalism of China's 'wolf warriors' and how Chinese students studying overseas can be forthright in challenging views they find unacceptable. This has never occurred in any class I have taught.

With the passage of time, the general ignorance that Chinese students have about the 1989 protest movement is now also true for most New Zealand students as well. A few might be familiar with the image of Tank Man, and this year one student said she remembered her parents talking about a 'protest movement', but most have little idea of why we should devote time to discussing these events. I have to remember that these students were not born in 1989 and there is so much that has happened since that demands their attention. Whereas in the case of the Chinese students their lack of knowledge is a product of state censorship, in the case of New Zealand students it is more just the casual amnesia that comes with distance.

We do, of course, discuss issues that generate more media concern in 2021, and hence are of more immediate interest to today's students, but as long as I am teaching about China I will return to the events of 1989. They have a personal resonance, and that makes it easier for me to engage students, but they also reveal a great deal about the nature of the Chinese Party-State and the resilience of China's people.

Winter (Season of Baby Mandarins, Apples): Spring Onion Oil Noodles 葱油拌面

NINA MINGYA POWLES

One weekend we sit huddled together on a bench in a narrow lane, eating noodles out of cardboard containers balanced on our knees. It begins to rain. It's March, the harsh edge of winter still present in the air at night, but this has the taste of summer rain: warm, fragrant, heavy. I'm with two of my classmates and we are deep inside a maze of picturesque lanes known as Tianzifang. The place is packed full of tourists, us included. We sit on one side of a sea of umbrellas and selfie sticks, blinking steam and rain from our eyes.

Where tourists abound in Shanghai, so does overpriced Western food. We could have picked anything — waffles, sandwiches, New York-style pizza, Chicago-style pizza, spaghetti Bolognese. We've taken one bus and three subway lines to get here. But when you are tired and hungry and it's starting to rain, there is only one thing that will do.

When I learned that *congyou banmian* (literally 'spring onion oil mixed noodles') existed, I had a feeling they might become a big part of my life.

The dish consists of a bowl of fine hand-pulled noodles tossed with spring onion-infused oil, dark soy sauce (the thicker, sweeter kind), and strips of spring onions that have been fried slowly in a lot of oil until dark and bittersweet, crisp and caramelised.

This is Shanghai's answer to *cacio e pepe*: simple, satisfying. And as with most Italian pasta dishes, the magic lies in the noodles-to-sauce ratio. Here, the ratio usually sits at an excellent 7:3. A modest amount of sauce, and an unspeakably huge amount of noodles.

The chef spoons the oil and the crispy onions over a thick wad of noodles. The smell reaches the table before the bowl does: rich, warm and bitter, a little sweetness in the tang of soy sauce. I use my chopsticks to mix it all together myself. Then I demolish it. With some practice, I learn not to regret it. I begin to think of those fried spring onions as a genuine part of my daily vegetable intake. I begin to prioritise joy.

Congyou banmian* are often called '*banmian*' for short. At breakfast and lunch (and dinner, if you're like me), people shout this across counters and tabletops all over Shanghai. The sharp, falling tone of each word makes me want to say them louder, give them more oomph, like a swear word. Sometimes the cashier knows what's up before the second syllable has left my mouth. She nods at me, serious and business-like.

It's become a kind of ritual. I ride my bike to the food mall at Wujiaochang after class, I order my noodles, I collect my chopsticks from the little chopstick washer and dispenser that hums pleasantly in the corner, and I sit at the bench full of people dining alone, more than half of them eating *banmian*.

Back in Wellington, I do things alone all the time during the day. I work, I eat, I write, I go for walks. But at night, things change. At night, aloneness in a public space means strange looks and unwanted attention. It means knowing the quickest, safest route home, pretending to talk on the phone and gripping my keys inside my pocket.

But here, perhaps like in all big cities, aloneness is part of the city itself. In Shanghai, I almost never feel unsafe. I walk long distances with my earphones in, never once needing to cross the road to avoid groups of loud, obnoxious men. I ride my bike through the campus without once glancing behind me. It's partly my white-passing privilege that affords me this feeling of freedom and safety, but I see many local students around me doing the same. I order my noodles and eat them in peace, and, for a little while, I feel less like an outsider.

Winter is nearly over and the downpours have begun. This is the beginning of the Plum Rains, Shanghai's infamous rainy season, named after the time when plums traditionally begin to ripen. *Plum rains.* I can taste the rain, sweet and full. At this time of year the sky is dark violet and gold at dusk. The Chinese for Plum Rains is 梅雨 *meiyu.* The end of the second syllable melts in my mouth.

In the early afternoon, during the third downpour of the day, I step out of my dorm building and wonder if I will make it to class. I have never seen so much water fall from the sky. I have never heard rain make so much noise. It streams down the sides of my umbrella and sloshes me in the face. Bikes and scooters tear through the water all around me, small waves breaking against the footpath. I set off into the underwater city, my boots instantly filling up. Just as I'm arriving, the rain suddenly stops and everything is still. The effect is dizzying: all the leaves shaking, umbrellas opening and closing. The air smells like mud and crushed flowers.

It rains a fourth time when I head to the nearest dumpling-and-noodle joint for dinner. It's not my favourite but it's the cheapest, which counts for a lot when you live in Shanghai on a student budget. The road is splashed across with pink and green from the neon lights above. Steam, or steamy smog, seems to be rising up.

Another benefit to eating alone is that the only person you can splatter with soy sauce is yourself. Like all best foods, *banmian* are messy. They are impossible to eat with any degree of restraint or elegance. With each bite I feel increasingly powerful and glorious, like some kind of fierce mythical creature who feasts only on soy sauce noodles. Out of the corner of my eye I see the man next to me devouring his *banmian* alongside a plate of six fluffy, crispy, soupy *shengjianbao* (pan-fried pork buns). This is a level of Shanghai hardcore I have not yet reached, but I'll get there.

Each time I'm at a new eatery where the menu is only in Chinese, I take a picture of it on my phone and look up the words I don't know later. This is how I discover new ways to eat.

The character 葱 *cong*, meaning 'spring onion', is one of my favourites. Complex and elegant, it is made up of 12 short strokes that fit closely together like a cluster of leaves. Or like the shreds of crisp onions left at the bottom of the bowl. When 葱 is combined with 绿, *lü* (meaning 'green'), it becomes 'lush green'. Bright green, verdant. A colour you don't see so much here in the middle of the city, except in food: handfuls sprinkled over dumplings, into bowls of noodles, over pieces of dough being kneaded and rolled out by the old man in the white cap. I can taste it.

Urumchi and the World in 2004

JOE LAWSON

In the mid-1990s, when I was 14, my German teacher, who would later briefly become a minister in a New Zealand Labour Government, took down a faded poster of Mao Zedong and put it on what I assumed was the recycling pile. I knew little about Mao other than that he was a Great Revolutionary Leader, and I asked if I could have it. 'Oh, you want Mao, do you?' he said with an expression I couldn't read, and handed it over. From then it had a place on my own wall until I left home when I was a student at Otago University. By then, reading my mother's copy of Jung Chang's *Wild Swans* had introduced another perspective on Mao. A further conversation, in which my naivety ran up hard against the lived reality of a classmate whose family were refugees from Pol Pot's Cambodia, had made me doubt the wisdom of being a global follower of communism.

Mao, Chang, and a final-year high-school project on Bertolucci's film *The Last Emperor* had not between them inspired a great ambition to live in China. A few Christmases in England, where I was born, had instilled an idea of living and working in the UK. That dream was gradually dispelled by the experience of living and working in Britain for a couple of university summers. I was a waiter in a pricey restaurant-bar, and then spent time wiping beer and fizzy drinks from tables at a bar in a bowling alley. My first post-university life plan was to teach English in Czechia. I went there at the beginning of 2004, but could only find a job that started in September. Not wanting to repeat the Lloyd Lanes bowling experience in London for the next six months, I got a job in China to tide me over, but ended up staying on for four years.

My knowledge of China had grown since leaving high school, thanks to excellent teaching on Asia at university. Fantasy visions now drew on Asian source material. I had started doing kung fu with a friend, and together we watched many Hong Kong martial arts films. I watched all the Wong Kar-wai videos from the local VHS rental. At my interview in London for a chain of English-language schools in China I talked about all this earnestly. Disappointingly, the interviewer seemed uninterested until I mentioned the pollution in Chinese cities. That was what she wanted to know I was prepared for. She was right to be attentive to this. The topic of smog was prominent in my first emails home. My father's Czech student — who knew what air pollution was from a childhood in a socialist Eastern European city — mentioned wryly in one email that he had heard about my 'fresh air surprise'.

I arrived in Urumchi in March 2004. What has happened there since around 2017 — the mass imprisonment and abuse of large numbers of Uyghur and other Turkic minorities — irretrievably colours my own memories of the city, and will shape the telling of its history in the early 2000s for a long time to come. In any context, when people narrate the past, on any scale from personal to global, it is natural to select details and events in a way that makes a coherent story. Often this imports a sense of prescience into the narrative. Of course, nobody knew beforehand that the Communist Party-State would adapt its traditions of extra-judicial detention and 'thought reform through labour' into a highly racist, war-on-terror-inflected campaign that would sweep so many people into the abyss. Some Uyghur and Kazakhs understood the possibilities for danger, and for them the prescience conveyed in narrating the past is justified. But for myself, and most of the foreigners I knew, there is a major disparity between the despair of the present reality and the optimism of the early 2000s.

Probably all humanities graduates from the 1990s and 2000s learned to dismiss Francis Fukuyama's *The End of History*, which held that Western liberal democracy was the endpoint in humankind's ideological evolution, and thus increasingly likely to be the prevalent form of governance in the long-term future. In retrospect, these dismissals were in large part unfair, as few had done so as a result of engaging seriously with his work. The most thoughtful discussion of it I have read was in the mid-2000s in the *Shanghai Review of Books*. Outside of university seminar rooms, most people I knew in the 1990s and 2000s actually shared Fukuyama's general interpretation of how societies were changing, although they usually articulated it more cautiously. When asked casually about what China's future might be like, one academic I knew said: 'Look at Taiwan.'

In Urumchi, many of the other foreigners I knew felt and admired the sense of dynamism in the city, which often extended to an appreciation of the Chinese developmental state. 'It took them about six months to put that up,' one colleague told me on my first night there as our taxi passed a spiralling bypass built over the street we drove down. Invocations of the city's energy were often made with a rueful contrast to what was perceived as the inertness of their own homelands.

Most of the Uyghur resentment we saw came about through discrimination in the labour market. 'Racial discrimination is very bad in Xinjiang, especially in the south,' said a secondary school teacher. He told me his degree from a university in the east of China would have led to a much better job if he were Han Chinese. The owner and manager of my own school employed Uyghur teachers on hourly paid contracts but was unwilling to offer them better contracts. The manager cited the spurious but often-used grounds that Uyghur employees' fluent but accented Chinese wasn't good enough. This was in an English training centre whose highest-paid foreign employees often could not have even a simple conversation in Chinese.

Han often viewed Uyghur with suspicion. While I was having dinner with students, a Han woman exhorted Uyghurs at the table to 'speak Chinese!' She didn't explain why Chinese and not Uyghur was to be the table's common language, and probably felt she didn't need to. What motivated her was probably nothing more than a sense that it was cliquey to speak a language not everyone understood, so people should speak 'the common language', Putonghua, when together. But at other times there was something more in people's minds. Urumchi always felt like a very safe city to me, but we also heard Han fears and rumours that punctuated development discourses like bad dreams. Were the small explosions that crashed a bus really 'gas explosions'?

Most of the complaints in Urumchi resembled the many resentments aired in unequal, multiracial societies around the world. I knew little about racism in New Zealand's job market, but when I heard Uyghur being told to speak Chinese, I remembered how, when I was working on the bar of a Dunedin restaurant in 2003, the owner told his friend over beers that 'there's too much of this kia ora bullshit in New Zealand', and complained about the 'darkies' he had encountered in London. I remembered anti-Asian graffiti on desks in the library at Otago University. Discussing the 2008 protests in Tibet and the Beijing Olympics, one New Zealander reminded me: 'The Olympics were in Sydney, and look at how Australians treat the Aborigines.' Given what has happened in Xinjiang since, this comparison might seem naive, but it was a point that was widely made among people I knew at the time.

Naturally, there was more to inter-ethnic social interaction than resentment. Urumchi was a city where different worlds tumbled alongside each other. An overriding impression was that most Han and Uyghur had few or no real friends from other ethnicities. Classroom interactions were often marked by curiosity, and a sense of surprise at how much they had in common. But the city's divisions were economic as well as ethnic. English lessons, like the classrooms and sports grounds of a few of the city's schools, were an imperfect social mixer, only available to a small elite of both Han and Uyghur.

Foreign teachers were often associated — among both locals and other foreigners who had some higher professional or academic purpose — with a stereotype of aimless indulgence. This was not so different to how Joseph Conrad depicted white people in Malaya in his novel *Lord Jim*. 'They led precariously easy lives.' This was fair in some cases, but many were also serious about their jobs and learning about the place where they lived.

English teaching offered a way of living in parts of the world otherwise only accessible to those with money for foreign study (or the academic wherewithal and the right nationality for a scholarship that might pay for it), or for those with the foresight to choose very specific pathways through a first university degree. English First in Urumchi was probably the most diverse workplace I have ever experienced, but it was still circumscribed in various ways. I later met Black people teaching English in other parts of China, where they faced formidable prejudices. A strong preference for native speakers — likely rooted in most students' and employers' inability to assess the language skills of a non-native speaker and a general fear of frauds and charlatans — also made it hard for continental Europeans, even though they typically had a better grasp of English grammar than their British, American or Kiwi colleagues.

What gets lost in a reduction of a city to contrasts between rich and poor, Han and Uyghur, local and foreign — as valid as they are in a broader perspective — are the galaxies of individual aspirations, passions and humour. In the street leading to our schools' apartments was the cheerful 'Backstreet Barber', who had a punkish aesthetic and posters of the Backstreet Boys on his shop's wall. He urged me through mime on my first visit to let him give me one of David Beckham's mohawk hairdos. More often than I had expected, the teenagers and adults we taught returned to topics related to queer identities in what they wrote to practise their English. By the standards of 2020s New Zealand, the tone would seem naive or problematic, but it did not at the time.

Less than five years earlier, I had graduated from a New Zealand high school where homophobic language was part of everyday life, and where it was unheard of for pupils to be openly gay. The teenagers I taught in Urumchi created alternative realities in their classes, where there were 'Sex Change High Schools', and where the walls of Number Four People's Hospital, the hospital for mental illnesses, were more permeable than they were in real life. When I learned more Chinese, I saw how these plays and stories often drew on the cheap ghost-story fiction that was popular among teenagers then. That was the youth of many who now still live in Urumchi, or are scattered around the world, or the desert; a spectre of a world now gone forever.

Chengdu:
12 May 2008

ANDREW WILFORD

5月12日 北京时间 14时 28分 04秒 (12 May 2:28pm)

A sudden surge of swirling movement propels plaster from the walls. Students, some dumbfounded, others screaming, are quickly marshalled down the darkened stairs of the twenty-storey building, thankful that the English school is only on level two and not on one of the higher floors. The ground heaves for two very long minutes. Buildings mimic the movement of the pavement underfoot as they sway back and forth. Some seek shelter under an overbridge, but quickly reconsider their decision as it begins to crack in front of the horrified students. It is a moment or two before I realise what is happening, an earthquake, a common experience for a New Zealander, but here in Sichuan it's on a scale that words fail to capture. Cries of 'di zen 地震, di zen!' (as pronounced in Sichuanese) echo through our group as shock turns to fear and screams ring out from the masses of people hastily fleeing the buildings.

Within the Hour

Spontaneous convoys of taxis and buses head towards Dujiangyan (都江堰), some 70 kilometres from downtown Chengdu, to help where they can. Drivers call to pedestrians on the street to ask if they can help them get home. Strangers help each other to their feet. People huddle and sob quietly in corners. Others scramble to get essential supplies from convenience stores and markets downtown, clearing the shelves of water inside an hour.

That Evening

As night falls, aftershocks strike and rumours swirl. The extent of damage at the epicentre is unknown; news reports with details of the destruction in the mountains surrounding the city slowly trickle in. Few dare to return home, congregating instead in makeshift tent villages, public parks, and university campuses. My Xiaolingtong (小灵通) phone becomes a vital means of connecting with families abroad. A quirk in the telecommunications system means these devices still call abroad, despite a limited ban on international calls for unregistered numbers and an overburdened network as people try to contact their loved ones. Colleagues and students from Canada, Russia, Australia and America gather at Sichuan University to call their families and assure them they are safe, while we frantically try to reach others who are away in the mountains near the epicentre.

A Week Later

'Landslides', 'Richter scale', 'aftershocks' and 'quake lakes'. We hastily add new vocabulary to the daily pronunciation classes. All become amateur geologists overnight in the hope that science might help us make sense of the unfolding tragedy. Children swarm around adult classmates who happen to be engineers, quizzing them on the cracks at home and the risks that quake lakes pose. The horrific number of casualties becomes apparent. A colleague lost her cousin, and others are still missing. Some students are eager to talk about the quakes; others become withdrawn and unresponsive. No one asks why. We know some of them come from villages near the epicentre. Premier Wen Jiabao appears on television to assure all that their hardships are shared, and that the central government will spare no effort to respond to the crisis. His visit is well received, with many

Beichuan 北川 (Sichuan province) in 2011, three years after the Sichuan earthquake. Destroyed buildings such as these have been preserved as a memorial to ensure that the calamity is not forgotten. In 2008 Andrew Wilford was living in Chengdu, about 200 kilometres from Beichuan. ANDREW WILFORD

touched by the 'down to earth' (接地气) man of the people. After similar pronouncements by CCP General Secretary Hu Jintao, some students note that, unlike Hu, they can't fly away in a helicopter afterwards. Numerous rumours of aftershocks and unspeakable horrors near the epicentre are spread by means of group text messages from a countless number of people. Foreign teachers ask students to translate their contents for them before returning to class.

A Visit to Beichuan 北川

More than two years pass before I can visit the worst-hit county. Beichuan, more than 150 kilometres from Chengdu, has been left as a monument to the horror wrought in those two minutes. In that city alone, thousands of inhabitants perished, and 80 per cent of all buildings were destroyed. Green shoots poke through the cracks in the shattered buildings, which are strewn about the area through which the Jian (湔) river flows. The tranquil river meanders around the town, roughly congruent with where the fault lines lie. The school has been consumed by an immense wall of earth cascading down from the surrounding hills. An acquaintance muses that only the children running late to class survived. Mr Hu, our guide, notes with some resignation the mass graveyard in the centre of 'old Beichuan', before shepherding us into his van to see a newly built city some 30 kilometres away. The new town of Beichuan is impressive, and many in the group remark with pride on the state's ability to rebuild after a disaster. We drive home in silence. Nobody mentions the students or others who perished.

事 Occasion

Memories of a Polisher in Beijing

PHILLIP MANN

It was a bleak winter's evening as our plane descended from the clouds into Beijing airport. I remember glancing out of the window at the snow wheeling down and the grey buildings passing beneath us, and thinking to myself: 'What am I doing dragging my wife, Nonnita, and our two children, Delia and Owen, away from the summer warmth of New Zealand to this grim world?' But there was no going back. This was the adventure I had wanted ever since I had become fascinated by the culture of China.

The plane was crowded, and the air thick with tobacco smoke. Most of our fellow passengers were military men in full uniform, and they wore their medals proudly. From the outset of our flight they had made us feel welcome, smiling and waving, and offering us cigarettes. I realised that, for most of them, the sight of a foreigner was a novelty; China had been closed for many years during the turmoil that was called the Cultural Revolution. Most of the warriors travelling with us were quite old, with weathered faces, and it appeared to me that some of them may even have marched with Mao Zedong during the Long March, when they were young men. Living history!

The plane landed smoothly and I was able to practise my limited Chinese vocabulary, saying *zaijian* ('goodbye') to the comrades who had travelled with us. They seemed delighted with this and waved goodbye. In truth, however, I was a bit worried. We were all tired from the journey, and the children were bewildered and kept close to us while staring at this strange new world. The arrangements for our arrival had not been clear. I did not know where we would be staying that night or who would be meeting us, and we had not expected to arrive in the middle of a snowstorm.

But I need not have worried. There, waiting to greet us, was a small committee from the New China News Agency (Xinhua) where we would be working. They rushed over to us, waving and smiling and calling 'Welcome! Welcome to China.' They had come well prepared, too, and threw warm, fur-lined overcoats around our shoulders and shook our hands like old friends. One picked up our son Owen in a warm hug. Another crouched down near Delia and put her arms around her shoulders. I felt a great surge of relief. We had arrived. All was well. The great adventure had begun.

My deep interest in China had started a few years earlier. I had always been interested in non-Western theatre, and one day, by chance, I had watched a video of a performance of one of the Monkey King stories: *Sun Wukong and the White Bone Demon.* I was completely mystified and fascinated by this effervescent mixture of music, dance and acrobatics. I wanted to know more. This led me to a study of Chinese literature, and ultimately to take a course in Chinese language. Then, one day, quite out of the blue, a Chinese friend informed me that China was 'opening up'. After the disastrous self-imposed isolation of the Cultural Revolution, the Chinese government was now looking for foreigners who would be able to help its development. Was I interested? I was indeed.

After a brief interview, I was informed that both my wife and I would be offered work at Xinhua in Beijing. We would be 'Polishers of Language'.

Our task was to ensure that the English texts published by the agency were grammatically correct and lucid. We would begin work immediately. We would be paid in yuan, and accommodation would be provided. It all seemed so simple and straightforward. We accepted. Victoria University, where I was teaching courses in drama, generously allowed me two years' leave of absence.

Xinhua was broadly divided into two sections. One section concentrated on information about Chinese life and cultural developments. This was the section in which my wife worked. The other section was more directly political, and concentrated on China's reaction to events that were happening in the world at large. That was my section. All in all, it was very exciting work and very new to me.

My section was busy night and day, and after a few months (that is, after I had proved that I could do the work swiftly and accurately, and that I was not a spy or a subversive) I was asked if I was prepared to work a night-shift, this being the time when China was asleep but the rest of the world was alert and at work. I agreed, and I am glad that I did so. I was told that I was the only foreigner working the night-shift in Beijing! True or false, I do not know, but I felt quite honoured.

The texts I was dealing with explained China's attitude to the events taking place in countries such as Britain, America, the USSR, etc. The year was 1978. It is important to remember that China was still at that point recovering from the dark period of the Cultural Revolution, and there were many contacts with the rest of the world that China needed to re-establish while at the same time being cautious not to betray its own revolution. There were many wounds left to heal. I will devote the remainder of this short essay to giving you a sense of what it was like to work what one of my comrades called 'the graveyard shift'.

It is a fact that working at night encourages a special kind of intimacy. People relax. There is a feeling of camaraderie, and I do not mean that in a political sense. For instance, one of my colleagues offered to teach me more Chinese language when we were not busy 'polishing'. People told jokes and expressed their hopes for the future and for their children. But they never, in my presence at least, talked about the Cultural Revolution. I suspect the memories were too painful.

To conclude, I have selected three moments that stand out in my memory on account of their humour, their human warmth and their political reality, respectively.

1. The Riding Lesson

In 1979 Deng Xiaoping visited America. It was an important, historic occasion, and our Xinhua office was on full alert. We had many documents flowing across our desks, especially at night. I received one urgent request to check an article that had to be published as soon as possible. It was an account of Deng's visit to a farm or a stable. It was not particularly exciting. But then I came to a sentence that read '. . . and Deng Xiaoping had an exciting time riding cowgirls'. That brought me awake in a hurry, and I must admit that, for a moment, I was tempted to let it go as the idea was so comic and outrageous. But no! Wisdom prevailed, and I added a 'with' and changed the sex to 'cowboys' so the line read '. . . and Deng Xiaoping had an exciting time riding with cowboys'. And that was what was published.

Later, I told one of my comrades about this change of wording, and he looked at me blankly, until I explained that the verb 'riding' could have more than one significance, especially if coupled with the improbable 'cowgirls'. I saw his jaw drop when he understood. 'But you did correct it?' he asked anxiously.

'Just in time,' I replied. 'Just in time.'

2. Music in the Night

One day, shortly after the night-time meal, I was walking back alone through the dark corridors to my office when I heard the faint sound of music. This was most unusual. I decided to investigate.

The Xinhua building was quite large, and had a wide central staircase which gave access to the upper floors and to an older building that had once been a magnificent library. As I climbed, the music grew louder. I recognised the tune. It was the 'Tennessee Waltz'. I moved down the passage until I came to a large door that was slightly ajar. The music was coming from there. I pushed the door wider and stepped through. I found myself in an old dance hall, and there, dancing, were some of my comrades. How extraordinary!

As soon as they saw me the music stopped. It had been playing from disc on an old wind-up record-player. Someone had lifted the needle.

I felt dreadful. 'Please,' I said. 'Don't stop. I heard the music, and it is one of my favourite dance tunes. I had not heard it for years. I love dancing, too. Please go on dancing.' The record player was wound up again, and little by little the music and dancing resumed. 'I was dancin' with my darlin' . . .'

I was about to leave when one of the men came up to me. He was not from my office, but I had seen him occasionally. He said, 'Please, Meng Feili [my name], I have a request. I do not dance, but my wife loves dancing. Would you dance with her?'

I was overcome. 'Of course I will,' I said. 'I shall be honoured, but . . .' There were no 'buts'.

And so, in a very formal and dignified way, arms outstretched but bodies not touching, we began to dance. She was not a tall woman but as light as a feather, and after a few stumbles we got it right and she seemed to float, as good dancers do.

And at the end, I bowed and thanked her. As I left, everyone was smiling, but I was close to tears. It was the beauty and the simplicity of it all that had moved me.

Later I asked one of my friends, in confidence, where the old gramophone would have come from. He looked at me shrewdly and said, 'Meng Feili, you do not understand. In the Cultural Revolution, we buried all our treasures deep under the ground, under our houses until it was safe to reveal them again.'

3. Washing the Wall

One night, at about 3.30am, I was told that as there was no more news coming in I could leave early. I gathered my things and went down to the parking bay where the cars and drivers were always on duty.

We had got to know the drivers well. Some never spoke; others wanted to try words in English. Sometimes I would buy American cigarettes for them as a way of saying 'Thank you for driving safely', even though I knew they were just doing their job.

On this night there seemed to be some tension in the air. Whispered conversations. No laughter. We set off for the Friendship Hotel where I lived, and I immediately noted that we were taking a different route.

'Why go this way?' I asked. But there was no answer. I knew that the road we were following would take us past Democracy Wall, and I noticed that as we approached it there were lots of lights shining on it and many soldiers and policemen milling about.

Let me explain. Democracy Wall was a celebration. It came into being after the fall of the Gang of Four, and was a place where anyone could put a message or express an opinion. Here you would find poems, political statements, requests for information about lost friends and relatives, or expressions of outrage and accusations of injustice. It was the people's voice. New texts appeared daily. It was not censored.

'So what is going on?' I asked, but my driver did not answer. We simply stopped and he turned the car lights off. I watched as a water cannon was brought into action. The powerful jets of water began scouring the wall and peeling off the messages. More water cannons and hosepipes came into play, and soon every message on the wall was gone, swilled away.

Then we were approached by some official, and the driver started the engine, and we drove on, straight past where the *dazibao* 大字报 (big-character posters, usually used as a form of protest) had been, and on to the Friendship Hotel where I lived. Not a word was spoken.

The next day I asked my colleagues what had happened, but no one wanted to talk about it. However, one official told me that the old chaotic *dazibao* had been replaced by a splendid new and official *dazibao* that was located in Moon Park. The only difference, he said, was that in the new location if you wanted to submit a comment or share information or display a poem, you had to sign your name.

Sic transit gloria mundi.

I loved the time I spent in China and my respect for the Chinese people is boundless, but I cannot help but feel that something has been lost in the mad race for economic prosperity. Now, in this age of coronavirus and lockdown, the one thing I can assert is that China will survive in one form or another.

Whakawhanaungatanga

MENG FOON

Chinese people have been in Gisborne or Tairāwhiti since the 1870s. Their main occupations were those they knew from their homeland: market gardening, selling produce, restaurants, laundries. In 1914, at the start of the Great War, Chinese people living in New Zealand wanted to go and fight for king and country. Initially, they were disallowed from doing so, but eventually the government did agree, and two young men from Gisborne, both from the Eng family, went to Europe to fight.

My parents both have roots in Guangzhou; Dad came to Gisborne in 1947, and Mum married Dad in Hong Kong and came to Gisborne in 1958. I was made in Hong Kong and born in Gisborne. I have two younger brothers. We were market gardeners and retailers.

I was first elected to the Gisborne District Council in 1994, and was elected mayor in 2001. Gisborne District Council already had a Sister City in China, called Rizhao (in Shandong Province). This relationship is still continuing.

My first visit to Rizhao was in 2002. Our delegation, accompanied by the president of the Chamber of Commerce, Anne Pardoe, was hosted in Rizhao. Tairāwhiti is a large grower and exporter to China of radiata pine timber, and this trade underpins the relationship. (Seventy per cent of the Tairāwhiti wood goes to Langshan in Hunan Province, and Gisborne and Langshan have exchanged mayoral visits.) Sister City relationships need to be sustained by projects and activities. It is hard to rely only on cultural exchanges, however important they may be.

Rizhao students come from their polytechnic to study at Tairāwhiti Polytechnic. One such student, James Zhang, graduated and went on to study at Waikato University. During his time with us, he also worked in the economic development department of the Gisborne District Council, helping to encourage more investment and export opportunities for Tairāwhiti.

We continued to have many exchanges in support of each other: Gisborne's fiftieth anniversary as a city in 2005, Gisborne's hosting of the *Beijing Olympic Art Exhibition* in 2008, and so on. I believe life is about relationships, even though some of our ratepayers have a different view. I believe that our Sister City relationships have been productive due to our economic activities.

I think I have had more Chinese delegations visit Gisborne than most other New Zealand cities because of my Chinese heritage, and I have been to many places in China. It is an awesome country. I admire the enterprise and the food culture, but I do worry about the pollution and imbibing too much Maotai during my visits. Many of our visitors want to establish Sister City relationships with us, but there has to be a limit; instead, I encourage economic activity and we have a few memorandums of understanding (MOUs) encouraging economic relationships.

In November 2008, I went with a team of engineers from New Zealand to Chengdu for about a week. They had had a major and catastrophic earthquake on 12 May 2008. Why was I selected to join this group? This was because Gisborne had suffered a medium-size earthquake in December 2007, which had badly affected the region economically, as it had struck at the height of our busy season. We are still repairing buildings in 2021. Four of us travelled to Chengdu, offering our various skills as road engineers, civil engineers and building engineers, and with me as Gisborne's mayor.

We toured Beichuan, Wenchuan and other places of devastation. Reports at the time told us that it was a 7.9 quake at its epicentre (measured as magnitude 8.0 by the Chinese), and was located near the city of Dujiangyan, about 50 miles (70 kilometres) west-north-west of the provincial capital, Chengdu, and it was at a depth of 11.8 miles (19 kilometres) below the surface. Almost 90,000 people were counted as dead, or missing and presumed dead, in the final official Chinese government assessment; the quake killed more than 5300 children, the bulk of whom were attending classes when the earthquake struck. In addition, nearly 375,000 people were injured by falling debris and building collapses.

By the time of our visit, it was the winter season and snow had just started to fall. We travelled in a minivan to many of the rural areas affected by the quake. I saw total devastation. As we visited the various cities and towns which the earthquake had flattened, I couldn't help but think that there were no more future generations from the families who had lost their children. I saw one primary school that had collapsed in Beichuan, and our support person said that 95 per cent of the children at the school had died that day. They indicated that the town was going to be left as a memorial as there were so many people buried there.

The roads were narrow in many places, and bridges and highways had collapsed. I couldn't help but see the indomitable spirit of the people; they were getting on with rebuilding. The government had delivered truckloads of bricks and left them in heaps at the various properties for the locals to start rebuilding. They were erecting their buildings with what seemed like mānuka poles. I'm not sure about structural integrity and building consents, but Chinese people are practical, and they needed to have shelter and to have it quickly.

The four of us delivered presentations at Chengdu University. We visited the panda nursery. I got to hold a baby panda — they are so cute! Sichuan food is spicy-hot. I had feared that I would end up with an upset tummy; given the lack of toilet facilities, what would happen if I got the runs? Fortunately, the worst did not happen. The food and company were exceptional, and it turns out I can handle hot, spicy food.

Given that my mandarin is *mama huhu* 马马虎虎, or just so-so, wherever I went in China and in Gisborne, I would start off my welcome speech to our host or guest in my Chinese dialect of Seyip (四邑). Mandarin speakers weren't able to understand what I was saying. And often it was acceptable to speak in English with the help of very able Chinese interpreters. The hospitality was awesome: huge banquets, some with thousands attending, and some intimate.

———

Gisborne District Council had been well supported by the Cultural Section of the Chinese Embassy. In 2005, they gave us a dragon and a drum set to support our Fiftieth City Anniversary. We don't have many Chinese youth in Gisborne, so I asked the pupils at Gisborne Boys' High, my old school, to perform the dragon dance. I told them to take a look at examples on YouTube. What a performance they gave! The Chinese–Māori dragon dance was a highlight of the anniversary.

In 2008, China hosted the Beijing Olympic games. I was watching TV one day late in 2007 and I saw that there was going to be an Olympic art exhibition exhibited in 12 cities around the world. I immediately wrote to the Beijing Olympic committee to ask if Gisborne might be the first city in the world to host this prestigious event. Within a short time, they said yes: if you don't ask, you will never know what the answer might be! Gisborne District Council was invited to Beijing to formally receive the invitation to host the exhibition. Councillor Burdett and I attended the event, and a grand ceremony it was. We also asked what the chance was of getting one of the full-size sculptures of the mascots created for the Beijing Olympics.

The officials indicated that they were going to auction them off after the Olympic games.

Our council artistic director, Nick Tupara, facilitated the whole exhibition: ka mihi, Nick. After a discussion with the New Zealand Olympic secretary-general Barry Meister, the Olympic committee arrived in Gisborne and stayed at Acton Estate, courtesy of the Nakamoto Family, with the help of Sheldon Drummond (general manager of eLandNZ). We had our first pōwhiri at Whāngārā Marae, hosted by Ngāti Konohi. The next day a pōwhiri was held at Te Poho o Rāwiri. The official opening of the exhibition was at the Lawson Field Theatre, but, because of the teeming rain, the event had to be moved indoors. In attendance was our then governor-general, Sir Anand Satyanand, who was also patron of the New Zealand Olympics. The event was a hit for Tairāwhiti and for all of Aotearoa New Zealand; 110 objects were on display for a whole month and received over 40,000 visitors. Dawn Brooking did a great job as host.

A year later we received a letter to say that we could have one of the full-size sculptures. All we had to do was pay the freight. Council was willing to pay for the installation, and one of my councillors, Councillor Wilson, whose wife had died in an unfortunate accident, said he would sponsor the freight and we would acknowledge this with a plaque that said 'In memory of Phillipa Wilson'. The sculpture, called *Evolution*, was gifted to the city of Gisborne. Designed by the Guangdong sculptor Lu Zenkang, the piece takes its inspiration from the sculptures of ancient Athens. It now stands proudly in the Rose Garden.

Lorraine Brown (the local MP at the time) called one day and said that Tū Te Mana Maurea, a well-respected kapa haka group from Manutuke-Rongowhakaata, was going to the 2010 World Expo in Shanghai. She wanted me to teach them a Chinese song. I arrived at the Manutuke Marae and suggested they learn 'The Moon Represents My Heart' (月亮代表我的心). As this was a famous and beloved song in China, I thought it would be appropriate. We went through the words and meaning, and I suggested that the group listen to YouTube for the rest. It was well received, and it is still sung today by Tū Te Mana Maurea.

In 2012 I was MC at the Beehive event marking the fortieth anniversary of the establishment of New Zealand–China Diplomatic Relations. The 2008 New Zealand–China Free Trade Agreement (FTA) was a major step forward for the relationship, and so has been the renewal of the FTA in 2019.

A key highlight for me was in 2012, when I was approached by the Ministry of Foreign Affairs and Trade (MFAT) and asked if I would be able to propose the toast to President Xi Jinping at a function hosted by then prime minister the Rt Hon. John Key at SkyCity. I said 'sure', but then thought: 'Oh, it's going to be in Mandarin.' But then the official said: 'We would like you to present the toast in Māori.' Whew! That'll be water off a duck's back. Te reo o Ngāti Porou is one of my proficiencies.

Before the event, I went to the Stone Studio in Gisborne and bought two pieces of pounamu as presents for the main guests. I knew the officials had said no gifts and I only had two minutes for the toast, but, you know, I'm from Tairāwhiti, and there we need to give a koha and no speech is ever short. I presented my toast with a quick promotion for Tairāwhiti, went up to the presidential table and gave the president and his wife our taonga.

I had the honour of being invited to China in 2015 to attend the Commemoration of the Seventieth Anniversary of the Victory of the Chinese People's Resistance against Japanese Aggression. It was a hot day in Beijing with an unusually clear sky. The Chinese government had closed all the factories in Beijing, and cars with odd and even numbers were only allowed on the road on alternating days. The sky was beautiful. We were fully hosted. The morning came and we were all on our buses, arriving early at the venue. After a few hours the parade started. What an impressive military parade. The touching part for me was that the veterans were acknowledged first, as they had paved the way for the current generation.

China and New Zealand mayoral forums were set up to foster cultural and economic exchanges. I attended forums in Wellington and Xiamen. The events were jam-packed with many activities, and, although each mayor was given only a five-minute slot for their presentations, there was ample time during the various breaks to discuss commercial opportunities.

Former ambassador Tony Browne is now chair of the New Zealand Contemporary China Research Centre, and of the Victoria University of Wellington Confucius Institute. I had first met him in Beijing at an event associated with the Auckland Philharmonic Orchestra tour of China. Through the Confucius Institute, he has facilitated Mandarin language-learning for students at 10 Gisborne schools. I believe that communication is very important to the social, cultural and economic wellbeing of Tairāwhiti, and I continue to encourage our young people to learn Mandarin, the language of our major trading partner.

In 2017, China's Premier Li Keqiang visited New Zealand. I was honoured to be asked to propose a toast to him. Right, I thought to myself, not a problem in te reo Māori. Then the official asked that I do it in Mandarin. 'Yes,' I said, 'all good.' I then sent a note to my Mandarin-speaking friend, Jackie. 'Mate,' I said, 'can you give me a few words in Mandarin for a toast to Li Keqiang?' I learned his toast down-pat. However, the day before the event in Auckland, hosted by the New Zealand Prime Minister John Key, they gave me a script of the toast I was to present. Okay, I thought, better get on and learn this one as well. Fortunately, it all went well.

I am grateful to MFAT for the honour of being invited to propose two major toasts to our important guests from China, and it has been an honour and a privilege to have played my part in building respectful relationships with China. Our region has benefitted greatly from these efforts, and the trade which Tairāwhiti has with China is second to none. Our economy has benefitted, more people are employed, many students are learning Mandarin. Our knowledge of both China and New Zealand has been enhanced through *guanxi* 关系, what Māori call whakawhanaungatanga. It's all about relationships, face-to-face.

The Poll Tax Apology and Reconciliation

ESTHER FUNG

It was a momentous occasion on 12 February 2002 when people — many from the Chinese community, and including the Ambassador of the People's Republic of China, Chen Mingming 陳明明 — gathered in the Grand Hall at Parliament to celebrate the beginning of the Chinese New Year, and heard these words spoken by Prime Minister Helen Clark:

> I wish to announce today that the government has decided to make a formal apology to those Chinese people who paid the poll tax and suffered other discrimination imposed by statute and to their descendants . . . The government's apology today is the formal beginning to a process of reconciliation.

She went on to recognise the New Zealand Chinese Association 紐西蘭華聯總會 (NZCA) for initiating and sustaining the foundational research and the work of informing the government and community about the issue. The apology was accepted by Kuan Meng Goh (吳光明), then president of the NZCA, myself, Esther Fung (馮吳瑞珍), president of the Wellington Chinese Association (WCA) and a direct descendant of poll tax payers, and Allen Chang (陳顧強), representing a group of Chinese organisations that had expressed reservations about the process. For many in the community, and indeed New Zealanders in general, the poll tax story and subsequent discriminatory, anti-Chinese laws enacted over the years were unknown territory; they were unpleasant and shameful acts, to be ignored and forgotten, or locked away and not confronted for fear of further hurt.

The story begins in the nineteenth century when the government passed the Chinese Immigrants Act 1881 to regulate the number of Chinese entering New Zealand. The provisions of the Act were that each Chinese passenger entering New Zealand by ship was to pay a poll tax of £10 (equivalent to $1,649 in 2013 dollar terms) to the Customs Department to legally land in the country, and the ship could carry no more than one Chinese passenger for every 10 tons of cargo. The ship's master was fined if his limit was exceeded, and the vessel could be forfeited. The Chinese Immigrants Act Amendment Bill 1888 raised the tonnage restriction to one Chinese passenger for every 100 tons of ship's cargo. The law was further amended by the Chinese Immigrants Act Amendment Act 1896, which increased the sum paid on entry to £100 (equivalent to $18,390 in 2013) and the tonnage ratio to one Chinese passenger per 200 tons of cargo.

These and other discriminatory measures — such as fingerprinting, education tests and certificates for proof of New Zealand residence — were imposed solely on Chinese migrants. The measure affected the ability of the Chinese to live and work in New Zealand, while causing great financial hardship and humiliation. Between 1882 and 1930, £308,080 (equivalent to $29,950,822 in 2013) was collected by the government from a community that was never more than 2 per cent of the total New Zealand population during these years.

When the poll tax was abolished in 1944, the deputy prime minister, Walter Nash, acknowledged that it amounted to:

> . . . the removing of the blot in our legislation. We are merely saying that the Chinese are as good as any other race, and that we will not in the future countenance any discrimination against them.

New Zealand had not been the only country to impose an entry tax and other discriminatory laws against Chinese migrants. America, Australia and Canada had similar patterns of Chinese migration in the nineteenth century and responded with similar measures.

The NZCA's awareness of these injustices was sparked in 1991, when Nigel Murphy (麥禮祖), of the Alexander Turnbull Library, informed my husband David Fung (馮智偉), editor of the WCA newsletter, of the campaign by members of the Canadian Chinese community to seek redress for the head tax (the Canadian equivalent to the poll tax) imposed in 1886 by the Canadian government on Chinese entering that country. This knowledge was to prompt the NZCA, under the presidency of Harvey Wu (吳義源), to pursue a similar goal of redress in New Zealand, with David as an indefatigable advocate of the cause.

The book *Turning Stone into Jade: The history of the New Zealand Chinese Association* (雕石成璧), published by the association with financial assistance from the Chinese Poll Tax Heritage Trust — which was established as an eventual outcome of the formal government apology — documents in considerable detail the lengthy and often fraught process whereby the association sought redress for the wrongs suffered historically by the Chinese in New Zealand.

Eventually, on 12 December 2001, the association's finalised submission was sent to the government. At the same time, other people were lobbying members of the government, such as Minister for Ethnic Affairs George Hawkins, about the poll tax issue, including Chinese Aucklanders who were members of the New Zealand Federation of Ethnic Councils. This exemplified the disparate interests within the Chinese community.

From this time, events unfolded at a rapid pace. While the NZCA prepared a strategy based on its submission, the government intimated that the prime minister would make a public announcement about past injustices to the Chinese community at a Chinese New Year function to be hosted at Parliament in February 2002. This would pre-empt further action by the association. The government appeared resolved on a course of action to deal with the issue of the poll tax.

Despite an unfortunate *faux pas* when the Chinese version of the apology was delivered in Mandarin rather than in Cantonese — the predominant language of the poll tax payers and the mother tongue of their descendants — the apology was a great coup for the government and was well received by the majority of the Chinese community. It also brought the whole descendant community into a discussion about the injustices of the past. Although many factions within the community claimed to be instrumental in achieving the apology, and certainly made a contribution in the latter stages, the research groundwork, the course of action, and the protracted negotiations with the government were all due to the efforts of the NZCA and its members.

The next stage in the poll tax journey involved the government making some form of conciliatory gesture towards the Chinese community in recognition of the past statutory discrimination and financial hardship imposed on the early settlers. The NZCA was joined by other groups in the descendant community for this part of the process. After extensive consultation, a Poll Tax Advisory Team recommended that the government set aside a sum of money, $5 million, to provide for meaningful activities

Esther Fung accepts the New Zealand government's apology 'to those Chinese people who paid the poll tax and suffered other discrimination imposed by statute and to their descendants' as president of the Wellington Chinese Association and as a poll tax descendant, 12 February 2002. ESTHER FUNG

for the Chinese community, and set up a community trust to distribute the money to suitable projects.

On 11 February 2004, during the celebrations at Parliament marking the Chinese New Year, Prime Minister Helen Clark announced the establishment of the Chinese Poll Tax Heritage Trust (CPTHT). Steven Young (楊瑞生), representing the advisory team, responded with a speech of thanks. A delighted prime minister was presented by the community with flowers and a Chinese scroll by the artist Stan Chan 陳康渭, which reads: *To the Rt Hon Prime Minister of New Zealand — herewith our thanks for the very sincere apology. With compliments from the Poll Tax Advisory Team, 11 February 2004.*

The objectives of the CPTHT are to promote the preservation of New Zealand Chinese history and the contributions of early Chinese settlers, and to provide tangible support for New Zealand Chinese history, language and culture, particularly of the early Chinese settlers.

The journey from discriminatory legislation to apology and reconciliation was a lengthy one, and the process was assisted by many friends and supporters of the Chinese community along the way. Nigel Murphy provided the first spark of awareness in 1991. His dedicated research, commissioned by the then president of the NZCA, Harvey Wu, and myself as secretary, unearthed and documented the circumstances of the New Zealand poll tax and the raft of anti-Chinese legislation that had been largely unacknowledged.

Concurrently, Harvey Wu and I had begun to engage extensively with government ministers in successive administrations to make them aware of the injustice of the past and the need for an apology. In 2003, while on the staff of the Alexander Turnbull Library, Nigel Murphy curated an impressive exhibition about the poll tax entitled *A Barbarous Measure: The Poll Tax and Chinese New Zealanders*. Held at the National Library, which houses many of the relevant resources, the exhibition documented and publicised the poll tax and the government's 2002 apology. After the exhibition closed in Wellington, the NZCA branches sponsored its display in other cities throughout the country. The NZCA can be credited with the persistent pursuit of the poll tax issue, resulting in the injustices achieving recognition and a government apology for the early settler community. The individuals concerned put a great deal of effort into the project over a number of years and saw it through, despite changes in personnel and governments and the multitude of views held by members of the Chinese community.

The reconciliation process that followed the 2002 apology was intensive, as the descendant community negotiated internally with its constituents and externally with the government. Finding an acceptable and amicable settlement was due in no small part to the wisdom, understanding, and negotiating skills of Sonja Rathgen, the director of the Office of Ethnic Affairs, who died in 2014. She expertly steered a large team from the community through a maze of community aspirations and bureaucratic constraints.

At the conclusion of the process, the Poll Tax Advisory Team presented Sonja with a specially inscribed scroll, also by the artist Stan Chan, which reads: *If it were not for the venerable fisherman, how could we behold the sea?*, and a small jade memento as a token of their gratitude and respect.

1989 Matters

BRENDA (ENGLEFIELD) SABATIER

'The students are too naive. They are too young to understand they will never be allowed to win,' my friend Alex remarked as we stood outside the Friendship Hotel at night. The roads were full of people, some en route to or from Tiananmen Square, others observing in solidarity or just curiosity. It was May 1989, and I had cycled down from Beida (Peking University) where I was an English teacher. Alex was a journalist, a Chinese-born New Zealander living at the Friendship Hotel, a place where many resident foreigners stayed. His father had brought his family back to China, answering the call for overseas Chinese to return to help rebuild the country after what the CCP called 'liberation', the establishment of a new China in 1949. But living under CCP rule had not been easy; Alex had been through much and was worried.

Another night in May, Alex had turned to two young men behind us. Alex was always aware of possible 'listeners' nearby. However, these two were from the countryside, poorly dressed in worn Mao-style jackets and canvas shoes. They were stunned that Alex spoke their dialect, which he had learned when he had been 'sent down' to the countryside for what the CCP called 'reform through labour', something many urban residents experienced in the 1950s and 1960s. They had heard about the events in Beijing, and had come not only to find jobs, but also to see if what they had heard was true.

I had arrived in Beijing towards the end of 1988, 10 years after first visiting on a New Zealand China Friendship Society student tour. Now it seemed that people were able to try some aspects of Western life. Mao-style clothing was not the only choice, with colourful, fashionable clothing freely available. Ballroom dancing was huge, with groups dancing in parks and on campus. Many places gave lessons, and I joined tango classes myself. On the streets, pool tables were everywhere, and seldom unused. I was struck by young couples entwined on buses, kissing, and Lovers' Corner in a park not far from Beida was a popular place. Perhaps these freedoms contributed to the hope that there could also be a loosening of the political system.

It was clear, though, that for many money was tight. My students submitted homework on scraps of paper; complete pages were rare. Food was expensive, and the food in the student canteen was basic, with meat infrequently offered and of low quality. My voluntary vegetarianism was puzzling, being the diet of the poor. Everyone urged me to eat meat for my health, and staff at local restaurants hid it in my dishes. I remembered this when many students became weak during the hunger strikes in May at Tiananmen Square and were attended by ambulances.

However, a strong belief in the communist system, which ostensibly provided everyone with an iron rice-bowl and a level playing field, persisted. This was proudly explained, sometimes along with a comment on the selfishness in the West. The iron rice-bowl, though, brought perplexing situations. When my light bulb blew, getting a replacement took days. Later I understood that everyone in the chain from my apartment to the light-bulb cupboard attendant had to be consulted, in the right order, and I could not fit it myself either.

In contrast to these communist ideals, a duality was apparent. People talked of the wealth and opportunities of cadres whose children attended foreign universities. There was a two-tier monetary system: renminbi, for those without privilege; and Foreign Exchange Certificates (FECs) for foreigners, which also allowed access to Western food and goods. Thus, there was a healthy FEC black market. Once, when talking with a student about it, he wept. He had been unaware of it, and was appalled that the leadership allowed an iniquitous black market to exist. However, it did, and when out at night looking for a taxi, often the drivers left after learning I carried only renminbi.

One difficult occasion was the night of 21 May, when martial law was declared. It was already dark and I had a 20-kilometre cycle-ride back to Beida from Tiananmen Square, which was then risky. Only a hefty amount of FECs, which I did not have, might have provided any possibility of getting a taxi. However, through his contacts, a journalist at the Beijing Hotel helped me get home.

The central organisation of the protest was at Beida. Initially, many students attended classes and went to Tiananmen Square afterwards, but they soon began to boycott classes to spend more time in the Square. Every day people crowded around the big-character posters near the dorms for the latest news. The Party controlled all official media, so these posters were a vital way to find out what was really happening. Some students at Beida and other universities went to the provinces to spread the word. Despite calls for students to return to classes, few did. Most days I cycled to Tiananmen.

May was an extraordinary month, with demonstrations, hunger strikes, martial law, the arrival of the 'Goddess of Democracy' (a 10-metre-tall statue, resembling the American Statue of Liberty, created by protesters in Tiananmen Square), and the visit of the Soviet leader, Mikhail Gorbachev. There were demonstrations of a million people, which seemed to form a solid block from Beida to Tiananmen Square. The student-led movement now included support from across society. The mood was one of elation, hope and comradeship.

A history of general mistrust, guardedness and 'me first' had been the norm throughout most of the 1980s. This was strikingly evident on the streets, for example, when the eddying of a multitude of cyclists meant frequent accidents, after which each rider would pick themselves up separately and go on their way. By May, however, the new spirit saw both riders and others nearby dusting down the fallen and checking the bicycles. Another example: in the busy retail district of Wangfujing, where people had previously rushed into shops, letting the heavy doors fall back onto those following, often now the doors were held open with a smile. Care for one another even went so far that some of my students pointed out the 'spy' in my class, a slightly older student who said little and was often near me when I was out on campus.

Just before Gorbachev's visit in mid-May, an idea emerged to write to him, as his *glasnost* policies — which encouraged more open discussion and transparency of government — resonated with the students. A group at Beida wrote in English, imploring him to advocate for similar reforms while in China. Twice, students asked that I proof read the letter, which I did, in the dorms. It was surreal to hold this letter to Gorbachev: anything seemed possible. The letter was duly delivered to the Soviet Embassy, but Gorbachev did not acknowledge it, nor, apparently, act on it. Even so, the Chinese leadership was embarrassed by the sit-in at Tiananmen Square during his visit. Martial law was declared soon after.

On the night of 4 June, Alex's words in May were vindicated. The news was shocking. Many, especially the young, had never believed the leadership would order the People's Liberation Army to open fire on them, or that the army would follow those orders. At Beida, groups gathered with little to say. In my building, we sat in the hallway, not wanting to be alone. We did not know which, if any, of our students had been killed. A Chinese friend came, and, unable to find any English words, sat slumped against a wall speaking only in Chinese. He could not process the enormity of the situation.

Eventually, we went to look at the big-character posters and found warnings that the army was en route to us. The university had been the nerve centre of the movement and there was genuine fear of being killed. Students and staff stood wide-eyed in shock, several were crying, many told me to 'tell the world'.

Back in my apartment, I managed after many attempts to ring my father in Blenheim, but I had no plan about what I was going to do. Later I called my friend Mervyn, a New Zealand journalist, who was at the time a 'polisher' for a Chinese newspaper; that is, a native English-speaker employed to make sure all reports in English were grammatically and idiomatically correct. From him I learned that the New Zealand Embassy had told him that Beida was at risk, but no one could get through to any of us at the university. Mervyn and Alex had been about to try to cycle over to get me when I phoned. Mervyn now advised me to come to the Friendship Hotel immediately, as he was concerned for my safety.

At the front gate, I walked my bike through as was the rule. A large crowd outside broke into uproar, shouting and waving their arms at me. The guards ran over to shoo me back. One said tanks had been seen on the road to Beida and I would be killed. This was the same road as the one to the Friendship Hotel, making the trip too dangerous. Shaken, I returned to my apartment building, where later a French Embassy car arrived to evacuate my French neighbours. This increased our anxiety, as clearly Beida was considered an unsafe place to be, but we did not know what was true.

The next day, when downstairs at my bicycle, an embassy van arrived to evacuate New Zealanders and Australians. I had 10 minutes to get my passport, and was told if I stayed there was no guarantee of anyone coming back. I stood in my apartment, paralysed. I desperately wanted to contact my Beida friends, but I knew it was impossible. As we drove through the campus, with a heavy heart, I could see the hundreds of staring Chinese students and staff we were abandoning.

The drive through the streets was distressing, with many burnt vehicles and concrete barriers from makeshift roadblocks in evidence. We went first to the New Zealand Embassy, a familiar place from Friday-night social events. Staff were busy preparing to leave, so I was put on reception to field calls from the New Zealand and other media, as the events of 4 June were now world news.

Later, some of us were taken to an apartment in a diplomatic compound. Instructions were to stay inside, but be ready to move. It seemed odd to be placed there, along the road to Tiananmen Square, which we could just see from the window. Soon a call came telling us to put mattresses against the windows to shield us from stray bullets, and put the bedding in the foyer, furthest from the exterior walls. We were to stay there night and day. Apparently, snipers were in the street outside and more tanks were expected.

The last call was for us to move, and we went to the Great Wall Hotel nearer the airport. Here embassy staff gave me a list of room numbers for other guests from New Zealand. I was to tell these individuals to be ready to leave if they wanted to join the evacuation. The second list consisted of telephone numbers of people to call elsewhere in Beijing, to whom I was to deliver the same message. In both cases, I had to advise them that this was the only chance they would have to leave for an unknown period. I recorded their answers next to the individuals' names.

The next day we were told we were leaving on an emergency Qantas flight. A van arrived with a large New Zealand flag draped over the top. We were apprehensive, a feeling heightened by instructions not to look at soldiers and to be ready to drop to the floor. There were many armed soldiers, but no gunfire.

In Hong Kong we were taken to a hotel and met by the New Zealand consul-general, who assured us we were now safe.

Sleep was elusive, though, and around midnight Alex, evacuated on the same flight, rang to ask me to go for a walk. We sat in a noodle shop, where Alex told me more about the night of 4 June. Woken by his media contacts, he had loaded his bicycle with medical supplies from the clinic at the Friendship Hotel and spent all night doing what he could. He was devastated by what he had seen, with 'blood running in the gutters'. Although he had feared this outcome, it made the reality no less horrific.

I, too, had been somewhat naive. I had gone to China with an interest in how the society worked, knowing that there was still a class system of sorts and that some had privilege and absolute power. I had not been prepared for the reality of 4 June, which showed that the leadership had no hesitation in using that power so brutally. Nevertheless, I consider my time in China as a gift: the people I met, the students I taught, the kindnesses shown, and the opportunity to live and work surrounded by an ancient culture in modern China, particularly at a time of struggle, of the forging of a future.

Crossing the 'Chinese Bridge'

THOMAS NICHOLLS

When I signed up for the fourteenth Chinese Bridge Speech Competition at the University of Auckland in 2015, I was in my final year of a Chinese degree. A Mandarin language assistant (MLA) working at the Confucius Institute approached me one day after class and recommended it as an opportunity to practise my spoken Mandarin. The description of the competition stated that participants would be required to perform a three- to five-minute speech in Mandarin, and that a (Chinese) cultural performance was optional, but could earn extra points. Not being much of a 'performer', I opted out of the cultural performance and focused on the speech.

The theme was 'My Chinese Dream'. Assuming we weren't expected to write a speech about the 'great rejuvenation of the Chinese nation', I decided to format my speech as a fictional dream in which a number of ancient Chinese philosophers advised me on how to study Mandarin. I practised every day leading up to the competition. I read my speech out loud every morning, made audio recordings and watched videos of myself to improve my pronunciation and delivery. Evenings were spent drilling double-third tones with my MLA over *Tieguanyin* tea.

On the day of the competition, I wasn't anticipating an award. I was the only contestant who didn't have a cultural performance, and some of the other contestants had done really well. As the third-, second- and first-place winners went up to collect their trophies, I sat in the crowd a little disappointed, but, overall, content with the experience. I started thinking about how much my Mandarin had improved and how I might go and have a chat with the Chinese tea store owner in Balmoral afterwards . . .

As my attention drifted back to the prize-giving ceremony, I noticed everyone was looking at me and clapping. The MC was waving at me to come on-stage. I looked up at the screen and saw my name in huge font above the words *Special Prize*. What sounded like a consolation prize turned out to be a return ticket to represent the University of Auckland at the international competition in China. In some kind of bitter irony, the first-place award was a return ticket to China to attend the final prize-giving ceremony as an *observer*. I was handed a trophy and a registration pack. My hand was shaken and photos were taken. With a mixture of confusion and curiosity, I made my way home to prepare for the trip.

About a week later, I received an email notifying me that the topic for the competition had changed and that I would need to: (a) write a new speech; (b) buy a gift for Chinese Bridge; and (c) prepare a *mandatory* cultural performance. I was also informed that the international competition would be broadcasted on Hunan TV, China's largest entertainment platform with a viewership of over 300 million. Needless to say, the weeks leading up to my departure were a bit hectic.

Coming off a 17-hour flight into 35-degree heat, I rocked up to the hotel in shorts and jandals. Before I could line up to check in, a Chinese guy with a lanyard grabbed my arm and ushered me away to a room at the far end of the lobby. Inside, the room was packed with university students from around the world, wearing traditional outfits, waiting to have their photos taken. From kilts to saris, hanbok to headdresses, lavalavas to soccer uniforms, the room was bubbling with colour and excitement. The competition that year had 133 contestants from 97 countries. Each contestant had gone through regional- and national-level competitions to get there, and their Mandarin was without exception very impressive. It was inspiring to be surrounded by so many individuals who had invested so much time and energy into understanding Chinese language and culture.

After the organisers had briefed us on the schedule for the coming days, we all went back to our rooms to practise our speeches and prepare our gifts. The gift I had chosen for the Chinese Bridge was a pikorua pounamu, which symbolises the weaving together of different peoples and cultures. Traditionally, pounamu is gifted, rather than bought for oneself, and it is custom for the person gifting it to wear it first to imbue it with their own mana. I felt privileged to represent New Zealand in the competition, and proud to be able to share a part of my culture with people from all over the world.

Finally, the day came for the Oceania contestants to perform. While the cameras were being set up, we huddled backstage waiting for our names to be called. Each time the curtain was pulled back, we caught a glimpse of the television audience. The crew was racing around frantically, tucking microphone transmitters under shirts and taping microphones to necks. When it was my turn to go up, my backstage nerves melted away and muscle memory took over as I recited my speech. I described the significance of the pounamu and explained the custom of wearing it first as I took it from around my neck and presented it to the Chinese Bridge competition.

Once all 133 contestants had performed their speeches and talents (mine was a beatbox rendition of 'The Moon Represents My Heart'), and had gone through quick-fire rounds of Chinese culture-related questions, the top 15 were chosen. To my sincere surprise, I was still among them. As the competition wound down for the day, the top 15 were escorted to a dimly lit room in the far corner of the building complex and told to wait for the director.

At around 11pm, as everyone began dozing off, I heard footsteps approaching down the corridor. A middle-aged Chinese man wearing light brown cowboy boots entered the room. The way he held himself indicated he was important. He wore a light blue shirt with clip-on buttons tucked into a pair of brand-new denim jeans. Despite being inside at close to midnight, he was wearing tinted aviator sunglasses. He sat down at the front of the room and kicked his cowboy boots up on the table. The resulting thump drew everyone's attention. After an awkward pause, the cowboy cleared his throat and said (in Chinese): 'Congratulations on making it into the top 15. This year, we're trying a new *zhenren xiu* format. At 6am, we'll be leaving Changsha. Pack your bags, and get some sleep!' Just like that, he stood up and walked back out of the room. 'What's a *zhenren xiu*?', I thought to myself. The contestant next to me, noticing the confusion on my face, smiled and said in English: 'reality TV show'.

That 'reality TV' format was a first for the Chinese Bridge franchise in its 14 years. In the early 2000s, the competitions were held in something akin to a school hall, with highlights broadcasted on CCTV (China Central Television). Over the years, the number of contestants had grown and the stages got bigger. By 2009, Hunan TV had taken over from CCTV as a partner organisation for the university-level competition, and over the next couple of years began experimenting with new ways of increasing ratings for the show, introducing challenges and activities outside of the traditional studio setting, and trying out new post-production techniques.

Our competition, however, was something else entirely. It involved being filmed 24 hours a day for three weeks. Cameras were installed in our rooms and in the buses we rode between locations. They were carried on the shoulders of the crew as we roamed through towns and villages, and they were strapped to our chests. It was an absolutely surreal experience.

Over the next few weeks, we travelled to Changsha, Quanzhou, Yunnan and Beijing, staying in custom-built *Big Brother*-esque accommodation along the way. In each location, we were tasked with a variety of activities and challenges. In one location, we had to devise and perform a show using marionette dolls for a crowd of children. In another, we were trying to convince customers in a store to buy ceramic crafts. One day, we were running a 'bubble marathon' while hundreds of people threw water balloons and sprayed us with water guns. The next day, we were having a *Master Chef*-style cook-off. At one point we were herding a bunch of donkeys down a maze of alleyways . . .

Every few days some contestants would be disqualified, based on examination scores and how they performed in each of the challenges. At the end of each day, we were taken aside individually to do an 'interview'. What started off as general reflections gradually became uncomfortable daily interrogations where the assistant directors would try to pry controversial soundbites out of us. What do you think about contestant X? Don't you think contestant Y is a bit annoying? Who do you think will be disqualified next?

There were aspects of the competition that were amazing and unforgettable. I met people from all over the world and got to learn about their unique experiences. I met the actor who often plays Mao Zedong in Chinese films, and saw him taking a nap on a golden prop throne. I ate all-you-can-eat Peking Duck in Beijing with a Chinese soap opera star. I got to speak Mandarin non-stop for a month and even had my first dreams in Mandarin. I got to experience what it's like to be a celebrity in China.

I also got food poisoning several times. By the end of the competition I had lost around 8 kilograms. I vividly recall that at one point during the competition most of the contestants had fallen ill with sore stomachs and fevers. We were at the airport waiting for our next flight when a 'slight delay' was announced. For the next 27 hours, we huddled together under jackets and sweatshirts, while the camera crew hovered around us trying to get shots for the show. These were later edited together with a sympathy-evoking soundtrack.

It took me a long time to figure out how I felt about the whole experience. When describing it to friends back home, the response was often: 'Well, what did you expect from the CCP?' While there were certainly elements of the competition that reflected a political agenda — like how the competition was framed in the context of the Belt and Road Initiative, China's global infrastructure development investment strategy aimed at positioning China in a greater global leadership role — it wasn't until I had time to reflect off-camera that I realised just how much Hunan TV had influenced the competition.

For example, early on in the competition, as part of a challenge, we were standing in a tiny store trying to barter with the store owner (who was employed by Hunan TV) to get a leg of ham and a bag of salt. After a bit of back and forth, the store owner said: 'What do you have of value?' The assistant directors came up behind us and passed us some packages. They were the gifts we had brought for Chinese Bridge. I couldn't believe it! The pounamu I had gifted Chinese Bridge had become a mere prop for the show. I confronted the assistant directors about it. Amid a somewhat heated exchange, the store owner said, 'Well, maybe if you perform something entertaining, I might give it to you.' So there I was, beatboxing for the cameras again, while some contestants danced and another did a handstand. Eventually we got the ham, but at that moment I lost respect for the competition.

Although I didn't realise it at the time, this (and many other) cultural *faux pas* were the result of the commercial interests of Hunan TV taking precedence over the Confucius Institute Headquarters' public diplomacy agenda for the competition.

That year was the first and last time the reality TV format was used by the Chinese Bridge competition. Not long after it was broadcast, the Hunan provincial government cracked down on Hunan TV for excessively pursuing ratings, stating it had 'deviated from its value orientation as a mouthpiece of the Party' and lacked 'political sensitivity'. From then on, ratings fell year-on-year as Chinese fans eventually became disillusioned by how the show was manipulating and coaching foreign contestants.

With the quiet disestablishment of the Confucius Institute Headquarters, the continued crackdown on reality TV shows in China, and the competition's transition to a virtual platform in the wake of Covid-19, the twentieth anniversary of the Chinese Bridge competition in 2021 was somewhat subdued. As border restrictions continue to keep Covid-19 (and international students) out of China, it remains unclear what the future holds for the Chinese Bridge competition.

Looking back, I don't regret the decision to participate in the competition, even if it was extremely challenging (and at times ethically questionable). It gave me a unique opportunity to experience the inner workings of the Chinese entertainment industry, and set me on a path to complete a Master's degree in China.

Although I fed into stereotypes and 'told the Chinese story well', it was also an opportunity to share my own culture with a Chinese audience and to be an ambassador for New Zealand. China doesn't lift the curtain for everyone. When it does, it isn't always clear what's on the agenda. For anyone who has the opportunity to see what's on the other side, my advice would simply be: make sure you know what you're there for and don't be afraid to stand up for yourself.

Where It All Started: The Class of '06 and the First China Field Study Course in Beijing

XIAOMING HUANG

Reflecting on the events, people and stories of my personal experience of the New Zealand–China relationship, I immediately thought of the New Zealand Contemporary China Research Centre and the Confucius Institute, which I had the pleasure of helping to set up and make work. But as I thought more on this, pondering on the things that led to these initiatives, and the growth of exchange and engagement by New Zealand universities in international education with China, I thought of one of the early initiatives we made happen that contributed to the rise of an era of New Zealand engagement with China in the 2000s and 2010s.

In the early 2000s, I had already been teaching at Victoria University of Wellington (VUW) for some years. Coming from an education background of mixed Chinese, American and European experience and training, I found Asian Studies at New Zealand universities thin and dominated by mainstream approaches and methods in the humanities and languages. Even in our faculty, the Faculty of Humanities and Social Sciences, there was little social science research on Asia, at least in the discipline of political science and international relations that I was in. Moreover, the study of New Zealand–China relations was largely formed around a towering figure, Rewi Alley, and the Gong He (Gung Ho) movement that he and other New Zealanders promoted in China in the 1930s and 1940s.

I organised some new courses at VUW on East Asian politics, Chinese political economy, East Asian international relations, and China and the world, to engage students with contemporary material and 'scientific' theories and methods related to the study of China. Field trips are a form of exchange and engagement in international education popular at American universities. I began contemplating organising a field trip for New Zealand students to go to Chinese universities so they could observe China's politics, economy and society in person.

In 2005, I was head of the Department of Political Science and International Relations at VUW. The head of the new School of Philosophy, History, Political Science and International Relations was Professor Stephen Levine. Stephen was keenly interested in learning more about East Asian countries. We designed a field trip as a VUW course, POLS/ INTP359 China Field Study, and operated it as a joint course between VUW and the China University of Political Science and Law (CUPL), our co-organiser in Beijing.

This was a summer course at VUW. The first half of the course was three weeks in Beijing at CUPL, when students would attend lectures by CUPL staff on Chinese government, the economy, society and international relations, and visit sites of interest for round-table discussions on select topics: local government, villages, business corporations, historical sites of government and politics, non-governmental organisations (NGOs), the Ministry of Foreign Affairs, the Ministry of Commerce, and the New Zealand Embassy. Students worked on their research paper and discussed and presented their research project in the second half of the course back in Wellington. We had a total of 28 students in the class of 2006.

There were significant institutional hurdles in both countries in organising this joint course. For example, VUW asked each student to sign a legal document detailing a fairly long 'yes/no' list in order for them to be able to study, live and travel in an Asian country. The university also had to work out regulations on how to ensure the quality of the content delivered at CUPL. For CUPL's part, what content was to be delivered and what field visits were to be arranged needed to be considered and organised. We had to figure out who should be responsible for the course fees and programme costs, and the costs of travel, accommodation, and three meals a day. In the end, we worked out these arrangements and satisfied the legal requirements in each country to meet the quality control requirements of both universities.

This set of arrangements became the model when offering this course every other year after 2006. A reciprocal programme was also organised for CUPL students to do their field study at VUW in the alternate year. The idea of a joint teaching programme was also used to create a double Master's degree programme in public policy with Peking University. Other attempts to develop joint degree programmes with Chinese universities faced more challenging regulatory requirements and did not develop further.

Our efforts to build co-operative degree programmes with Vietnamese universities were based on the same model, and these programmes are also still operating today.

To ensure the quality and effectiveness of international education programmes, and indeed to ensure that exchange and engagement in international education by New Zealand universities fit well with the imperatives of the overall development of the New Zealand economy and society, the idea for a New Zealand China Research Centre focusing on contemporary issues became desirable. Professor Neil Quigley, then deputy vice chancellor at VUW, was an enthusiast in connecting the national economy, the public sector and international education, and an important initiator for the China Centre project.

I believe the underlying rationale behind this project was the belief that the most efficient and effective way for New Zealand universities to compete for enrolments was to attract students from outside, rather than redistribute the fixed numbers within. This required substantive institutional innovation and investment to achieve. The China Centre was designed to serve as a national platform to enable our research and teaching to gain an international reputation.

The class of '06 had a great time on the China Field Study in Beijing. The weather, though, was a serious challenge. If you can survive the cold weather in late November and early December in Beijing, you can survive any cold conditions imaginable. All 28 students, and Stephen and I as supporting staff, managed well. Students attended daily lectures in English by CUPL professors, and passed a test at the end of the three weeks of lectures on Chinese history and culture, contemporary Chinese diplomacy, contemporary Chinese government and politics, and the Chinese judicial system.

They attended a court session to see a bit of how the Chinese legal system works. They had round-table discussions with local government staff to see how local government works. They had a seminar with Greenpeace China to see how NGOs worked in China. We managed to organise a session with Ministry of Foreign Affairs staff to learn how Chinese diplomacy works, and a session with Ministry of Commerce staff to see how trade policy works in China. We had the opportunity to meet with New Zealand Embassy staff to gain insight on how New Zealand Ministry of Foreign Affairs and Trade staff work in Beijing.

Students also had a great time outside the classroom. Some students made daily trips to traditional markets near CUPL's city campus where

Victoria University of Wellington students visiting the Temple of Heaven during their China Field Study course in 2006. XIAOMING HUANG we stayed. One student ordered several suits for himself from a tailor at the market, and this became a tradition for classes in subsequent years. Students went to the most notable places in Beijing. We also organised an overnight trip to the ancient capital of Xi'an. I am pretty sure students also went to a lot of different places on their own in and around Beijing outside of our plan, and, judging by their reactions, they had a wonderful time.

One of the most memorable extracurricular activities I recall is the farewell party the class had at a Xizang [Tibetan] restaurant in Beijing. We ended up having the farewell party at this particular place by chance. The whole class had come out on a site visit somewhere close to Sanlitun and were looking for a place to eat. As we were wandering along the wide boulevard in the dark evening, we found a place hidden from the wide street with a sign indicating Xizang-style food. No one was quite sure what would be inside.

This turned out to be the most memorable experience for everyone over the entire field study. We were served authentic Tibetan food and drinks. Tibetan students from universities nearby worked at the restaurant. They provided food, as well as music and dance, and well into the middle of the night everyone was cheered on to get up to dance and sing something that the rest of us could dance along to. Even I found myself picking up Tibetan dance steps for the very first time in my life, and Stephen and I became primary targets for a song contest that lasted for hours before we headed home through the freezing-cold Beijing night.

This beginning led to many New Zealand students staying on or returning to Beijing, to explore their life, career opportunities and further study there, and to CUPL students travelling to Wellington to pursue their study at VUW at different levels. Other programmes were subsequently set up for a broad range of exchange and engagement of New Zealand students with China and Chinese students with New Zealand. Most importantly, as everyone in the class would agree, the class of '06 in Beijing was one of the best learning experiences these students had at VUW and in their personal journey to engage with the world.

Poets
on Yellow
Mountain

MURRAY EDMOND

On Huang Shan, Yellow Mountain, there is a rock shaped like a writing brush, with an ancient pine tree perched on its tip: the rock is called 'Li Bai's pen'. The dominant pine on Huang Shan is *Pinus taiwanensis*, the Taiwan red pine. As a traditional image in Chinese painting and poetry, pines can be read as 'strong, brave and eternal'. This is what I was told by Deng Mingyan, who was part of the Chinese English Poetry Festival held on the mountain and in nearby locations in Anhui Province between 16 and 21 October 2007. Deng Mingyan was an active participant in the festival, and blessedly fluent in both Mandarin and English (as well as engaged in writing a doctoral thesis on Nietzsche), and she helped me make a translation of a poem by Zang Di.

One of the exercises that was undertaken during the festival was mutual translations of each other's work by the English-language and the Mandarin-language poets. The night we stayed on Huang Shan, Zang Di showed me this poem of his, which had already been translated, but he remained unhappy with the translation. With Deng Minyan as our intermediary, there on the mountain, we composed a new version, changing its translated title from 'A Poem on Things' to 'A Charm About Things'. Pines and pine cones (as well as fists, pagodas, squirrels and fur coats) are all 'things' in the poem, which opens:

On a windowsill, three pine cones.
The size of each
is almost the same.
But they vary from dark to light.

By the time we reach the poem's conclusion, the cones have entered the poem as an active voice:

I am writing poetry, secretly in love
with the clear structure of the cones.
It asks me to take it to where I picked them up.
It asks to be placed on top of the Red Pine.

This translation has been published in the anthology *Chinese Writers on Writing* (San Antonio: Trinity UP, 2010) edited by Arthur Sze, and then in *Jade Ladder: Contemporary Chinese Poetry* (Hexham: Bloodaxe, 2012) edited by W. N. Herbert and Yang Lian. Bill (W. N.) Herbert, Arthur Sze and Yang Lian were all participants in that Chinese English Poetry Festival in 2007.

The Chinese poets at the festival were Chen Xianfa, Wang Xiaoni, Yan Li and Zang Di, all living in China, plus Yang Lian, then living in England as he still does as of 2021; and the sixth Chinese poet was Luo Ying. Luo Ying, graduate of Peking University and enthusiastic poet in his own right, was most notably a highly successful real estate businessman (not to mention mountaineer conqueror of Himalayan peaks). It was through Luo Ying's generous sponsorship that the conference proceeded. For instance, the hotel where we were housed for most of the conference, in a small-town, semi-rural setting in Anhui, belonged to Luo Ying. None of the English-language poets could provide such input, although the British Council had come to the party as well.

As mentioned already, Bill Herbert from Scotland and Arthur Sze from the US were attending, joined by Odia Ofeimun from Nigeria, Robert Minhinnick from Wales, Pascale Petit from England, and myself. We were welcome guests and thoroughly cared for in what was essentially a small and intense interface of poets, with occasional forays into public outreach.

The local Party officials joined us at the hotel one night for a rather restrained 'banquet' — both sides were doing their duty. One was made aware that the official interpreters did not hold their positions without approval from above, and therefore they might later be asked for their interpretations of events.

When Mao broke China's isolationist foreign policy in 1972, leading to Nixon's visit to China, he chose *Pinus taiwanesis* as the symbol of the change, but, in order to evade any mention of Taiwan, the pine was re-christened 'Welcome Guest Pine'. In a charming and presumably deliberate confluence of sound, this new name sounded like a transliteration of Nixon into Mandarin. *Pinus taiwanensis* exudes an organic acid, which mixes with water and dissolves the rock on which it grows on Huang Shan, allowing the tree to create for itself new soil from bare rock.

Our first plenary was held in Hongcun, a Song dynasty village Luo Ying's business was developing for cultural tourism. Later we visited a construction site: a 'fake' Buddhist temple was being built where once an old temple had stood. Would 'fake' monks find employment when the job was done? Xi Chuan, poet and critic and university teacher, told me that Roman Catholicism was the growth religion in China: the Pope was an infallible leader of an ideology seeking global dominance, which was not without precedent in China. Xi Chuan was one of the two presenters for the first plenary. He told me: 'I love fakes'.

When he spoke at the first plenary — which addressed the question of the pressure that Classical Chinese poetry forms exerted on contemporary innovation — Xi Chuan sought to demolish the myth of the totality of 'the classical' in China. He argued that the 'rhetoric of tradition' had actually been put to use to effect change, emphasising that rhetoric was essential to renovation: what is now called 'Classical' involved 'conflict and diversity and generation against generation'. (Where I use quotation marks, I am citing notes taken during the live sessions.) Taking an opposite point of view, Yang Lian combined a High Modernist stance with a pitch for the persistence of the Classics: 'the destiny of Chinese language is in its writing system'. For him timelessness and totality are the space of writing, and he cited then, as I had heard him do before, the lack of tense in Chinese verbs.

Along with Robert Minhinnick, I was one of the speakers at the second plenary session, held in the very Ming Dynasty family hall in which Ang Lee shot some of the early scenes in *Crouching Tiger, Hidden Dragon*. Since the festival brought together the world's most widely used language (English) with the world language with the greatest number of native speakers, it was timely that Robert Minhinnick addressed the fate of the Welsh language, and I was able to say something about the precarious position of te reo Māori. I stretched Roman Jakobson's idea of the 'axes of language', from the metaphoric axis to the metonymic axis, and applied it to the existential politics of language, the great power stacks of metaphor versus the democratic reach of metonymic combination.

These plenary gatherings led to workshop sessions in small groups, reading individual poems, providing translations, pitching and fighting questions and responses, exploring the blank spaces of incomprehension and the moments of seemingly serendipitous insight. I was called away from one of these 'tutorials' to be interviewed for an arts programme on Anhui Province TV. 'Why is modern poetry so incomprehensible to ordinary people?' I was asked. I asserted that I knew 'ordinary people' who

Poets engaged in a workshop session during Chinese English Poetry Festival, 16-21 October 2007, Anhui Province, in the grounds of Zhongcheng Mountain Villa hotel. From left: Zang Di, Pascale Petit (obscured), Murray Edmond, Shao Xueping (interpreter), Yan Li, Arthur Sze, Yang Lian. MURRAY EDMOND

took great pleasure in difficult poetry, while I also knew professors (I could have named one or two!) who thought modern poetry all nonsense.

We also bussed out on excursions. One of these was to meet students at Huangshan University. We had face-to-face meetings, with readings and questions as well as small-group discussions. The students were lively and engaged. It was the local Party secretary, present for the occasion, who asked the question: 'Why is modern poetry so incomprehensible to ordinary people?' The ritual nature of this challenging question had been quickly revealed.

One poet who occupied an interesting position in the festival was Arthur Sze. He had been born and brought up in New York, in a Mandarin-speaking house, and had studied Classical Chinese at Berkeley. He was the one English-language poet who had a substantial knowledge of Chinese. (He said to me that when he arrived he was picking up 30 per cent of what was being said, and by the end of the week, 50 per cent.)

His great-uncle had been one of the Chinese representatives who had refused to sign the Paris Peace Treaty of 1919 because of its betrayals of Chinese interests to Japan. It was the student protests of that time which had influenced the delegation's refusal, and which then led on to the May Fourth Movement, with its slogans 'Struggle for Sovereignty' and 'Throw Out the Warlord Traitors'. The May Fourth Movement had no Chinese written character for the concept of a political 'movement'. Yang Lian told me that the activists telegrammed Japan for advice, because there were lots of political movements in Japan. One of our interpreters told me that this character had been first used in a newspaper in an elegy for those killed in May Fourth protests. This interpreter went on to say that China had never been so unified in its entire history as it was now;

that the history of China in the twentieth century could be read as one bloody march to unification. And that dread of losing that unity was a powerful force in the country.

My rather random presence at the Poetry Festival owed everything to the presence of the poets Yang Lian and Gu Cheng in Auckland in 1989. They, in turn, were there because John Minford held the professorship of Chinese at the University of Auckland at that time. The exile of these poets reached crisis point with the 4 June massacre in Tiananmen Square. I organised a memorial concert on 17 September 1989 at the Maidment Theatre in Auckland called *China: The Survivors*. The memorial stone that stands in St Andrew's Church grounds in Alten Street, Auckland, was installed at that time.

While Yang was in Auckland I used to be the English half of his poetry readings, for then he spoke little English. That was a time of heightened awareness, hope and despair, and I think my invitation from Yang Lian to be one of the poets on Huang Shan came because of that time. In 1968, as a first-year student at the University of Auckland, I had taken (and passed!) the two first-year courses of study required to earn what was called 'Chinese One' in the old structure of the BA degree. The head of department then was Professor Lancashire, I think the first professor of Chinese at Auckland.

One of the Chinese poets at the 2007 Festival in Anhui was Yan Li, who, like Yang Lian, is numbered as one of the 'Misty' or 'Obscure' poets of the 1980s, as well as being an equally prominent painter. In Arthur Sze's anthology, mentioned earlier, *Chinese Writers on Writing*, Yan notes that: '. . . people who don't have power . . . just follow the system. But poetry lets those people speak out.' His poem 'Thanks for that' was written in 2001, but the first time it could be published was in 2007, in the rather handsome publication that accompanied the festival, *2007 Pamirs Poetry Journey: The First Chinese–English Poetry Festival* (Beijing: Pamirs Academy, 2007). The first two lines of Yan Li's poem read:

> The state has occupied all geographical surfaces
> I can only construct my inner world downward

10,000 Lights Across the City 万家灯火: Lantern Festivals and Their Role in New Zealand– China Relations

JAMES TO

As a New Zealand-born Chinese, my links to China run through my family, community work and education, and now at the Asia New Zealand Foundation. Over the past few decades, I have seen the relationship between Aotearoa New Zealand and the People's Republic of China growing and evolving, ebbing and flowing, and in a range of different spheres, particularly in social, cultural, economic and strategic contexts.

When I was a child, there were around 200 families of ethnic Chinese heritage across the wider Canterbury region; it was a relatively small, tightly knit community of long-established clan or village groups that had been built up over two, three or even four generations. They were joined by scores of Southeast Asian Colombo Plan students, who, in the decades after the Second World War, came to study at New Zealand universities; in addition, skilled migrants and their families, harking mostly from Guangdong and Hong Kong, bolstered overall numbers. My parents arrived in Christchurch as part of the latter.

Being 'Chinese' while I was growing up meant many things; it did for us, at least. For example, in addition to English, it was Cantonese, Taishan or Seyip dialects that were spoken within our cohort. It was rare to hear Mandarin (*guoyu* 国语), which was used mainly by the few Taiwanese families, or among the handful of mainland scholarship students around town. In short, the Chinese community back then was very much a niche minority in a nascent bicultural society still strongly tied to its colonial roots. That's how we perceived New Zealanders in pre-earthquake Christchurch, which was often described as the most English city outside of England.

It was not until the late 1980s when immigration policies were relaxed that we saw the arrival of large numbers of new families from Hong Kong, Taiwan, Singapore and, in later years, mainland China. This period began a significant evolution in New Zealand's demographic profile; specifically, it was a shift away from a population comprised predominantly of people of Anglo-Saxon origin to one in which people from the Asia–Pacific constituted a growing part of contemporary society. Acknowledging this development, and the potential implications for New Zealand's future in the region, it was 1994 when then Minister of Trade Philip Burdon and Foreign Minister Sir Don McKinnon founded the Asia New Zealand Foundation (initially established as the Asia 2000 Foundation). The Foundation's early mandate was to increase New Zealanders' knowledge and understanding of the countries of Asia and their peoples and cultures so that they could develop relationships in the region more comfortably and effectively. In other words, its aim was, and is, to 'equip New Zealanders to thrive in Asia'.

The many opportunities offered by the Foundation have helped me grow my own connections with China and things Chinese. For example, a scholarship in 2002 enabled me to study in Beijing; in 2009, I led the first NZ–Sino Youth Exchange Delegation in partnership with the Chinese People's Association for Friendship with Foreign Countries; and my current role is running Track II exchanges with think tanks in Shanghai and Beijing.

In addition to providing offshore experiences in Asian countries to New Zealanders, the Foundation initiated the annual Lantern Festivals as a way of bringing China to domestic New Zealand audiences. The first was held in late February of 2000, timed to mark the end of the Chinese Lunar New Year period. Involvement in these festivals over the years has enabled me to appreciate the important role that interpersonal engagement and experience can play in building mutual understandings and strengthening relationships with international partners.

My former colleague Jennifer King (Director of Arts and Culture at the Foundation from 1995 to 2017) recalled that for many New Zealanders these Lantern Festivals were the first 'encounter with China' they had ever had beyond their Friday-night takeaways or what they might have read about China in the newspapers. And for those of Asian heritage such as myself, the festivals offered an opportunity to share our culture, history and lifestyle with other New Zealanders. It's fair to say, therefore, that the Lantern Festivals play a key role in deepening the New Zealand–China connection.

Jennifer's memory of that first festival in 2000 was that over half of the huge crowd was made up of people of Chinese descent. In addition to the long-established local Chinese community I mentioned earlier, participants included recently arrived Chinese mainlanders, Malaysians, Singaporeans, Taiwanese and Hong Kongers. They joined with Christians, Buddhists and other groups that shared links with China and Chinese culture. School children made their own lanterns, and community groups sponsored prizes to whip up support.

These events have helped make those of Chinese ancestry feel at home and valued as Chinese in New Zealand. Furthermore, as host cities of the festivals, Auckland and Christchurch have increasingly become self-confident, vibrant multicultural cities. Pākehā, Māori and Polynesian families have brought their children to the festivals to enjoy the displays, the music, the dancing and exquisite lanterns while drinking bubble tea and eating dumplings together with festival-goers from a wide range of ethnic communities.

The origins of the Lantern Festival can be seen as reflecting the 'can-do' attitude for which New Zealanders are well known. It all began back in the late 1990s when sponsor AIA (the insurance company) asked the Foundation to hold a 'Chinese' event. The Foundation suggested a Lantern Festival. HSBC bank immediately came on board as the major sponsor. With the help of the RNZAF and Singapore Airlines, 300 second-hand lanterns were flown over from Jurong Gardens in Singapore. The Embassy of the People's Republic of China in Wellington supplied 30 traditional lanterns, and the Taipei Economic and Cultural Office provided lantern giveaways. This was the humble beginning of what would eventually become New Zealand's largest public event.

A serendipitous boat trip across Wellington harbour a few months later resulted in Jennifer being brought together with official representatives from Zhejiang Province. The misfortune of the boat breaking down actually turned into a stroke of good fortune, when, to fill in time, Jennifer got talking to the group about the Festival. Zhejiang, it transpired, is a leading manufacturer of lanterns. The following year, the provincial officials sent a delegation to New Zealand that included craftspeople and a gift of 13 large feature lanterns. Zhejiang also promoted the festival, sending TV crews to New Zealand, and heavily subsidising the travel costs of performers from China.

Long-term relationships such as that which developed between the Foundation and the Zhejiang provincial government are built on trust and mutual benefit. Once that trust had been established, negotiations relating to the sourcing of performers were handled by a chain of Chinese officials from national to provincial to municipal levels, in turn spawning a large number of broader connections. Cultural attachés at the Chinese Embassy in Wellington helped with useful introductions to people in Shanghai agencies and organisations, such as the Shanghai Cultural Exchange Agency, the Shanghai Performing Arts Agency, the Shanghai Municipal Administration of Culture, Radio, Film and TV, and the Yuyuan Garden.

In time, the embassy also encouraged the Foundation to deal with Zigong (自贡) city officials in Sichuan Province, the traditional capital of Chinese lantern-making. Initial relations with local authorities in Zigong proved problematic. Things changed when the Foundation was approached by the lantern-making company Haitian, one of the city's top businesses. Like the Zhejiang provincial government, Haitian also took a strong interest in the festival in New Zealand; its representatives came up with its own set of ideas specific to the needs of the organisers.

As the festival grew in scope and size, the Foundation sought even wider relationships. Officials in the Chengdu Foreign Affairs Office in Sichuan, the Department of Culture in Guangzhou, and the External Exchange Division of the Shaanxi Provincial Cultural Department in Xi'an all helped to find new talent. Over the years, performers who might be invited to New Zealand were chosen by means of, for example, reading and research, discussion with partners in China, or attending their performances. Over 1000 performers have been brought to this country; they have included everything from stilt walkers to jugglers, puppeteers, fire eaters, magicians, dancers of all descriptions, rock bands and acrobats. Highlights included Lao Qiang (老强), a group from Shaanxi that plays 'ancient Chinese rock 'n' roll' or 'old tune' music, a Mongolian *khoomei* throat-singer, and the Xingguang Acrobatic Troupe.

Thanks to my bilingual ability, my early days at the Foundation included helping Jennifer and her Arts and Culture team with the communications, visa and travel arrangements of visiting artists and performers. I even helped pick up band members and all their equipment at the airport. For me, this was all a very 'hands-on' introduction to how *guanxi* (关系) works as key to a strong relationship.

New Zealand's Lantern Festival has been in growth mode ever since its inception, when an estimated 50,000 people packed out Auckland's Albert Park; people were standing shoulder-to-shoulder back in 2000. The organisers had to cancel the children's lantern parade that afternoon because there was simply no room for it. The festival was moved from its original site to the Auckland Domain in 2016; then, in 2021 it moved to the Captain Cook and Marsden wharves on the Auckland waterfront. Likewise in Christchurch, the event began in Victoria Square but then spread out into Hagley Park. In 2021 it was rescheduled as the South Island Moon Festival. The Covid-19 pandemic, of course, disrupted plans in 2020 and 2021.

With more than 200,000 visitors annually in Auckland alone, the festival is the biggest celebration of Chinese culture in the country. And a consequence of the growth in attendance numbers is that city councils have taken on bigger and broader roles; the Lantern Festivals have become iconic 'city events'. The waters of Auckland harbour and the vast open space in the Garden City will become backdrops to new features such

Visitors admire a wonderfully lit menagerie at the 2017 Auckland Lantern Festival, Auckland Domain. ASIA NEW ZEALAND FOUNDATION

as fireworks displays and poetry recitals. And in these new settings, the festivals will take on even more of a local flavour. While seeking to retain 'authenticity' as a Chinese festival, and at the same time opening its doors to a very culturally diverse audience, can the festivals remain 'Chinese'? Or are they now shaped by Aotearoa New Zealand's own evolving national identity and culture? From my perspective as a New Zealand Chinese, my answer to both questions is simply 'yes'!

Each year, more than 800 lanterns are delivered to the Auckland and Christchurch festival sites in 20 shipping containers. And in China every year, new lanterns travel by road from the inland city of Zigong to a port in Chongqing; from there they are barged down the Yangtze River to Shanghai. Then the lanterns are shipped almost 10,000 kilometres to New Zealand. That long journey not only reflects the breadth and depth of the story behind the Lantern Festival, but also my own journey as a member of the New Zealand Chinese community, and now as a member of staff at the Asia New Zealand Foundation.

This story illustrates the value of making global connections, whether on a personal level or at official or institutional levels. It is a story that tells the importance of establishing mutual interest and building trust for growing a better New Zealand–China relationship. As for the Lantern Festival, it has become a symbol of the integrity and strength of New Zealand's multicultural social fabric. Its embrace of diversity and inclusiveness gives promise of an illustrious future for Aotearoa New Zealand.

Making Friends: A China Journey Spanning 30 Years

GARTH FRASER

My first visit to China was at the invitation of All-China Federation of Trade Unions (ACFTU) in 1979. For the next 30 years I led delegations from New Zealand to China, and in New Zealand received delegations from China. I have served on the executives of both the New Zealand China Trade Association and the New Zealand Taiwan Business Council. That this was possible in the 1990s is a tribute to the pragmatism of Chinese authorities and to the foresight of New Zealand business and political leaders such as Mike Moore, who developed trade mechanisms that separated trade and politics.

A highlight of my China years has been my involvement in the development of the new Shandan Bailie School. Rewi Alley founded the school back in the early 1940s, and its revival and expansion became his all-consuming passion in the 1980s. The new Shandan Bailie School of Agriculture, Forestry and Animal Husbandry was formally opened eight months before Rewi's death in December 1987. The New Zealand government that year gifted NZ$150,000 to the school, and in numerous other ways New Zealanders have had a strong connection with it, particularly as teachers. Courtney Archer, who taught at the school in both the 1940s and the 1980s, deserves special mention. So, too, do Tom Newnham (1987) and Karen Wilson (now Karen Lang; 1989–90).

Particularly crucial was the support and activism of local Chinese officials, of course, and especially that of the former deputy-governor of Gansu, Li Qiyang.

By 1990, it became evident to me that the Rewi Alley Scholarship was being awarded only to New Zealanders and not to the Bailie School's Chinese personnel. Who won the scholarship each year seemed to be the result of a cosy relationship between officials in the Gansu provincial government, the Education Commission and whoever made the selection in New Zealand. There was nothing underhand or ill-intentioned in the arrangement, but it could have served the Bailie School better than it did. I was determined to see the wrong righted. I sought the assistance of Wang Xinzhong, chairman of the ACFTU, our old comrade Li Qiyang, the New Zealand Embassy, Lu Wanru (Rewi's former secretary) and Li Xiaolin (the new director of Youxie 友协, Chinese People's Association for Friendship with Foreign Countries). Together we set about 'running some interference', to put it bluntly.

Our scholarship nominee from the Bailie School duly began his journey to New Zealand by travelling from Shandan to Lanzhou. There he was told by the Education Commission to go back to Shandan and await further news. I told him that if he ever wanted to get out of China on the scholarship, he was to remain in Lanzhou until he had heard from me, even if he had to resort to begging on the street corners. This is how the first Shandan Bailie School teacher, Zhang Xinhui, got to come to New Zealand. At the same time, Tom Newnham arranged for a Bailie School student, Cao Yujuan, to study in New Zealand for a year.

That was the beginning of a three-year battle of wits. We knew that it was unwise to make mortal enemies of the Education Commission (we were sure to need their co-operation and support for the future good of the Bailie School), but we were determined not to let go of the gains we'd made. Helped greatly by the New Zealand Embassy, during the tenure of Michael Powles, we were able to broker an arrangement that would allow the Education Commission and the Shandan Bailie School to each nominate the Rewi Alley Scholarship recipient on alternate years.

Another step forward was in 1991, when New Zealand's United Food and Chemical Workers Union presented to the Workers' Cultural Palace in Shandan a Māori carving depicting two figures: a Chinese dragon and a manaia, a spiritual messenger of Māori mythology. The carving depicts the people of both countries together holding three kete.

Not long after this it seems that someone decided to give me, the upstart from New Zealand, a lesson. I had been enquiring in my usual subtle way about the whereabouts of some alkathene water pipes that had been sent to the school, and had been mislaid or gone missing. I was summoned to a meeting that took the form of a good old-fashioned criticism session, the kind that had been common practice during the Cultural Revolution. I was given a thorough dressing-down about my unorthodox way of going about things, and lectured about how many totally useless items arrived in containers from New Zealand. I was particularly surprised by the gusto with which Li Qiyang, whom I considered a good friend, joined in the criticisms.

Adding insult to injury, the hotel manager insisted that I pay for the room in which the criticism session had just taken place! The argument occurred when I was leaving the hotel for the airport. I reminded the manager in no uncertain terms that the authorities in Lanzhou had far more money than I had, and if he delayed my departure any longer, causing me to miss my flight to Beijing, and Youxie officials learned why, the room fee would be the least of his worries.

I should add, however, that Li Qiyang and I remained good friends after this incident. Furthermore, she continued to be a great supporter of the Shandan Bailie School and teacher Karen Wilson. Shortly after this the alkathene pipes reappeared at the school farm, and were put to good use by headmaster Liu Guozhong. The incident reminds me of Deng Xiaoping's famous saying: 'It doesn't matter if a cat is black or white as long as it catches mice.'

Another high point of my China years was participation in the 1994 conference of the ICCIC (International Committee for the Promotion of Chinese Industrial Co-operatives), a movement with which Rewi Alley's name is indelibly linked. Senior members of the New Zealand China Friendship Society, including Jack Ewen, also attended. The conference was addressed by Vice-Premier Zhu Rongji in the Great Hall of the People; he urged participants to ensure the progress of Gung Ho (工合) co-operatives, which he saw as a contributor to economic growth, particularly at the village and township levels.

I continued to lead and receive delegations to and from China through the 1990s and up to 2010. Delegates included High Court judges, trade union leaders, farmers, educationalists and others from a range of different enterprises. I was also fortunate enough to be included, at the invitation of Mike Moore, in one of the biggest and most successful trade missions to China. Taking groups to China resulted in many friendships.

One visit led to a request from the Chengdu government's foreign affairs director, Wang Heyong, to offer advice about choosing a New Zealand city with which Chengdu city might negotiate a 'Friendly City' relationship.

In the end, on the advice I provided, they decided on a region-to-region relationship and signed a memorandum of understanding (MOU) with the Waikato region. The signatories were the Waikato Chamber of Commerce, Waikato Regional Council, Waikato Federated Farmers, Waikato University, Waikato Polytechnic, Tainui, Hamilton City Council, Waipa District Council and Waikato District Council.

Signing on behalf of Chengdu was Tao Wuxian, who went on to become the Sichuan Provincial Party Secretary. Wang Heyong had successfully put together most of the 17 Friendly City relationships that Chengdu city has with cities in other countries. The Chengdu–Waikato relationship flourished, and it was perhaps because of this that I received the title of International Friendship Envoy and, a decade or so later, International Friendship Cities Work Representative.

In 1997 I was invited to arrange for a Māori cultural group to be one of just three performing groups at a huge trade fair sponsored by the four southwest provinces; the fair focused heavily on tourism that was environmentally and ecologically friendly (around this time the United Nations bestowed on Chengdu an award for cleaning up pollution in the Xia River). Attending the fair were mayors from 17 cities worldwide, and the event had coast-to-coast television coverage nightly. For the best part of a week the Māori culture group was the centre of attention wherever it went.

The New Zealand tourism industry had been invited to send representatives to the fair and was offered free display space, and free interpreting and translation services. Regrettably, that invitation was not taken up. The good news is that the New Zealand government opened a consular office in Chengdu in 2014. Bill Sharpe had been pushing

The carving that was presented in 1991 to the Workers' Cultural Palace in Shandan (Gansu) by the United Food and Chemical Workers Union of New Zealand to commemorate the palace's opening.
GARTH FRASER

for this as early as the 1980s. Bill was one of our earlier hardworking trade commissioners, and a field agent of what was the forerunner of New Zealand Trade and Enterprise.

A final word about friendship. One of our dear Chinese friends, Wang Heyong, a friend of New Zealand, was taken ill in the early hours of the morning; he had been visiting the Waikato and had arrived in Auckland. He insisted that he could wait until a more civilised hour before calling an ambulance, but we insisted that he allow himself to be taken to hospital immediately. The hospital later assured us that had we delayed his admission for even just an hour, he probably would not have survived. Now, however, we had to figure out how to get him back to China; he could not fly without a carer, and the rest of his group was in Western Australia. Rather than having one of his group fly from there to join him, we arranged for one of our people to accompany him back to China. There is another happy ending to this story. Not only was a region-to-region Friendly City protocol signed, but a Sister City relationship between the cities of Hamilton and Chengdu was eventually finalised. To this day Wang Heyong is teased for loving New Zealand so much that he had to leave a part of himself here forever.

New Zealand has been fortunate in having a series of ambassadors to China who, since 1972, have built on and strengthened the foundations of a New Zealand–China friendship that were laid well before 1972. Rewi Alley's friendship-building was only tangentially related to trade, and was primarily in the area of people-to-people relationships; this is the sphere into which I fit most comfortably. Rewi was a prolific writer. It is in large part due to the persistence of Anne-Marie Brady that a large collection of his writing came to be deposited at the National Library of New Zealand. This happened in the late 1990s, towards the end of Chris Elder's term as ambassador to China.

I have been fortunate, and feel honoured, to have had very rich engagements with China and Chinese people since the late 1970s. The 'reform and opening-up' policies since 1978 have resulted in extraordinary changes in mainland China. I feel privileged to have often been a first-hand observer of some of the changes, to have friendships with some wonderful change-makers, and to have sometimes been a participant in change-making initiatives.

Revisiting China for the First Time

JASON YOUNG

起

I have lost count of the number of times between 2006 and 2019 that I travelled to China for academic events. Most focused on international relations debates. I have recently participated online (2020–21) due to government-mandated travel restrictions and increasing sensitivity to a growing carbon footprint. I have had the pleasure of meeting interesting and friendly people, although, as with anywhere, some were distant and cold. I have heard new ideas and a form of argumentation that flows from worldviews and social experiences that differ from my own. These experiences have stimulated my research and thinking.

There are many stories in these visits, and I apologise to the reader because they will not appear on these pages. I could entertain you with tales of mayhem, mishap and funny misunderstandings, or bore you with the tedious monotony of airport waiting rooms, long flights, formal speeches, and academic presentations with arguments so buried in statistics that one is left shellshocked by the experience. I could recount the fabulous scenes of big cities and futuristic buildings, pristine rural villages with land leases bundled up by migrant businessmen made good, or of creeks that flow purple and smog-laden industrial cities that would make Dickens cough. Each visit presents something new. After visiting

China many times, I have come to appreciate the challenges and the value of these discussions, however hard they become as the 'chilly war' (涼戰) between China and the West beds in.

承

Growing up in a small town in New Zealand no bigger than a small village in China, I was as free of the overbearing intellectual traditions of the West and China as I was of the training needed to understand them. The tireless wit of broadcaster Kim Hill began my training in one, and the good people of Xinzhuang (新莊區) planted the seed for the other. Small-town New Zealand taught me the value of listening and maintaining dialogue even when, or especially when, one does not share the same view. This is a lesson all in Aotearoa New Zealand have come to grapple with as we confront our colonial history and acknowledge the diversity of viewpoints, worldviews, political norms, and cultures here. As I have discovered time and time again, it is an essential skill for maintaining dialogue in China, especially on contentious issues, the list of which continues to grow.

I have experienced Chinese academia as dynamic and eclectic, packed full of intelligent scholars and officials. Some are more official than scholar, but all are steeped in a tradition that sees value in pursuing knowledge. Bounded by institutions and funding streams, as we all are, I have felt the environment more constricting in China than in New Zealand. The assumptions that underpin the political orthodoxy are foreign to me, and therefore appear more evident. I have met good academics who have suppressed their views, and others who have modified their speaking and writing. Most academics there are adept at presenting their arguments within the political 'formulations' (提法) of the Communist Party. They have shifted seamlessly from 'peaceful development' (和平發展) to 'Xi Jinping diplomatic thought and the new era of Chinese diplomacy' (習近平外交思想和新時代中國外交).

The overly formal academic discussions too often, but not always, create an environment as dry as sawdust, making them unsurprisingly hard to swallow. The formalities play out in drawn-out formulaic presentations that reinforce the central themes of the event. These appear to outsiders as homage to an ordained worldview, replete with political rituals and hierarchies. Speeches from senior academics or officials have little daylight between them and the official line. But there are always other talks that present alternative views. These are signalled not in confrontation, but through a lack of enthusiasm for the prevailing political line and subtly critical interpretations of the guiding formulations.

The participation of academics from a broad range of countries provides the opportunity to hear a wide range of views. Having been taught that international relations scholarship should strive for objectivity, I struggle with representation at academic events where, not unlike the Olympics, foreign academics appear as national representatives and tend to behave as such. Our (Western) intellectual tradition did not train me, nor even fully acknowledge, that scholarly differences come about due to national affiliations. At first, I found it off-putting to watch academics employ the same theoretical approaches and empirics but come to radically different conclusions to accord with their country's national interest and worldview. Now I view this as a regular part of international relations discussions in China.

In recent years, I have witnessed a closing down of space for academic debate in China. That, combined with the hardening of China's relations with Western nations, has rounded the edges of Chinese academia. There is now less space for free, frank and fruitful discussions. A more confident and articulate academic community, and one more comfortable embracing China's new-found great-power status and the overriding formulations of Chinese politics, has changed the type of discussions now possible. Some conferences have felt like show conferences put on to articulate the correct political line on a particular issue, such as the Belt and Road

Initiative (一帶一路倡議), or to socialise and test new political thinking, like a 'new type of international relations' (新型國際關係). This creates dilemmas for those trained in the West, where academia is more contested, more distant from government policy, and where, for better or for worse, scholars still present Western interests and worldviews as universal.

轉

This has led me to consider what value there is in continuing to participate. I continue not because I am blind to geostrategic concerns or unmoved by the plight of democracy activists in Hong Kong and the diverse communities in Xinjiang, Tibet and other parts of China prevented from practising their way of life. I persist because we should take every opportunity to present and hear alternative views and attempt to resolve issues. We seek to achieve this in academic settings in China, just as academics from China continue to present their arguments in the West.

I have met more and more academics who have turned away from visiting China for academic events. For some, it is frustration with the stifling academic format. For others, horror at the politics. For others still, it is a conviction to highlight and push back on China's more assertive and concerning foreign policy behaviour. I respect these positions and value the scholarship that underpins them. I also think it would be a mistake for all academics to take this position. There is value in exposure to different views, including those of China's political élite, and attempting to have one's arguments heard, even within a highly constricted academic environment. Chinese academia can appear as a hermetically sealed vault, but our shared history has shaped China just as it has shaped the world. The growth of environmental scholarship is a case in point.

I have seen academics visiting China and imitating the political positions of the Chinese state by using their formulations. The first time I saw this, I was in a meeting discussing China's overseas investment. A think-tank representative from a smaller nation that is dependent on China for trade and security read a speech that had no argument but resonated with Chinese policy, hitting all the right talking points. Their address was made more significant for me when I shared a car with the speaker to the airport, and he told me tales of fighting China-sponsored Maoist rebels during his youth, making clear he was not a fan of China's growing influence in his country. While I understand this strategy, it is not one that I employ. Concepts and ideas should not be valued for political favour, but should stand alone on their analytical merits.

Between the two extremes, I have had the opportunity to participate in discussions of international issues and to present my analysis in an academic setting where views are seldom aligned. While my colleagues in China often disagree with my framing and conclusions, they have noted and listened to them, just as I have listened to theirs. My goal has been to learn as much as I can about how they frame a given subject, to present my views on the issue, to identify the discrepancies, and, where possible, to seek areas of common ground. I do not consider this a search for truth *per se*, which would require independent evidence to verify, but rather an exchange of worldviews.

合

Each visit is a new opportunity to exchange views with familiar and new characters against an ever-changing backdrop. The visits rhyme but are never the same, and each reminds me of the possibility I felt visiting China for the first time. Each plays a small part in our collective pursuit of knowledge, and each now brings a sense of familiarity. At a time when engagement is under assault, attending academic discussions in China, however frustrating and problematic they can be, remains a window into the worldviews of a country that plays an increasingly influential role in the world. When the border closures brought on by the Covid-19 pandemic end, I will be looking to revisit China for the first time.

轉 Transformations

Crows, Ducklings and Kiwis: New Zealand in Chinese Minds

PAUL CLARK

Between my first visit to China in 1973 and today, the place of China in the world has been transformed. The place of China in my life has similarly grown from an academic fascination to a broad obsession. But what of New Zealand's place, if any, in Chinese consciousness? Several incidents from almost 50 years' engagement with China may give some inklings.

On the Bund, Shanghai, July 1973

Surrounded by curious locals on a sultry evening, a visiting group of New Zealand university students was surprised when a Shanghai gentleman pressed forward and asked, in precise English: 'Do you know Mr Wilcox?' Rivalling Rewi Alley as the best-known New Zealander in China, Vic Wilcox was in the habit of at least annual appearances on the front page of the *People's Daily*. On occasion, he would be standing beside Chairman Mao. A non-entity back home, Wilcox received this attention as the general secretary of the tiny but determined Communist Party of New Zealand. Unlike all other communist parties, except Albania's, our nation's party aligned itself with Beijing, not Moscow.

Shangnian Production Brigade, Beixiaoying People's Commune, Shunyi County, April 1976

Two elderly men, living in a shack in the middle of a field on the outskirts of Shangnian village, a bumpy hour-and-a-half bus ride northeast of Beijing, got into conversation with a couple of the Peking University history department students. We were there to work for two weeks in the fields (open-door schooling) and billet with commune families. When I explained that in New Zealand our houses faced north, a look of concern crossed the old men's faces: 'How do you keep warm in the winter?'

In a Peking University car on empty Beijing streets, May 1976

The look on my Peking University roommate's face was priceless: a mix of little-boy wonderment and slight embarrassment as we sped past the night-time cyclists. For one of the few times in his life, he was being driven in a car, not an army truck or a three-wheeled tractor. Earlier, in the Great Hall of the People he had seen the newly elevated leader Hua Guofeng (but only New Zealanders were allowed to shake Hua's hand), had a 10-course meal with 200 other guests — the simple winter-melon soup was the best dish — and seen Robert Muldoon. To this political instructor in a People's Liberation Army artillery unit based in Zhangjiakou, our prime minister was the least of his delights that evening.

Zhang Heng was one of three soldiers in our class of 20 worker-peasant-soldiers and 24 foreign students. Growing up in a village halfway between Beijing and Tianjin, he had 'seen' Chairman Mao in 1966. Standing among a million Red Guards and high-schoolers like himself, he thought he had made out a tiny figure waving from the platform of Tiananmen. Just a month before his encounter with Prime Minister Muldoon, my roommate had gone into the city on the day after the Qingming demonstrations in memory of Zhou Enlai. He excitedly returned to our dorm that evening with a notebook of poems and declarations he had seen pasted up in the square. Our classmates shared the frisson of this moment of popular resistance. My roommate had borrowed my Flying Pigeon bike to make the trip into town and back. In those days each bike was registered with a small license plate affixed to the back mudguard. This soldier had risked being caught on a bike that was registered to the New Zealand Embassy.

In the hills south of Xi'an, Shaanxi, May 1986

Probably not many New Zealanders have travelled with a gun in China since 1949. We were about 40 kilometres south of Xi'an, climbing the zig-zag roads into the mountains looking for birds to shoot. The other double-barrelled shotgun was in the hands of our host, Wu Tianming, the enterprising head of the Xi'an Film Studio. He pointed it at any tiny bird that flitted into view. All without success, and there were few birds to be seen. Snowflakes began to fall as we drove on. My chance came from a large, sleepy crow sitting on a bare tree branch close to the road. Pointing my shotgun through the back window of the now-stationary van, I hit the target, much to the distress of the other foreigner in our party of six, an Englishman.

It was soon time for lunch. Zhang Yimou, then a cinematographer, almost an actor, and soon to become a director, busied himself gathering dry wood and scooping water from a tiny stream. Soon the unfortunate bird was boiling in an impromptu soup. The moment of my eating crow from the enamel rice bowl is immortalised in a photo Zhang took. He had it printed onto a small white, lattice-edged plate as a surprise gift a couple of days later.

Ducklings at Xisi, Beijing, June 1989

On the Sunday morning I heard the news on my shortwave transistor radio and started walking about 12 kilometres from my hotel, just beyond the Third Ring Road, towards the city centre. Unlike the evening before, the intersections on the road down to Xidan were littered with buses dragged across to block traffic. Some food shops, the state-run ones, were open and people were wandering about, dazed. At Xisi, just past the crumbling

Peking University classmates at the Badaling section of the Great Wall in 1975.
Zhang Heng is on the left, next to Paul Clark. PAUL CLARK

Chinese-style two storeys of the old Xinhua bookstore, a country woman was crouched on the pavement with a basket in front of her. A half-dozen tiny ducklings sat in the basket: future Peking Ducks to anyone who thought that far ahead on this particular day.

Going east on Chang'an Avenue at the crossroads at Liubukou, the southwest corner of Zhongnanhai, the leadership compound, the way to the square was blocked by armoured personnel carriers. Soldiers sat on top with machine guns pointed at the 15 or so people standing there, one cursing heatedly. A few hundred metres away on our side was the first dead body I had seen in my life: apparently a soldier, burnt and naked beside yet another burnt-out bus. Retracing my steps and heading north, at Deshengmen came another body, that of a young boy on his mother's lap on the tray of a small, duck-egg blue Toyota pick-up. She was driven beside the line of army trucks that had been blocked the night before by locals at the old city gate. Under canvas canopies over the back of each truck, young soldiers were being spoken to by civilians in the crowd of citizens. Tears flowed on both sides. As I made my way further north to the Third Ring Road, a family sitting on the pavement at the front door of their home greeted me: 'Does this happen in your country?'

The New Zealand Centre at Peking University, May 2007

I was lucky enough to attend the launch ceremony of the New Zealand Centre at my old school in May 2007. In front of a crowd of students recruited to fill the hall, Foreign Minister Winston Peters unveiled a plaque with the name of the Centre and date on it. We had earlier been warned that we needed to vacate the hall immediately to allow for the next ceremony. 'The Bulgarian Centre opening?' I wondered cynically. A workman strode up to the easel on which the brass plaque sat and quickly lifted both up together. The plaque slipped and crashed to the floor. When the room of the Centre finally became available in 2008 in a building just south of No-Name Lake on campus, the bent top-right corner of the plaque remained. It is still there today.

Supported by all eight New Zealand universities and three Wellington ministries or agencies, the Centre since 2008 has offered visiting fellowships and a course on New Zealand history and culture. Undergraduates from across all faculties at Peking University each fall semester attend classes taught by visiting New Zealand teachers. To most of the students (numbering in some years more than 60) this is simply an English-language course offering the credits in the language that they need for their degrees. The attraction is a course taught entirely by foreigners. To the visiting lecturers each week, the content about New Zealand is rather more important. But knowledge of a distant country and an appropriate emphasis on our nation's indigenous origins can confuse. In a survey of students at the end of one year's version of the course, a student asked: 'What is the proportion of the Pākehā minority in New Zealand?'

New Zealanders like to think that we have a special relationship with China, a country 35 times bigger than us and 270 times more populous. For perspective we would do well to remember the place of our country in many Chinese minds, at least from the 1950s until the late 1980s. In that period new graduates of high schools and universities were assigned jobs by the state. To many Chinese in those decades 'New Zealand' was a pun. Our name was short-hand for a remote place, the back of beyond, the boondocks. *Xinxilan* 新西兰 (literally 'New West Orchid', a flattering conceit) is our Chinese name. But in the well-known pun used about work assignments, the three syllables are broken down: *Xin* as in Xinjiang 新疆, *xi* as in Xizang 西藏, the Chinese name for Tibet, and *lan* as in the severely polluted city of Lanzhou 兰州 in Gansu, the remote province where Rewi Alley founded his school. 'Why are you looking so upset?' 'I've just heard about my work assignment. Bad news, I'm off to Xinxilan (New Zealand).'

Two Decades of Development Work in West China

DAVE BROMWICH

I have been going to China since 1991 and have now made over 50 visits, with a total of more than 10 years spent in the country. From 2001 on, a firm focus of my work has been in the area of poverty reduction, predominantly in the western provinces of Guangxi, Guizhou, Sichuan, Gansu and Shaanxi. The projects have been financed partially through NZAID and the New Zealand China Friendship Society (NZCFS).

From 2006 to the present, I have been involved in rural community and economic development projects in Gansu and Shaanxi Provinces, where we worked with local government institutions from provincial level down to townships, including Women's Federations. This work was promoting co-operatives as the tools for development, and was a perfect synergy between Rewi Alley's three key legacies: the Bailie education system, the Gung Ho co-operative movement (ICCIC, the International Committee for the Promotion of Chinese Industrial Co-operatives, for which I have served as a vice-chair since 2010), and the NZCFS, where I served as a vice-president, and since 2013 as national president.

From 2008 to 2010, with the NZCFS, I was involved in four rehabilitation projects after the Sichuan earthquake, where we worked with various local government institutions and Women's Federations. The response to rehabilitation by the various local governments was most impressive, with efficient assessment and implementation of rehabilitation projects, through to emotional support in the form of community gatherings. In one county, weather permitting, every night there was dancing in the street to help relieve stress. The NZAID approach to development has always been at the background of this work, using participatory approaches and targeting outputs to the needs of the beneficiaries. The most important stakeholder was always the beneficiaries, the households, the smallholder farmers, the women involved in handcraft work to supplement meagre incomes from farming.

Two key issues facing the poorer areas are scale of production and remoteness from market. In provinces like Guangxi and Guizhou, the landholding entitlement for households is around 0.2 to 0.4 hectare, often stony hillslopes. The sale of goods produced has traditionally been in the township markets, where farmers must travel to different localities with their basket of produce, competing with others for sales of the same product. The co-operative enabled members collectively to achieve a much larger scale and reach a broader market. Marketing has now been further enhanced through establishing a brand name for internet sales through the co-operative. Introducing a co-operative to a group of households in a village was a step-by-step process. In any community, there are natural entrepreneurs who can conceive of the value of collaboration within a co-operative structure. Others quickly followed when they saw the benefits the co-operative brought.

Democracy is alive and well in the village setting when the leadership of the co-operative is elected! I was fortunate to be present on several such occasions. First, a small group of men would go into a back room and fill it with smoke. I would suggest that they needed to augment the name list with nominations from the floor. And where were the women? Out in the meeting room, crammed so full that people were leaning in through windows, the election process would start. The enriched list of nominees was written on a blackboard, and all those present wrote their selection on a voting paper. A recorder was appointed, someone to call out the names, and a further scrutineer to check that the names were correctly called out. The participants reacted enthusiastically and noisily when an error was made. Invariably, several women were elected. In fact, democracy exists at the grassroots of Chinese society, whether in a co-operative, a village or in workplaces at all levels; leadership positions are democratically elected. It was sometimes disconcerting to us visiting the project site to find that the person or persons we had been working with had been changed by the election cycle. Fortunately, this only happened at predetermined intervals, and new partners became participants in our teams.

The approach we brought was from the grassroots up, encouraging collaboration with all stakeholders. An example of how this worked came from a township in Guangxi. In our pre-project evaluation, we identified that a vast number of plum trees of one variety had been planted by several villages on the firm recommendation of the local Fruit Bureau technicians. The farmers reported this to us as a problem. Not only had the plum trees taken up valuable land area, but they were not fruiting after several years. Had they fruited as predicted, it would have been a logistical nightmare to harvest and get the fruit to market, having no cool storage and limited market infrastructure. The farmers knew this. After five years, when still no return was evident, the farmers took it upon themselves to take the trees out. One of the outcomes of this project, from the four different sites we worked in, was reported at the end-of-project evaluation with the various

Inspecting the reconstruction of an irrigation canal in 2009, after the Sichuan earthquake. The New Zealand China Friendship Society contributed to the cost of this project. DAVE BROMWICH

participating institutions. Technicians all stated that they had learned how to talk to the farmers, learnt to respect their knowledge and respond to their needs, rather than merely instructing what should happen.

If there was a major success, it was this aspect of participation between all stakeholders. This could be seen filtering up to work at a provincial level. Different institutions which competed for development funds to promote a technology or training programme said that it was easier to pick up the phone and talk to other institutions to better co-ordinate their work. Our projects usually involved a training session for technicians in participatory approaches. The overall success of the work was achieved through local buy-in at all levels, and collaboration.

A key element that we as outsiders brought to our project communities was increased awareness of gender issues. It was my challenge at an inaugural project meeting to encourage the women to speak out and take a leading role, and for the men to respect the strengths that women can bring, and to encourage and support them in leading roles. At one project's mid-term evaluation meeting, the participants were asked to introduce themselves. When one woman gave her name, there was much laughter. On asking what the issue was, I was informed that the woman had given not her name but that of her husband, and they all knew I would not approve! Having a reasonable level of Chinese language added to my engagement in these meetings. Local dialects and accents were sometimes a challenge to my Chinese colleagues, too!

On another evaluation exercise, we initiated a role-reversal discussion. The men, pretending to be women, complained that the men spent the family money on tobacco and alcohol, not leaving enough for daily necessities, health and education for the children. The women, pretending to be men, complained that they did not have enough money for their own pleasure, and had to ask for an extra allocation of money to buy tobacco. This was quite a degrading activity for a man in a traditional household! With great merriment, it became clear that the domestic affairs were understood, and there came commitment to overcoming issues based on traditional gender roles. With membership of the co-operative, sale of goods was managed by the co-operative and income deposited in a family bank account, and it was usually the woman of the household who managed this.

The west of China lags behind the eastern areas of China in development. The stage of change in social attitudes is slower to reach the poorer, more remote regions. But through these kinds of exercises, it was clear to me as an outside observer that the seeds of change were already implanted. We perhaps played a very small role in encouraging them to be established.

During a visit to meet with the director of Shaanxi Women's Federation in Xi'an, I was a little early so was given a magazine in English put out by the Women's Federation, and referred to an article written by the chairwoman I was about to meet. She proclaimed that Xi'an and Shaanxi Province, having been a major centre of government in the Tang dynasty (618–907), was slower to respond to change than the more open and progressive regions to the east. The Tang dynasty is often considered the pinnacle of conservative traditional social culture. It is interesting to observe the influence that this still exerts today, some 1100 years later. But to see change happening, not only in policy direction but also in people's thinking, shows the dynamics of modern China at work. Yet there is continuity with ancient wisdom. This is expressed in the willingness for collaboration, with a foundation in the value placed on community over the individual. In Guizhou Province, at forums on rural revitalisation and eco-civilisation, I compared the Daoist principle of man and nature with current policy for sustainable environmentally sound agriculture, and the value of the co-operative in this paradigm.

Over the 20 years of development work, we observed significant changes occurring with the livelihoods of smallholders, and also with their aspirations. Once, on asking project participants 'Where do you see yourselves in five years' time?', a common response was modern houses built and car ownership, good indicators of optimism. We can claim some contribution to this in the local areas where we worked, but policy filtering down from Beijing provided the environment for success.

As previously mentioned, the projects implemented by NZCFS in conjunction with partners in China are linked to the legacy of Rewi Alley. The significant contributions that Rewi Alley made to the establishment of a new China show that he was ahead of his time. He was highly respected by the top level of leadership. In China, he recognised the need for change, appreciated the character of ordinary Chinese, and had a vision for a new China and a peaceful world. But he also had an innate understanding of participatory and sustainable approaches to development, respectful of the ordinary people, working with them to achieve goals together. The high esteem with which he is still held today plays an important part in the New Zealand–China bilateral relationship.

Myths of Dumplings, Business and International Relations: Is it Time to Demystify?

HONGZHI GAO

Kiwis, at least those I meet, love dumplings! Whenever I go to a dinner party or gathering, I always bring a plate of pan-fried dumplings with me. No surprise! People are always thrilled by the taste and texture of the food. I then brag about how important it is to get exactly right the cooking time and temperature. But I never reveal (without prompting anyway) that the dumplings were actually bought from an Asian grocery shop, and what I did was just the cooking bit (of course the most important bit).

From a marketing perspective — I was trained to be a marketing academic — the secret recipes inherited from my mum, and the 'sacred' process of cooking (focusing your mind and breathing slowly and deeply), were all important parts of the story I told people. We always had great fun and laughter after talking about the secrets of dumplings at the dinner table. It had to be mystical (with a bit of Chinese whispering when you talked about food).

Food is often cultural, but people's love of food is cross-cultural. Of course, my New Zealand story is more than dumplings and food. Kiwis welcome new food cultures, but also have open arms to people who are inspired by peace, freedom and quality of life. It has been a transforming experience for me living in Kiwi-land over the past 20 years. Kiwi-land has taught me so much! Including many values I thought that I had known long before: Why individual freedom is so important to the collective good of a country. How you should show respect to others who you do not like personally and even 'culturally'. What integrity means to people living in a high-trust country. Even something about love! 'Love your neighbours' in Christianity. And greet, and show your care to, the strangers who you may just meet on the street!

Kiwis' engagement with Chinese (immigrants, visitors, traders and investors) in recent years has been interesting and encouraging, for the most part. Unfortunately, some things, especially issues of international relations and human rights in recent times, have required some troubleshooting. Many Chinese Kiwis, including myself, enjoy living in a free, multicultural environment in New Zealand. Yet these people are still connected closely with family, friends and communities in China. Many of us have witnessed the fast development of the political, economic, social and cultural ties between New Zealand and China, but have been caught in the middle in debates about politically sensitive topics such as human rights and civil freedom, in relation to China.

Many Chinese, especially those who have grown up with a rising China in the past 30 years, see China very differently from those of my generation and older. My generation has seen at first hand the economic and ideological struggles that China had been facing during the early years of the economic reforms and 'open door' policies. How fresh and precious it was to people living and growing up in the 1980s and 1990s, those concepts and ideals of economic freedom, private ownership and free market competition.

There is no doubt that Chinese people are always very proud of their country: a history of thousands of years, a very rich food culture (you bet!), and amazing economic development over the past two decades (thanks to globalisation and China's entry into the World Trade Organization). However, many Chinese I know personally have started to realise that, along with all the great things that Chinese people have achieved in recent years, there have also been paradoxes.

The paradoxes of living in a city in China can be seen from being spoiled by an unprecedented level of availability and variety of choices that older generations could never even have imagined (loads of food at the dinner table, spectacular shopping malls, thrilling theme parks, karaoke houses everywhere, housemaids, after-school tutoring), and a desire for peace and nature that is so distant from city life. People increasingly desire individual freedom and social justice, but they know their security and protection actually come from tightly knit family and social groups that favour the incumbents at the expense of out-group members.

The Chinese constantly struggle between the ideal of 'being rich is glorious' as a way of living, and the increasing worry of losing their wealth due to the lack of sufficient legal and political protections. While people are filled with national pride from high-speed trains, gigantic harbours, and bridges within and between cities, they have also seen those struggling with rural lives in villages, families separated between cities and rural homes, and abandoned farmlands. People are in a search for spiritual richness, and are seeking ways to deal with all the pleasant and unpleasant changes that intertwine as China grows its economy and embraces governance paradoxes.

At the very beginning of my academic journey in New Zealand in 2002, I had decided to study something unrelated to China, just for a break from

313

the country that I thought I knew so much about. Building on my past work experience in China, for my Master's study I investigated the impact of biotechnology firms' product strategies on initial public offering (IPO) pricing (over or under) on Nasdaq. While it was fun and rewarding, I found out quickly after the research that my real passion was still for China, my motherland, a country I love so much, and care so deeply about, wherever I happen to reside. Throughout my life in New Zealand, I have always been asking one question: How can I contribute to a rational, sensible and genuine Kiwi–Chinese relationship?

For the most part of the 50 years' history of New Zealand's engagement with the People's Republic of China, globalisation has been the main theme. A decade ago, I wrote a piece that talked about 'changing the rules of the game in the new era of global competition the Chinese way'. Fast-forward, and we are now living in an increasingly deglobalised era. This is not an exaggeration: the rise of China has brought both opportunities and challenges to the world. I have researched how Kiwi exporters have smartly crafted China-entry strategies, how Kiwi exporters have tapped into the relational connections, skills and experiences of 'gatekeepers' in entering into the Chinese market, how they have mitigated the political risks in China, and how they could have analysed Chinese consumer responses to food scandals and product-harm crises. Most recently, I have started to write about the risks of the world's over-reliance on China in manufacturing, and advocate, from an Australian and New Zealand perspective, a dynamic balancing in the shift of global value chains in response to the global pandemic Covid-19.

Upon reflection, I find that my own engagement with communities in both countries has also changed significantly; the people with whom I have developed new relationships, the people I have gradually kept distant from, the topics of research that I have chosen, got bored with, put aside, and found a new love with. While my love of this island country and my faith in its liberal democracy have grown stronger and deeper,

I have developed new worries and concerns about the two countries I am emotionally affiliated with, as the world that shapes New Zealand and China has come to a new phase.

Indeed, New Zealand's engagement with China has shifted its focus over the past 50 years, through the initial immigrant and cultural ties prior to the early 2000s, to the bubbling international relations throughout the first 20 years of the twenty-first century, and the booming economic and commercial exchanges between the two countries after the signing of the Free Trade Agreement in 2008. Most recently, New Zealand has been walking across a tightrope in relation to China, amid growing US–China political tensions and the increasing strategic rivalry between democratic countries and authoritarian countries around the world.

The dumplings are still the same dumplings. But is it time to know a bit more about what is inside the dumplings, how they are made, and to demystify the cultures and institutions that Chinese-made dumplings come from. Extending the dumplings analogy to a wider context in the New Zealand–China relationship, should Kiwis know a bit more about how products are made in China, how labourers are treated, how the environment is protected, how intellectual properties are treated, how Chinese consumers perceive outside ideologies and foreign ways of living, and how these perceptions influence their purchasing behaviour?

It is dangerous to be focused only on trade and to ignore other important topics. Where are Chinese political institutions heading? Where do Kiwis stand with regard to those politically sensitive topics such as Hong Kong, Xinjiang, Taiwan and other religious, freedom and human rights issues in China? Transparency, fairness, freedom and democracy are things taken for granted by many Kiwis, but in fact they have all been fought for in

New Zealand. They can be taboo topics in China, and probably in the realm of New Zealand–China relations as well. From an international business perspective, the benefits from manufacturing and importing from China and attracting Chinese inward investment in New Zealand are all great — so long as the systems, values and norms of Kiwi-land are not diluted and compromised as a result. Remember what had attracted so many immigrants, including myself, to come to Kiwi-land in the first place.

When the world is becoming increasingly uncertain and volatile, we might learn some wisdom from Taoist philosophy, take a yin–yang perspective on life. In business terms, we call it 'dynamic balancing'. The reality is that New Zealand is being increasingly caught in the middle of a tug-of-war between the United States and China. In this context it must be recognised that despite New Zealand's unprecedented economic ties with China over the past 20 years it is the United States, Australia and other allies who will remain the most important partners for New Zealand in security, defence, IT and financial services, and also innovation. Despite its openness in recent years, China is still considered an extremely complex and 'insider-controlled' market for foreign businesses, including Kiwi exporters.

A yin–yang perspective of relationships with China and the United States appreciates that both countries will remain important to New Zealand in different areas, but that the key to success is to get the priority right when dealing with each of the two superpowers in each specific area. This involves always considering a response to one country in conjunction with how it impacts the other, and keeping balancing in focus at all times. This perspective might offer a solution to a divided, deglobalising world in the years to come.

A few years back, I coined the term '*Guanxi* gatekeeper' and proposed a relational gatekeeping model in international exchange relationships involving Western businesses, including Kiwi companies, and their partners in China. Despite the challenges faced by the firms I interviewed back then, I have to say that, in retrospect, it is considered something of a Golden Age. Now, it is time to rethink the yin–yang approach that accepts paradoxical conditions and embraces dynamic network momentum (*shi* 势), resources and capabilities, and the importance of relational gatekeepers in strategic planning.

The keys to dynamic balancing in business relationships are (1) selecting, (2) leveraging and (3) retaining relational gatekeepers, either within a company or as agents of the company. In my view, there is even a greater demand for relational gatekeepers in the sphere of international relations, beyond government-to-government interactions today. They are the people who can span the boundaries of communities in China and communities in democratic countries during a time of conflict, facilitating dialogue, looking for deeper institutional causes for differences, and exploring new ways of responding to these institutional and cultural differences — and ultimately seeking rational, sensible, legitimate and peaceful solutions to disagreements.

It is time to rediscover, rethink and rebalance the ties between Kiwis and the Chinese. If we can demystify the dumplings, can't we demystify business in China and international relations between the two countries? I believe we can. We need more gatekeepers, though. The question then is: where are they?

Understanding Grandmother's Buddhism: Lessons for Respecting the Beliefs of Others in China

AMY HOLMES-TAGCHUNGDARPA

'I am interested in the study of Buddhism, but not my grandmother's Buddhism. I don't think my grandmother knows what Buddhism is, but she spends all her time praying,' said Jenny. Many students around her nodded in understanding, adding that they have similar relatives in their own families who bewilder them due to their piety and dedication and, more generally, their superstitious (*mixin* 迷信) beliefs.

It was the first night of a two-week seminar I was teaching at a large university in eastern China in 2016. The seminar's topic was 'Western Presentations of Chinese Religions'. The American university where I taught had circulated a call for guest faculty to teach at a Chinese university as part of an exchange programme during the summer. I enthusiastically applied, seeing it as a great opportunity to meet with local scholars and learn more about what religion looked like in China in the 2010s.

I was also motivated by my frustration at the inadequacy of approaches and materials available for the teaching of Chinese religions in the United States, and in English language studies more generally. I had received my undergraduate degree in religious studies in Aotearoa and my PhD in Australia. After moving to the United States to take up a teaching position,

I had tried to adapt to American approaches to the study of religion, which I found focused on American theoretical models and histories that were deeply entangled with colonial legacies. Over the years, I had worked to acknowledge these legacies in my classes and, in particular, to attempt to bridge the chasm between the lived experiences of religion in contemporary China and how these are presented on the page.

Some available textbooks are focused entirely on the past, with no acknowledgement that people still participate in these traditions. Other texts are fixated on what scholars seem to see as the cognitive dissonance of China, a communist country where people flock to temples on weekends to pray for family, prosperity and success in their studies and careers. While there is an excellent emerging body of more nuanced scholarship, I wanted to position the seminar as an opportunity to think more about how to develop classroom resources that would be engaging for students from diverse backgrounds, and that acknowledge the experiences of Chinese communities as sites of authority, as opposed to 'debased traditions' or as of purely theoretical academic interest.

On the first day of the seminar, I acknowledged the absurdity of a New Zealander with no Asian heritage attempting to teach Chinese students about Chinese religions; instead, I expressed my hope that the seminar would focus on issues of representation and an exchange of perspectives of how Chinese religions have been categorised in global scholarly communities. The students were excited by this inversion of classroom hierarchies, and we had lively discussions around China's main 'three traditions' (*sanjiao* 三教) — Confucianism, Daoism and Buddhism — and the terms and texts used to understand these traditions, as well as popular translated resources and the terms used in these translations.

The students told me about how their own experiences with these traditions had been greatly affected by their own historical experiences and positions as educated elite. Their own positions had come out of over a century of struggle over concepts and terms that had attempted to categorise Chinese religions as part of the multiple national projects that have created modern China.

We intentionally used the term 'tradition' (*jiao* 教), due to the problems with using the loaded term 'religion' (*zongjiao* 宗教). When I first lived in China as a teenager at the turn of the new millennium, people who I visited temples with often explained what they were doing as 'covering all bases' as opposed to enacting religious belief. As one friend told me at the time, 'we are not sure if anything is there in the temple, but it is good to give offerings anyway, just in case!' Visiting temples was an opportunity to spend time outdoors, eat snacks and take photographs. At the same time, however, it didn't appear that people were merely participating in these visits as tourists; the aspirations around these visits were connected to people's hope for better futures, and for prosperity and happiness in a rapidly changing world.

Religious ideas and activities were also present in other parts of life: the impact of Confucian ethical systems on family interactions was clear; my friends learned Confucian and Daoist texts in their classical literature classes; and Buddhist prayer beads were becoming popular as fashion items among young people. As a young New Zealander from an atheist family, I was fascinated by the long histories of these traditions, and also how they were categorised variously as cultural (*Zhongguo wenhua* 中國文化) and/or religious as they gave meaning and reassurance to the people I met.

One form of categorisation I became especially familiar with was that of what constituted a 'cult' (*xiejiao* 邪教), since around that time Falun Gong was frequently in the news. Fed by a reading diet of *China Daily* and limited internet access, I was simultaneously horrified and fascinated by this evil group that was intent on splitting up families and setting people on fire. It was only when I returned to New Zealand and had access to information about the persecution of this group, that I was able to understand this media representation in a broader context.

The complicated intersections between culture and religion continued for me when I returned to China to study Buddhism formally at Peking University (or Beida) in 2005. There, the classes were entirely text-focused, and mostly revolved around translating *sūtras* between classical and modern Chinese languages.

Many of my classmates did not approach these *sūtras* purely as aesthetically beautiful pieces of literature. Wen Shifu, for example, was a monastic, and saw her Master's studies as part of her monastic curriculum and spiritual training. Her close friend Xiaorong was a layperson who had a day job as a publishing executive in Beijing. For her, the courses at Peking University were intellectually engaging and spiritually meaningful. She had grown up during the Cultural Revolution, but her grandmother had remained a devout Buddhist throughout, doing her prayers in hiding. When the Cultural Revolution ended, Xiaorong had been busy with schooling and professional development. But as the years went on, she had re-engaged with Buddhism as part of her heritage and for her own peace and wellbeing. Xiaorong learned about Buddhism from many other sources.

At the end of evening classes, students would trade with each other CDs with recordings from Buddhist studies scholars and famous masters. On the weekends, Wen Shifu and Xiaorong attended other courses at local monasteries. They kindly included me in a number of these excursions, including to a Prakrit class, led by an 80-year-old monk who taught from a photocopied manual from Taiwan and from his memories of classes he had taken back in the 1940s.

A number of students took part in these classes: older women from the local neighbourhood; Li, a man in his forties who wore a sweatshirt that depicted planets of the universe and talked about the spiritual teachings of aliens after class; and middle-aged professionals who also frequented Beida seminars. These students also traded CDs of teachings, along with small booklets published by Buddhist associations, mostly in Hong Kong and Taiwan, which contained teachings on a wide variety of Buddhist-inflected ideas, and postcards featuring famous Buddhist masters.

Even within this small collective of Prakrit students, there were many motives for and modes of engagement with Buddhism. Some students stayed behind to cook vegetarian food for the monastics at the temple, and others would go into the temple's main hall after our classes to undertake prostrations and chanting practice. There were multiple pathways of engagement, and many of the group did not necessarily 'believe in Buddha' (xin fo 信佛) more than any other tradition; some of the professionals were also active in Christian prayer groups and other Daoist-influenced practices, which were still abundant in the capital even after the crackdown on Falun Gong several years before.

Our Prakrit class operated under any government radar, as did these other study groups and prayer practices. However, not all Buddhism was seen as innocent: I also participated in a Tibetan–English language exchange with Tibetan students from the Minzu University of China, who told me what were acceptable forms of expression of Tibetan culture and religion (particularly singing and dancing), as opposed to what was deemed as 'sensitive' (min'gan 敏感) and therefore problematic.

At Beida, I was grateful for the opportunity to learn more about Chinese Buddhism, but had hoped to focus my studies on Tibetan and Himalayan Buddhism. Although some professors and scholars at the university were encouraging, among my classmates this was seen as eccentric and potentially problematic. Additionally, studying the past, from the supposedly safe space of texts, was much more straightforward than attempting to study contemporary movements that were subject to shifting political categorisations.

Since I have completed my PhD (which focused on the history of a Tibetan Buddhist lineage and its contemporary practice throughout the Himalayas), and have spent time in China away from university campuses, I have found that the category of *min'gan* has expanded. Tibetan Buddhism has become increasingly fashionable, and Orientalist engagements with Tibetan culture among university students in China is similar to that of their peers in the United States: they hang up prayer flags in their dorms, participate in meditation classes, and plan backpacking trips across the Tibetan plateau. Researchers have shown how, among Chinese Buddhists, Tibetan Buddhism has become seen as a pure, uncorrupted form of Buddhism, in contrast with Han Buddhism, which has been polluted by political interference.

However, actual Tibetan people, along with Uyghur Muslims, are not treated with the same deference and fascination. In travels throughout the Tibetan Autonomous Region, Sichuan, Yunnan, Qinghai and Gansu, I found thriving Tibetan Buddhist communities living and negotiating with severe government surveillance and restrictions on a daily basis. On the pilgrimage route at Samye — the centre of Tibetan religion associated with the foundations of Tibetan Buddhism — a group of middle-aged Tibetan women offered me tea, and spoke about their hopes that the pilgrimage would clear obstacles not only from their current lifetimes, but their future lifetimes as well, in their dedication to the teachings of the Buddha (Tibetan: *nang pa sangs rgyas kyi chos*).

Near the grassland tourist centre of Lhagang (Chinese: Tagong) in eastern Tibet (contemporary Sichuan), thousands of stones have been etched with the mantra of compassion by a diligent and dedicated artist, and placed into the river to carry these aspirations far beyond the plateau. And in Lhasa in 2018, under the supervision of cameras and patrols of armed military officers, dozens of young Tibetans wearing aprons, kneepads and gloves prostrated themselves around the sacred pilgrimage route of the Barkor. Tibetan topics may be sensitive as Tibetan communities live within a colonised environment, but Tibetan culture and religion are vibrant and remain as crucial sites of autonomy and sovereignty for Tibetan communities.

Throughout my experiences in China, I have seen the multiple layers of religious traditions and concepts, and their position in everyday life. In 2016, I had intended to brainstorm ideas with my students about how to more successfully cultivate understanding about Chinese 'religions' across different cultures. However, this had a limitation: I could not talk to my seminar in China about non-Han religious traditions. Before I arrived in China, I received an email asking me to focus on the 'Chinese Classics', due to the faculty's concern that students 'may not know how to respect the beliefs of others'.

The students actually did not have any such problem. Over the course of two weeks, we debated, laughed and shared our engagements with Confucianism, Daoism and Buddhism in our academic and social lives. In our short time together, we could not deconstruct and decolonise all of the representation of Chinese religions in English-language scholarship. However, my perspective on how to present these topics with nuance and respect, and appropriate deference to the multiplicity of these traditions and their complex political and historical contexts, was greatly enriched.

At the end of the course, I asked Jenny again about her grandmother. She told me that the discussions in the seminar had led her to question her own ideas about what Buddhism was, and that she had resolved to spend more time with her grandmother the next time she went home, so she could learn about the Buddhism of her heritage. Other students similarly expressed their hope to think more about categories of religion and culture in contemporary China as they participated in festivals, meditation classes and temple visits. Clearly, the aspiration of the Communist Party, that people would eventually grow out of religious belief, is not yet on the horizon.

Hopefully, we can continue to have conversations across nation states and communities like these, as these traditions remain central to, and important for, many Chinese people and communities. I also hope that in future discussions we can include a full spectrum of the diversity and complexity of what are often called religions, and the many elements of culture that have historically been associated with religion, in the People's Republic of China. Young people often have unique talents for respecting the beliefs of others and for cultivating tolerance, benevolence and care. These discussions can forge new worlds.

Bridges and Rainbows: Teaching Chinese Students in New Zealand

ELLEN SOULLIÈRE

When I arrived in New Zealand in 1975, I was looking for ways to make use of my academic background in Chinese Studies. I had studied Chinese history, language and art history at Wellesley, Middlebury and Princeton in the United States, and had taught at the Chinese University of Hong Kong from 1970 to 1972. But in those years it was still not possible for citizens of the United States to travel to China. After the establishment of diplomatic relations between China and New Zealand, and as the Cultural Revolution drew to a close, China and New Zealand initiated the reciprocal China Exchange Programme (CHEP), which allowed small cohorts of students to study in each other's countries. When I learned that some of these students were studying at Victoria University of Wellington, I was keen to explore the possibility of making contact and working with them.

I began by volunteering to join in translation sessions that Dr Jock Hoe was holding for the five Chinese exchange students who were then studying English at Victoria. We met for a couple of hours on Friday mornings in Jock's office and worked on the practicalities of Chinese to English translation. From memory, we translated only from Chinese to English, and most of the texts we translated were from official sources, including the *People's Daily*. In 1977 Jock Hoe and Helen Wylie, who had been working with the Chinese students, both went to China for the year. At this point, I began to work with the students on a more formal basis, and in 1978 I took up a junior lectureship at Victoria's English Language Institute, where all the Chinese exchange students studied.

In those years, the education officers at the Chinese Embassy in Wellington provided guidelines on how they wanted us to teach the exchange students. We were asked to focus on translation and interpretation, and to design and deliver a practical curriculum with a minimum of theory. We were also asked not to have any formal examinations, and not to rank the student performances in relation to each other. As part of our practical work, I arranged visits to Wellington hospital, Wi Tako Prison in the Hutt Valley, the Botanic Garden and Parliament, among other places, and worked with the students to develop vocabulary and other exercises around the experiences we had there.

The texts that we translated from Chinese to English were rather formal in style and content. Encouraged by H. V. George, who was then head of the English Language Institute, I started work with the students on a lexicon to assist us with the practical translation tasks that were the basis of much of our classroom work. Our Chinese–English lexicon contained many vocabulary items that were heavily loaded with political and cultural content. Literal translations of some of these words made them difficult for an audience of English-speaking people to understand. They included:

Running dogs 走狗
The capitalist road 资本主义道路
Socialist construction 社会建设

The development of this lexicon highlighted the linguistic and cultural gulf between China and New Zealand in the 1970s — and the potential for heat to be generated by political differences. The students and I had to construct bridges across this gulf, giving careful attention to how to communicate when the differences were great, while respecting each other's backgrounds, feelings and potential sensitivities. The students often contributed insights into our work that surprised and delighted me. I began to think of these contributions of theirs as rainbow moments, when light and colour unexpectedly shone onto an apparently mundane classroom task.

In the 1970s and early 1980s, most of the work I did with the Chinese exchange students focused on linguistic matters but, in addition to the cultural explanations associated with our reading and our excursions outside the classroom, we undertook other activities that required us to cross cultural boundaries. Sometimes, we sang. I remember that once I decided to teach the students a folksong. I chose one called 'The Foggy, Foggy Dew', because the tune was simple and the lyrics had multiple repetitions that I thought would make it relatively easy for the students to learn. I had not thought much about the lyrics, which tell of a love story between a young man who worked as a weaver and a fair young maid whom he nightly held in his arms, 'just to keep her from the foggy, foggy dew'. At the end of the song, we find the weaver back at work, accompanied by his son, who reminds him of the fair young maid. When one of the women students asked what happened to the fair young maid, I had no answer. I remember this as a rainbow moment, because this cogent lesson on the feminist analysis of discourse was delivered to me by one of my students.

Thirty-five years later, in 2012 and 2013, I was again working with translators and interpreters at Massey University with small groups of People's Liberation Army (PLA) officers. This time, I had free rein on the choice of texts and teaching approaches. I selected texts on a range of subjects that I thought would be interesting to the students and relevant to their needs, and set up feedback loops that helped me to incorporate their views and initiatives into our work. A colleague and I developed

Ellen with the CHEP (China Exchange Programme) students to whom she taught English in Wellington in 1978–79. From left: Wang Yu-chiung, Ling Hunghsiang, Wang Chih-kao, Ellen Soullière, Hsu Ming-chiang, Wu Hung-po. ELLEN SOULLIÈRE

a pattern for our translation activities that seemed to work well. The students worked both ways, from English to Chinese and from Chinese to English. I chose texts in English that I thought would be appropriate. I workshopped the passages for translation with the students in class, and then they prepared polished Chinese versions which they submitted to my colleague, who was a first-language speaker of Chinese, for evaluation. Meanwhile, my colleague selected texts in Chinese, workshopped the translations with the students in class, and they then submitted their polished English versions to me for evaluation.

Lively bilingual classroom discussion ensued, covering issues of form, meaning, style, equivalence, collocations, connotations, audience and the principles of translation. A few examples of the English vocabulary items for which we sought Chinese equivalents included the following: mission creep, clout, interoperability, cyber warfare, a layman, a regime, a revolt, a politician, host (as a verb).

Like the CHEP exchange students I had worked with decades earlier, the PLA students went on field trips, and on one of these we attended Question Time at Parliament. The students asked searching questions about what they heard there. They wanted to know what it means to 'hold somebody's feet to the fire'. They asked for an explanation of what it meant when one male Member of Parliament said that another was 'follicly challenged'. After I had explained this small insult, they then asked why MPs displayed such high levels of verbal aggression towards one another.

After watching the Speaker of the House in action at Question Time, one of the students observed that the Speaker's role is rather like that of a teacher or a judge who ensures that rules are followed and that questions are answered. The student followed up by asking whether MPs can ask *any* question at question time. In preparing my reply, I discovered that a minister can be asked and must provide a satisfactory answer to any question that falls within his or her ministerial responsibilities. The students then wanted to know if government MPs ever ask questions that reflect well on their own party. Again, the answer was yes, and there is even a special name for these: 'patsy questions'.

I remember that the students of the 1970s had arrived with the expectation that because more-formal language in Chinese often makes use of set 'four-character phrases' (*chéngyǔ* 成语), so too would English. This often led to difficulties when students unwittingly used a set phrase that was not frequently used in English, or changed the form of a set expression in a way that made it hard to understand. For example, one student said about a New Zealand woman who had hosted him in her home: 'She was over 60, but she was in her pink.' In those years I recall that the students often asked me to suggest set phrases, and I struggled to explain that collecting and memorising these phrases might not be the most useful learning strategy.

The students whom I taught in 2012 and 2013 arrived in New Zealand with a greater depth of previous experience of learning English and much more exposure to knowledge of the world outside China than the exchange students of the 1970s. As a result, linguistic and cultural bridge-building was easier in many ways. One of the students asked me about the English phrase 'hoist by your own petard' and I tracked it to *Hamlet*, Act III, Scene 4, v. 207.

> For 'tis the sport to have the engineer
> Hoist with his own petard.

Another student asked about 'the writing on the wall'. This led to locating the incident in the New Testament Book of Daniel 5:25, where the prophet Daniel interprets the words 'Mene, Mene, Tekel, Pharsin', predicting the imminent end of the rule of Belshazzar, King of Babylon, and the division of his kingdom.

For resources, in the 1970s, we had bound dictionaries, newspapers in Chinese and English, and textbooks prepared for second-language learners. All other class materials, we had to make ourselves. In 2012 and 2013, we had paper copies of Wellington's *Dominion Post* and access to a wide range of online sources. These included online dictionaries, *Stuff*, the BBC, Al Jazeera, CNN, Reuters and YouTube. Radio New Zealand provided in-depth interviews on topics that interested us. After we listened to Susie Ferguson interviewing Admiral James Stavridis, who was then Supreme Allied Commander of NATO, one student observed that, at that level, senior military officers were also politicians. Kathryn Ryan's interview with retired New Zealand Major General Lou Gardiner led to a discussion of leadership and the structure of the military. Wikipedia was a first line of access to concise and reliable information on many topics, and, whenever we wanted to go more deeply into a topic, we could sit in the classroom and access the electronic resources of the university library. These changes in the range and depth of resources that were available for teaching and learning were transformational.

Near the beginning of my work with the PLA students, we undertook a memorable exercise in translation and interpretation. When the first cohorts of these students had arrived at Massey University in around 2010, they brought with them a gift: a handscroll bearing the magnificent calligraphy of Liu Xianhua, a PLA general.

I designed a role-play task in which I asked the students to take the roles of interpreters on the occasion when this scroll was presented to the university. We prepared for this by researching the source of this text. We found it in Chapter 14:1 of the classic text by the philosopher Mencius, written during the Warring States period in the fourth century BCE.

The phrase appears in a conversation between King Hui of Liang and Mencius. The king told Mencius about the challenges that beset his kingdom from all sides, and asked about the approaches that would lead to successful governance in the future. Mencius replied that the king should base his governance on *rén* (仁), a term that is usually translated into English as 'humaneness' or 'benevolence'. If the king were able to govern in accordance with the principle of humaneness, Mencius explained, he would succeed: 'There will be no opposition to the humane person' (仁者無敵 rénzhě wúdí).

The students developed their interpretation task from the ground up, explaining the place of calligraphy in Chinese culture and the meaning of this calligraphy for a New Zealand audience. The beauty of the calligraphy was a powerful incentive for us all to persevere in the enterprise of translation and interpretation, and to integrate the virtue of humaneness into our lives and our work. For me, this exercise seemed to be a robust linguistic bridge and a cultural rainbow, among the most beautiful that I have seen with Chinese students in educational settings over the past 50 years.

A taniwha and a dragon are integrated as one entity as it circles a lone frangipani. This image is offered by the author as symbolising her identity and research journey as she explores China and New Zealand geopolitics and their aid to Pacific countries.

JUZZAH IOSEFO

Between Imaginaries: Interconnections of a Samoan New Zealander with China

ASHALYNA NOA

I am.
Born and raised in Aotearoa New Zealand – the land of the long white cloud.
The land of milk and honey. The land of opportunities.
I am.
A descendant of one of the first twelve Chinese entrepreneurs
who chose to call Samoa home.
I am.
A descendant of a Chinese settler who arrived before over 6900 Chinese
labourers set foot in Samoa under German and New Zealand colonial rule.
I am unsure.
'Saiga.'
A term proudly used in familial (hi)stories about my
maternal grandfather and great-grandfathers. Yet a term used
to 'other' my mother and her siblings in Samoa.

I am unsure.
Struggling to make sense of what I am learning in school.
It does not reflect where I come from. Unknowingly yearning for
knowledge of my whakapapa. A journey ignited by learning te reo.
I am unsure.
If my great-grandfathers are from China, is it even
appropriate to say that I am part Chinese?
How Chinese do you have to be, to be Chinese?
People don't believe me when I say it anyway.
I am Samoan.
'But you can't be full Samoan, you must be something else.'
I am 'many things else' but should that take away from being Samoan?
I am Samoan.
In a beginners Mandarin class. I have to say
where I am from in one sentence, but how?
I don't look like a typical Kiwi — whatever a typical Kiwi may look like.
I am Samoan.
Delving into China–Pacific research, there aren't many Pacific people. It has
surprisingly taken me around the world as part of New Zealand delegations.
Should I say I'm from Samoa or New Zealand?
I am a New Zealander.
Surrounded by Samoan elders. Respectfully
soaking up their wisdom and assumptions.
'You are lucky. You don't need to worry about what is happening in Samoa.'
'She wouldn't care about Samoan politics.'
I do care. At times I feel invisible.
I am a New Zealander.
In Samoa. My soul feels at home. I look Samoan
but I dress and sound like a Kiwi.
I am searching for hints of inclusion and exclusion
while conducting my field work.

I am a New Zealander.
In Shanghai. Strolling along the Bund captivated by the grand architectural designs before me. Intriguing glares from Chinese tourists and locals, whispering, pointing and laughing. A friendly local practises his English fluently while I reciprocate in broken Mandarin.
I am a New Zealander.
In Beijing. Travelling alongside a Canadian/Hungarian with New Zealand citizenship. A shocked local is perplexed that *I, Too, Am New Zealand.* I am more perplexed about the deep fried spider in sight.
I am a Samoan New Zealander.
In Bournemouth, England. Visiting a cousin from Samoa after my first solo presentation at an international conference. We are asked, 'Are you both from Samoa?'
I am a Samoan New Zealander.
In Qingdao. Dazzled by its light show and the city's connection to Fisher & Paykel.
Exhilarated by the knowledge and confidence I have already gained participating in dialogues dominated by men. I am out of my comfort zone. I see the power and strength of just being me.
I am a Samoan New Zealander.
In Chengdu and Xi'an. Marvelling at treasured artefacts, ancient sites and their authentic cuisine. Impressed by the lavish hospitality. Accustomed to WeChat and its translating function.
I am a Samoan New Zealander.
In Beijing again. I am given a business card with the left hand. My heart sinks a little.
A fellow Kiwi is visibly displeased at the slight.
They unknowingly make me feel reassured.
Note to self: your presence here is *valid* and *valuable*.
I am a Samoan New Zealander.
At an international conference standing with New Zealand, Australia and US delegates.

One delegate claims that one of the worst postings
is to a particular island in the Pacific.

I am.

Proud of where I come from and the stories of my ancestors. Enriched and
empowered by learning to negotiate various spaces. Privileged to be on this
journey paved by those before me.

I am.

Waiting. Observing. Covid-19 rapidly rupturing the status quo. A hiatus on
international travel. An increasing flurry of commentaries about China —
amplifying the good but mostly the bad.

I am.

Constantly evolving in my identity — ever changing like a braided river.
My engagements with China are interwoven channels
of family (hi)stories, research and travel.
It flows as part of me.

I am.

They Aren't Going to Take My Organs, Mum

ADAM OSBORNE-SMITH

I had just finished working a long shift at BNZ and walked in the door. *Seven Days* was blaring on the TV, and my folks were on their second bottle of Sav. Mum dragged her gaze away from Dai Henwood's impish grin.

'Darling, are you sure you want to move to China?'

I had been planning it for years, but nobody believed I was actually going to follow through. Then to everyone's surprise, I'd attained a cheap teaching certificate off the internet, cobbled together some meagre savings and was about 90 per cent there. I had also secured a job teaching English at one of the many after-school training centres in China.

'One-point-four billion people seem to live there happily enough,' Dad stated matter-of-factly, but with doubt behind the eyes.

'I was reading on the internet that they take people's organs. Your friends went to Germany . . . Why can't you go there? I'd feel much happier if you went *there*.' This was partly wine, partly understandable motherly concern.

'They aren't going to take my organs, Mum,' I thought to myself for a moment.

'I'll be fine, I think,' I said out loud.

It turned out that the biggest threat to *my* organs in China was the Ningbo expat community and a few young men from Shandong, who, looking to impart some cultural knowledge, taught me how to open a beer bottle with a pair of chopsticks. The only other New Zealander I met in Ningbo was repulsive and tried to goad me into smashing a guy's head against a bar, just because he was passed-out and easy prey. I pretended to go to the bathroom and quietly slipped out the door.

There have been a few times I've looked around *laowai* (foreigner) bars in China and thought of Donald Trump's infamous comment about Mexicans moving to the USA: 'They're not sending their best.' Some are very impressive people; but many do not even pick up basic Chinese, and the worst develop a deranged superiority complex to justify the relative privilege Western foreigners enjoy compared with the locals they work with. They do this unironically and in full knowledge that their higher salaries derive mostly from their skin colour. Quite a few won't need to be embalmed when they die.

I am subject to some of the criticisms listed above, and, while I've done nothing criminal, I'll admit I have not always acquitted myself in ways that make me proud. Nor am I highly fluent in Chinese, yet. What needs to be emphasised is that the bar is generally low for foreigners engaged in China's teaching profession.

Once, during a job interview for an English school, a middle manager remarked that he got promoted solely on the basis that he was observed taking notes during a meeting. It would seem this is proof enough that you take your job seriously. Another acquaintance saw her career advanced because after a happy school-night binge-fest she swerved up to work on her electric moped, went straight into a parked car and fortunately managed to break a leg. The school had no choice but to promote her straight away; her immediate competitors were impeded by their ability to actually teach children. Given the length of time it takes to get a visa and the fierce competition between schools for anyone remotely passable as a native English-speaker, making somebody else a manager would mean fewer classes and wring less money from terrified parents trying to get their tired children through national examinations. My friend would hobble into class with a spring in her crutches to assess other people doing work.

What is astonishing is how such an incredibly degenerate mishmash of foreigners is placed in charge of young children in a sprawling system of international schools, somewhat international schools, kindergartens, public schools and, of course, the brightly-coloured and poorly named private training centres looking to cash in on China's educational arms race of parent against parent. Altogether, we educate millions of children. For those fresh out of university looking to explore China from the 1990s onwards, these training centres were often our ticket in.

When I first arrived in Ningbo in late 2016, it honestly failed to register that being a teacher was what I was mostly going to do. I thought I'd be a Sinified version of Lawrence of Arabia with a New Zealand accent (I had not yet read about Rewi Alley), or a protagonist from one of my favourite dystopian novels, despite how thoroughly ridiculous both notions are. Teaching young children was only a pretence to get in. A side gig. My friends were going to be boring bureaucrats in Wellington; I had escaped my predestined middle-class path. Naturally, I was an atrocious teacher in the beginning.

I still remember being thrown in front of 12 seven-year-olds, in a fluorescent green room with blue chairs, white tiles, nausea-inducing office lights, a whiteboard and peeling decals of zoo animals all over the walls. It was my first class. There was no sound. I had no idea what to say or what to teach, so decided to go with mumbling a series of unclear commands. The students sat there understandably confused. A very small boy, with an incredibly round head, let his face fall, and slapped it with his tiny palm, somehow making a noise loud enough to reverberate around the awful room. My Chinese teacher aide kindly found another teacher to relieve me and them.

Nothing can accurately capture the sheer misery of being hauled out in front of primary-school children for 25 to 30 hours a week with minimal training, if any, and the BBC's mandate to 'inform and entertain', with entertain being by far the more important of the two. Essentially, every foreign teacher needs to adopt the persona of a Disney talk-show host, and roll out speaking game after speaking game. Without exaggeration, I have about four different games to amuse a child and get them to speak English using only a paper cup. If this was all a secret Chinese plot to get revenge on the English-speaking world for the sins of the Opium Wars, it does something to balance the ledger. Just ask any ex-training schoolteacher (few are stupid enough to stay more than a year) when they're a couple of mojitos deep. To this day, anything resembling the image of a lazy, fat cartoon dragon called Leo (a recurring character in our textbooks) makes my stomach feel empty.

The training centre I started at is called Shane English, and is part of a large chain. Training centres are places that teach children after school and on the weekends. The industry had seen a big boom since the 1990s as parents sought to gain an advantage in China's highly competitive university entrance exam, the *gaokao*. Many of these training schools try to inject fun into their courses, mainly to give parents the impression that their children are getting some semblance of a childhood. Usually, the

The World in a Magic Building. YUJIA GONG

schools can be found in glittering colossal shopping malls or scattered around office blocks. Mine was in a tall, black tower on the sixth floor. Parents would line the narrow hallways looking to score a nap where they could. It is common for middle- to upper-class students to attend around four or five extracurricular classes a week and get swamped with homework from all their respective institutions.

From the perspective of any child, anywhere, it's a raw deal and they know it. A lot of these training-centre children are brilliant, but it comes at a heavy cost. By about 12, they all universally slump in their chairs, any childish energy scoured from their bodies after years of over-schooling.

Angela (I have changed all the names mentioned here) was one of the brightest children I have ever taught, and, being about 10 years old, had not yet reached this point of lethargy. At my 193 centimetres, she was roughly the same height as my legs. She had short hair, a narrow face, and large, bright eyes. She moved with slow, clumsy, sloth-like movements and had strangely long limbs for her stature. A genuine pleasure to talk with, she would often join me and the other foreigners in the teachers' office after class.

'So, Angela, what do you want for Christmas?' asked Jeremy, a balding teacher from California, about 30 years old.

'Hmmmmm . . . I don't know.'

Jeremy, another teacher from South Africa, John, and I smiled at her, as adults confident in their superior knowledge of the world always do.

'It's normal to not know what you want for Christmas.'

Angela's eyes lit up and she started to smile.

'Actually, I know what I want for Christmas.' She paused for effect.

'I want Taiwan for Christmas!'

We all laughed. Apparently, 'Taiwan' was one of the words we were never supposed to mention here at risk of being turfed out. Isn't everyone in China supposed to be brainwashed?

'What do you think the Taiwanese children want for Christmas?' asked John.

'Maybe some of them want to be with China.'

We nodded our heads cautiously in agreement.

'Yes, maybe some.'

Her eyes lit up again and her smile became sly.

'Of course, if Santa Claus gives all of the Chinese children Taiwan for Christmas this year, next year they might ask for America.'

Now we really laughed. I doubted that she needed me as a teacher.

'Angela, you're too brilliant,' I said.

In every school in China that I have worked at to date, I have met children this impressive — as well as a fair number of doorknobs. Although I had studied China a little before coming, my perception of it as a place inhabited by people waving around little red books was rooted deep. I didn't expect jokes.

I often see this belief in people who have never been to modern China. There are certainly a good number of nationalistic Chinese ideologues, and they are scary, but how representative they are is anyone's guess. For some of us who come here, we do observe what should be a striking and obvious fact: there is no amorphic blob known as 'the Chinese people', no matter how often 1.4 billion people allegedly get outraged at star alignments on flags used in the Olympics or the latest tactless comment made by a Western politician.

In a way that better fits perceptions on the outside, China's training centres have recently been targeted by a government 'rectification' campaign. I have heard reports from friends all over the country that stringent regulations have forced many centres to close. Part of me thinks this is for the best, as I seriously query whether many of my foreign compatriots should be teaching. I genuinely hope that children here catch a break. My organs weathered my first year much better than my dignity. Training centres are filled with overworked children and alcoholic performers; their owners drive new Teslas bought with fear money. There is a case for change.

Yet for all their faults, and there are many, private training centres are often the first impression that many young foreign travellers have of China in the twenty-first century. So with the closing of these centres, I can't help but feel sad to see what seems to be the end of an era; although people here are incredible at finding a workaround, I doubt it will be the same. No matter the future of the sector, it was a direct contact point for millions of China's youngest generations and an eclectic group of outsiders. In this period of estrangement, that may be something sorely missed. My first experience of China will forever be defined by a tasteless fluorescent green room, tired children, and a wall covered in peeling images of zoo animals.

Middle Kingdom, Middle Earth, My Adventure

LUKE QIN 秦瞳

Tihei mauri ora.
Matua te tihi. Matua te kaha. Matua te āio. Matua te mana.
Whiua te hā kino. Tokia te hā ora.
Ki rua. Ki raro. Ki waho. Ki roto. Hui ē, tāiki ē!
Ko 峨眉 Emei te maunga. Ko 沱江 Tuojiang te awa. Ko 龙 Long
tōku taniwha. Nō 四川 Sichuan ahau. Ko 秦瞳 Luke Qin Tong
tōku ingoa.

Kia mau ki te tokanga nui a noho

I was born in Sichuan, the 'Land of Abundance', growing up watching *The Monkey King: Uproar in Heaven* and *Black Cat Sheriff*, and TV series based on the four great classical novels of Chinese literature: *The Romance of the Three Kingdoms, Water Margin, Journey to the West* and *Dream of the Red Chamber*. I read *The Art of War, I Wonder Why* and my fair share of history books. I played table tennis, badminton, basketball and football at school, and vaguely heard that the 'olive ball' was a 'brutal' sport. I was a religious follower of the Sichuan Quanxing football team; and my parents would have loved to have had in place back then the current rule for the gaming industry stipulating that minors can spend no more than three hours per week playing video games. I learned to play a bit of guitar, and was the class representative for 'arts and entertainment' throughout my school years. I had a good voice as a child, so was often picked to lead the school choir to sing songs like 'Defend the Yellow River' and 'Where is Spring?'.

I was not a fan of the large amount of homework we were given at the time, but am now most grateful that my primary-school Chinese class was the 'experimental class' for our school, as we would learn an extra advanced Chinese textbook per semester, and there was intensive reading every evening as homework. I am proud that I can read, write, speak and think in Chinese, as it carries the culture, history and collective wisdoms of the Middle Kingdom. I learned to think independently, and that truth and enlightenment will be found when all perspectives and criticisms are considered, however uncomfortable they might be 兼听则明. I am grateful that I was brought up with traditional Chinese virtues that have stood the test of time 仁义礼智信, 温良恭俭让, 忠孝廉耻勇. He aroha whakatō, he aroha puta mai.

Two roads diverged in a yellow wood

I remember when I was at intermediate school, much to my annoyance at the time, a fortune-teller told my grandma that I would end up somewhere 'far, far away'. I thought that was just a standard proclamation for kids of my generation, as China was opening up to the world at an extraordinary speed. I did wonder, though, what lay beyond Sichuan, beyond China, and I always knew I would follow my own path to see the world for myself. As a famous Song dynasty statesman and poet from Sichuan, Su Dongpo, wrote over a thousand years ago: 不识庐山真面目, 只缘身在此山中 ('if you are in the mountain, you can't see the mountain'). I knew I would one day stand at a distance to be able to truly appreciate the significance of the mountain, and to learn where bridges can be built within the mountain and to the outside world. Thanks to the video games I played, I was a believer that countries of the world would one day drop their differences to address the common challenges facing humanity, and together sail the combined terrain fleet to 'the sea of stars' 星辰大海.

The first time I heard of New Zealand was when we were deciding on a country for me to study in, as many students of my generation looked abroad for options. New Zealand ticked all the boxes for us, being English-speaking, safe, accessible, 'clean and green with lots of sheep'. Little could I imagine when I first arrived in New Zealand in late 2002 what I would experience in Aotearoa. Many years later, the penny dropped when I watched Bilbo Baggins sprinting out of the Shire raving joyously 'I'm going on an adventure!' To tick it off my bucket list, I re-enacted this famous scene at exactly the same spot when visiting Hobbiton in the rolling hills of Middle Earth New Zealand with my family.

Kia ora, Aotearoa

I stayed with a host family upon arriving in Christchurch, and my homestay dad, Brian, was an avid rugby fan. We wouldn't miss a single All Blacks game, and I learned that the 'olive ball' was actually not a single sport, because Rugby Union, Sevens, Touch, Rugby League, Aussie Rules, American Football and Canadian Football all use the oval ball. I quickly learned that brute strength alone would not win you the game, and the All Blacks, with its unique combination of flair and discipline thanks to its diversity, were the team to beat.

As a teenager I had no fear, so curiosity drove me to put my hand up for a trial with the school rugby team. Surprisingly, I was selected to play for the First XV on the blindside wing, as I had serious wheels back then. The problem was, I had to learn all the rules from scratch. My teammates were really supportive, especially our captain/head boy, Josh, who took me under his wing. But I knew I had to prove that I deserved to take the field to represent the school. I remember the overwhelming emotion when I was handed my jersey in the changing room before my first game, with all my teammates and coaches applauding and nodding approvingly.

I remember during one game, as I was tackling my opposite wing, our own flanker, a strapping Samoan boy, ran over and smashed the both of us. I felt something hot dripping down my forehead, but charged straight back into the ruck, only to be dragged off by Mr Edgerton who took me to the hospital to be stitched up. After that, I truly became one of the boys, as I had earned my respect through blood and sweat, and I remember the commotion at the school assembly when our principal, Mr Burrough, handed me my First XV Rugby Blazer Award.

I had a great time at Linwood, and it was an excellent introduction to the New Zealand way of life. The lessons and opportunities I enjoyed there gave me self-belief and prepared me for what was to come. I was chosen to represent the school in the Lion Foundation Young Enterprise Scheme, and won the Excellence Award for Commerce, sponsored by Lincoln University. A decade later, I was honoured to give back, as I mentored the Hutt Valley High School team to take out the Wellington Regional Young Enterprise Scheme Company of the Year in 2014. I broke four electronic dictionaries learning English, reading politics and sports pages while jotting down every new word I'd come across. I taught my accounting teacher, Mrs Carr, Chinese, and she became my first mentor and answered all my questions on anything Kiwiana.

After graduating from the University of Canterbury, and a couple of jobs in bilingual journalism and business development, an opportunity to join the banking industry took me to Wellington, then Auckland. This work has meant that I have been able to travel the country to support many hardworking and innovative businesses that generate export earnings for New Zealand and bring in goods to ensure New Zealand's living standards. I am convinced that New Zealand's future prosperity depends on its liberal and pluralistic society, a fair and transparent international system, and its ongoing ability to invest in productive assets to provide value to the world.

Nā tō rourou, nā taku rourou ka ora ai te iwi

Over the past two decades, I have been blessed to work with and learn from many amazing people of various backgrounds who call New Zealand

Luke Qin leading the dragon dance during the Chinese New Year parade, Wellington waterfront, February 2018. LUKE QIN

home. The Asia New Zealand Foundation took me to Japan and Waitangi, and afforded me the opportunity to connect with and learn from New Zealand's future leaders. It helped broaden my horizon to better understand and appreciate Asia's diversity and its importance to New Zealand's future prosperity.

I was appointed to serve as national treasurer and standing committee member of the New Zealand Institute of International Affairs, and was later elected to serve on the board. I had the opportunity to attend state luncheons and public forums welcoming foreign dignitaries, and was invited to attend many celebrations, seminars, roundtables and cultural exchanges hosted by the United States, Japan, India, Australia, China, the United Kingdom, Hungary, the Netherlands, Vietnam, Malaysia, Singapore, Indonesia, the Philippines, Thailand and Korea at public venues, embassies, high commissions and official residences.

I was elected to serve as a board director of Transparency International New Zealand, and regularly attended the Public Sector Leaders Integrity Forum at the Office of the Auditor-General. I have served on the executive committees of the New Zealand China Council, the New Zealand China Trade Association, and the New Zealand China Friendship Society.

Even though I wasn't born in New Zealand and my Cantonese is scratchy at best, I was entrusted to lead the Wellington Chinese Association and serve on the national executive of the New Zealand Chinese Association. I was elected by fellow panel members and city councillors to chair the Hutt City Council Community Funding Panel, and was selected to serve on the panel of the Ministry for Ethnic Communities Development Fund.

I have learned both All Blacks haka, and an off-the-cuff video featuring my then five-year-old and me jamming 'Tūtira mai ngā iwi' to celebrate the 2020 Māori Language Week had nearly 14,000 views and over 900 likes on Twitter. The Friends of Waiwhetū Stream taught me how to distinguish weeds from native plants, and the White Ribbon Trust nominated me to serve as a White Ribbon Ambassador. The Hurricanes Super Rugby

Team named me as its cultural advisor, and two senior All Blacks held up Chinese couplets with me to wish the Chinese community a happy Dragon Boat Festival.

Fire and Emergency New Zealand trained me as a volunteer firefighter, and supported me to complete the Sky Tower Stair Challenge to raise funds for Leukaemia and Blood Cancer New Zealand. I will never forget the look on my son's face when our fire truck visited his kindy, and the kids performing the 'Fire Truck Song' to thank us, before we had to dart away for a real call-out.

I take pride in being able to go home whichever way I travel between my little shire in Sichuan and New Zealand. I am grateful for the many opportunities and adventures New Zealand has given me. I can't wait to share my experience and lessons with my son, and introduce him to the world just as I was taught and inspired by my family, colleagues, friends and mentors, who have helped me along the way. When I am feeling down, unwell or unconfident, I just have to reflect back on the many opportunities I have received and the challenges I have overcome, as it gives me renewed strength to pursue my current assignments and the quests that lie ahead.

Nō reira, waiho i te toipoto, kaua i te toiroa. Kua tawhiti kē tō haerenga mai, kia kore e haere tonu. He tino nui rawa ōu mahi, kia kore e mahi nui tonu. Kua pari ngā tai, kua timu ngā tai, he tai ope, he tai roa e kūmea mai nei i te tai nui kia eke panuku, eke tangaroa. He toka tū moana. Haumi e! Hui e! Tāiki e!

咬定青山不放松
立根原在破岩中
千磨万击还坚劲
任尔东西南北风

Reflections of a NZUSA Delegation Visitor, 1971

PHILIP S. MORRISON

On the morning of 3 August 1971, I opened the window of my hotel room in Guangzhou and looked down. Single-storey, narrow brick houses with tiled roofs, joined wall-to-wall, ran both sides of a narrow lane as far as I could see. Men and women were walking briskly, almost invariably dressed in blue, while the children played in the few available open spaces. It was summer and five years into the Cultural Revolution.

On 23 October 2013, over 40 years later, I again opened my hotel window and looked down, this time from a hotel on the campus of Xiamen University in the neighbouring province of Fujian, less than seven hours drive northeast from Guangzhou. It felt like summer again, and I had a weird sense of *déjà vu*. But the air was hazier, there was a cacophony of car horns from the neighbouring city of Xiamen, and the buildings were much taller. Dozens of cranes dotted the horizon, and people walked around in casual Western dress.

In 1971 the PA system exhorted the citizens to work harder and to read the works of Chairman Mao. Forty-two years later, each morning the PA system on the Xiamen campus delivered the daily news, including regular updates on the progress China was making in catching up to the USA. The subtext was the same two generations later: work hard and we will continue to progress; remember, a man can move mountains.

I was 23 years old in 1971 and a member of the New Zealand University Students Delegation to the People's Republic of China. In Xiamen I was 65, accompanying my wife while she taught a six-week course in academic English for Massey University. Her students were preparing to travel to the West to do postgraduate studies.

I was both fascinated and deeply moved by the contrast in views from the two hotels, 42 years apart. I felt caught in a vortex, my head spinning against the tide of change. Those walking to class on the Xiamen campus were the grandchildren of the adults whose peers we'd interviewed throughout China over 40 years earlier. Back then, after a tumultuous decade, their grandparents were dreaming of peace and prosperity for their children. Now, two generations later, their only children could dream of a graduate degree from America, of well-paid jobs, status, and owning a nice apartment in the city.

When an undergraduate student in geography at Victoria University of Wellington in the late 1960s, China had been presented to us (along with India) as a failure of development. In his 1960 book *The Stages of Economic Growth: A non-communist manifesto*, Walt Rostow found China a particularly challenging case. He was unable to countenance a planned economy raising standards of living in the way a decentralised, open, free system could. Ironically, nor could our first-year geography lecturer, Professor Keith Buchanan, whose own *The Chinese People and the Chinese Earth* and *The Transformation of the Chinese Earth* extolled the virtues of a command economy. Even in the face of exaggerated production figures and the human cost of the Great Leap Forward, Buchanan saw in the Chinese 'model' a way forward.

The contrast of Buchanan's rendition of state socialism with the capitalist road advanced by Rostow could not have been more stark. In a world of opposites, neither foresaw a felicitous combination of socialism and capitalism that China was to meld from 1978 onwards through a series of experiments that Deng Xiaoping believed would strengthen the Chinese Communist Party. As we now know, China was able to double the size of its economy in real terms every eight years (on average). Notwithstanding continuing debate on the effectiveness of the government's poverty reduction programme, the deterioration of access to basic education and public health in rural areas, and the widening of income disparity beginning in the mid-1980s, progress on almost all indicators since our visit in 1971 was remarkable.

China was not my first exposure to 'Asia'. In 1966, as an 18-year-old school-leaver, I had been posted under the Volunteer Service Abroad scheme to a primary school carved anew out of the jungle a few degrees north of the equator near the small bazaar town of Serian in Sarawak, on the island of Borneo. By the end of that year I had seen stark poverty, vast inequalities in wealth, precarious living in a volatile rural economy, and a quite different social order. I had stood with other volunteer teachers from the USA, Canada and India in the searing heat on the concrete forecourt each morning as we sang 'Negaraku' with the students, directed by a Chinese headmaster in compliant allegiance to the newly formed State of Malaysia. In terms of daily life — the shops, houses, hawkers, and the general bustle — China in 1971 did not appear that different.

The University Students Delegation of 1971 was a PRC initiative under the broad banner of 'people-to-people diplomacy'. It was organised by the New Zealand China Friendship Society, which, Alister Shaw wrote, in his PhD thesis *Telling the Truth About People's China* (VUW, 2010, pp. 162–163), was dreamed up in China by Rewi Alley and Shirley Barton, a CORSO representative in China. The delegation he suggested was a 'hugely significant trip. At the time very few New Zealanders had been to the PRC,

Above: A scene outside a railway station, south China, 1971. PHILIP MORRISON

Below: A rural family in north China, 1971. PHILIP MORRISON

other than Communist Party members and China Society fellow travellers. The trip was seen as an opportunity for New Zealanders to get an objective image of the PRC, and would, according to then NZUSA President David Cuthbert, change the way that New Zealanders saw China.' For the Chinese, young New Zealanders were the best conduits for their message. For their part, the selectors of the delegation 'chose what they regarded as a balanced tour party, representing each university campus and a variety of political perspectives. There was a clear agenda to ensure that their findings would not be written off as those of the already converted.'

The visit took place in August 1971, and, after an initial stop in Hong Kong, followed a south-to-north route that included Kwangchow, Chiuchow, Shanghai, Nanking, Sian, Yenan, Tachai and Peking. As Paul Grocott summarised it in his 'Report by the leader of the NZUSA delegation to the People's Republic of China in August 1971', the group's tour included 'approximately six days visiting historical places and taking part in tours on fourteen separate occasions; nine factories visited; three and a half days spent on three different communes; seven opportunities spread over about four days for learning about aspects of China's adult and child education programmes; at least three formally arranged discussions with government and military officials concerning their work; three main visits to social services, concerned with housing and health; attendance at nine public performances of concerts, acrobatics, films and opera; and . . . six banquets.'

Alister Shaw referred to our collective 'struggle to express the state of mind of the Chinese people and the way in which this was reflected in Chinese society', noting that our accounts are very matter-of-fact and, for the most part, simply consist of repetition of what we were told. In retrospect, any attempt we might have made to sum up a nation's mood, aspirations and disappointments would have been heroic in its naivety. We were travelling in a country where freedom of expression was severely constrained, where even an accidental departure from the accepted word was dangerous. Self-censorship was paramount and pervasive.

I found I'd expressed this challenge in a letter I wrote to colleagues, after just three days, on our train ride to Hangchow. 'One of the most frustrating difficulties for us, and I should say for any social scientists who would do work in the future here, is to try and get past Mao's thoughts which are on everyone's lips and serve as an answer to any question we choose to ask. So when we ask a question too often we knew exactly the answer we are going to receive. Mao's answers were right and unquestionable.'

The observations we made as we travelled through southern China were possibly more telling than the conversations we had, and in the same letter I'd written: 'We were all impressed by the intensive land use and the absence of machinery and therefore the hundreds upon hundreds we have seen working in the fields. Even those of us who have visited similar agricultural systems elsewhere in Asia are impressed by this.'

In 2021, as I look back at China, I do so from two perspectives simultaneously: a macro perspective involving changes in aggregate indicators, the general sequence of which we are now familiar with. The complementary perspective is a micro one, in which change is viewed from the point of view of particular individuals. These stories are of course much more complex and heterogeneous, and depend greatly on the person's social and economic standing, notwithstanding a Cultural Revolution designed to reduce their significance. My own impression of both levels, the macro and the micro, has been of a sense of mission, of drive to restore pride in a unique country, and in being a citizen of a nation which one day will lead the world, as it already does in many respects. Those of us in New Zealand watching from the sidelines can only hope that this mission will be respected and supported for the good of all.

In August 2021, 18 of the original 20 members of the delegation who visited China in 1971 reassembled at Victoria University's Rutherford House in Wellington, in person or via Zoom. It was a delightful, life-affirming event in which we all expressed gratitude for the opportunity the New Zealand Union of Students' Associations had given us to learn, and then to share our impressions of China with hundreds of New Zealanders across the country. Television New Zealand's *Q and A* programme captured the spirit of 1971 and 2021 in their coverage of our reunion.[1]

---

1 The views above are mine alone and are not intended to represent those of the delegation or any members of it. For coverage of the delegation's reunion, see www.tvnz.co.nz/shows/q-and-a/clips/rare-video-of-life-in-china-in-1971-from-intrepid-kiwi-students

A Young China-watcher's Take on a Changing China

ALEX SMITH

When I lived in Shanghai in 2014, I developed an obsession with the Peace Hotel. Located on Shanghai's famous Bund along the Huangpu River, I'd drag visiting friends and family in through the lobby's revolving door and under its oversized chandelier to the hotel's jazz bar. It is a shameless throwback to the opulence of a bygone 1920s Shanghai, and one that somehow embodied the nostalgia I had come to feel for this period, and for China when it was still only a place I'd read about in high school.

My interest in China was first sparked while studying Chinese as a 13-year-old in Wellington. This fascination was cemented, along with a somewhat counterintuitive association of China as a place of escape, through a carefully managed, Chinese government-funded experience four years later. After coming a joint second place with two other New Zealand students, we were sent to China to form the 'honoured audience' of the televised Chinese-language speech competition, Chinese Bridge.

At the time we joked and wondered about whose crazy idea it was to put dozens of privileged foreign high-school runners-up in four-star hotels and bus us around Beijing's and Chongqing's most impressive tourist attractions every day for two weeks. It was 2009 and China still seemed to be basking in its post-Olympic glow. The students who had actually won the competition in their home countries, meanwhile, spent hours each day rehearsing elaborate talent routines and memorising facts from thousands of years of Chinese history in preparation for the televised spectacle. To us runners-up, it felt like we'd managed to pull off an elaborate scam, albeit through no genius of our own.

Only now do I realise that the joke was on us. For many of us who went on that trip, China has become the focal point of our careers, or at least a central feature of our adult lives. It is what social policy makers would describe as a successful intervention in the life course of the individual.

After finishing my undergraduate studies in Wellington, and with the seed of my China obsession firmly planted, moving to Shanghai — a city itself celebrated as a place of refuge and notorious for its escapist trappings — seemed like a natural decision.

My year of studying Chinese at Fudan University proved to be the escape, from what felt like the monotony of post-adolescent life in Wellington, I had been hoping for.

Many a carefree muggy evening was spent chatting, and on occasion eating watermelon, with the security guards tasked with monitoring the comings and goings of the international students' dormitory. The guards were gruff at first, gesturing for us to present an ID card before letting us in through the dorm's gates without so much as a 'hello'. But after a few months, they'd start to nod us through without asking for ID. The first night one of the guards stopped us as we were coming in through the gate in order to share her watermelon felt like a real milestone. After that the guards would often joke with us as we passed in and out of the dorm's gates. I grew accustomed to these rhythms that formed the flow of my new everyday life.

Much of Shanghai's appeal rests on its ability to conjure nostalgia

A man stops on his riverside stroll to enjoy one of the views that led the Qing rulers (1644-1911) to build their summer holiday resort in Chengde 承德. Alex Smith lived in the city in a local homestay in 2019 while she worked on her Chinese. ALEX SMITH

among its visitors for the glamour of its treaty port days. And as a 22-year-old, I was quick to fall into this nostalgia trap. My classmates and I would spend lazy weekends traipsing around what remained of Shanghai's old *longtang* alleyways, or window-shopping our way along the upscale *qipao* boutiques on Huaihai Road in the former French Concession. Shanghai's roadside antiques markets became another frequent stop on the itinerary. The highlight, however, remained the Peace Hotel.

I had become a cliché, hankering for a romanticised version of the city's colonial past, and seeking out a history that seemed accessible only in the fleeting glimpses of tucked-away spaces. And like my colonial predecessors, I took for granted the easy access, friendly reception, and the strange sense of freedom that came with being an anonymous Westerner in China.

While my student loan called me back to New Zealand, my interest in China, and desire to write about it, failed to subside. After a couple of years in the public service, I eventually plucked up the courage to apply for graduate school in the United States to continue my China studies.

The unappealing prospect of spending an oppressively hot New York summer, in 2019, awaiting work authorisation after completing my Master of Arts, provided the perfect excuse to escape back to China. This would be the first decent length of time I would spend in China since leaving at the beginning of 2015. I stayed a month in a small city outside of Beijing, living in a homestay and working on my Mandarin.

But it was on this trip that China started to feel less like an escape and more like a reality check, long overdue. It was August 2019 and swells of protestors were taking to the streets in Hong Kong. Being naturally conflict-averse, I found discussions with my new Chinese friends, with whom conversation otherwise flowed seamlessly across topics, jarring and confrontational whenever Hong Kong inevitably found its way into the conversation. Pangs of anxiety began punctuating our discussions as my teachers-cum-friends expressed sympathy for the naive young Hong Kongers somehow conned by America into protesting against Beijing and ruining their futures.

The same was true when my young, liberal and otherwise like-minded friends would mention in passing that they didn't think that racism was a problem in China. I would feel myself fumbling, trying to steer the conversation in any other direction.

Alone and scrolling on my phone provided no respite. Chinese news sites were filled with stories about the so-called 'black hands' and 'ruffians' behind the Hong Kong protests, and I quickly came to regret promising myself that I'd read only Chinese media for the duration of my trip.

My anxiety only intensified in the latter half of my visit when I was interviewed from New York for an internship at International Crisis Group, a conflict-prevention organisation. Since December 2018 their East Asian advisor, the Canadian Michael Kovrig, had been detained by Chinese authorities — a move widely considered to be a political retaliation for the arrest and detention of Huawei's CFO in Canada earlier that month. We talked about Michael's situation in the Skype interview. I remember being struck by the ordinariness of it all: that Michael's colleagues still had to go to work despite this rupture in the course of their normal lives, and that this could happen to someone who worked at a place I, too, could work. I accepted the position in New York four days before flying out. At Beijing airport, waiting for my flight, paranoid thoughts kept circulating their way through my head: what if I, too, was detained for reasons unknown?

After a few months back in New York and eager to step up a rung on the China research ladder, I took an internship writing copy for a daily newsletter covering China. One of the earliest newsletters I worked on marked the first anniversary of Kovrig's detention. But in the months that followed, and as relations between China and much of the West deteriorated, helping curate the day's political news became an increasingly depressing exercise. China clamped down on visas for US journalists, and long-time China correspondents were forced out of the country in droves. An Australian journalist was also detained, while two others made a quick escape with the help of Australian Embassy staff after being accosted by Chinese intelligence officers in the middle of the night. If a Western passport once felt like it granted a degree of privilege and immunity in China, it now felt like a liability waiting to crystallise.

While the idealised China of my teenage years and early twenties may have never really existed, there is no doubt in my mind that China has nevertheless changed. The China of 2021 is not the China some China-watchers now fondly recall in the comparatively liberal era of Hu Jintao and Wen Jiabao that I first encountered in 2009. A friend told me recently that the security guards at our old university have been replaced by a more professional cohort less inclined to banter, and aided by freshly installed facial-recognition software. The politics have changed, and so too has much of the minutiae that once comprised my day-to-day life in China.

But an undeniable part of my changing relationship with China is my own getting older and having to reckon with the irreconcilable aspects of something that has shaped much of my own life trajectory and made my world infinitely larger.

Having started studying Chinese at the age of 13, I have always felt lucky to have known what 'my thing' was. My younger self probably assumed that I would be progressing nicely along the China career track (whatever that means) by now. But starting a full-time career dedicated to researching and writing about Chinese politics also increasingly feels like either a sure way to end one's own access to China or to accept an uneasy personal compromise. Even for young researchers willing to make this compromise, the line demarcating what one can safely write about — known by some China scholars as the 'anaconda in the chandelier' — also seems increasingly blurry. For now, the easiest option appears to be avoiding committing to the China career whatsoever, or at least delaying it to a hypothetical future when one is better equipped to deal with its consequences.

Sinologists often point out that there is no singular China. It exists in multitudes and infinite possibilities. History is contingent, and no one knows what China will look like in the future. But the China of the present no longer represents for me an easy escape, and if I was once nostalgic for the Shanghai of the 1920s, I'm now nostalgic for the China of the early 2010s and my own simpler understanding of the world.

About the Contributors

Diana Bridge has published seven collections of poetry, the latest, *Two or more islands*, in 2019. She has a PhD in Classical Chinese poetry from the Australian National University, and is the first foreigner to have taught in the Chinese Department at Hong Kong University. She has written essays on the China-based poems of Robin Hyde and William Empson, and completed a collaborative translation of a selection of classical poems. Her essay 'An attachment to China' won the *Landfall* Essay Competition. She has been the recipient of the Lauris Edmond Memorial Award, and in 2015 won the Sarah Broom Poetry Prize. She lives in Wellington.

Nick Bridge is a retired diplomat whose career centred on Asia. Six of his seven postings were in the Indo/Pacific region. China was the central theme, with assignments in Beijing, Taiwan, Hong Kong and Singapore. Almost five years as New Zealand High Commissioner in India provided a fascinating counterpoint, revealing the pervasive and different cultural influences that these two great Asian civilisations have had throughout the region and the ages. A cricket tragic, his memoir *The Boat that Brought Me* was published in 2019. He lives in Karori, Wellington, with his wife, poet and Sinologist Diana Bridge, who closely monitors, and improves, his writings.

Dave Bromwich has been national president of the New Zealand China Friendship Society since 2013, and vice-chair of the International Committee for Promotion of Chinese Industrial Co-operatives (ICCIC) since 2011. Since 1991, Dave has spent an accumulated total of more than 10 years in China. His main work has been in community development projects in rural poverty alleviation. He has travelled extensively, and has reasonable fluency in Chinese language. He has also taken many educational tours and delegations, and facilitated various exchange programmes with partners in China, focusing on youth. In recent years, he has addressed international forums. In 2019, he received a Chinese Government Friendship Award.

Tony Browne, having joined Foreign Affairs in 1973, made his first visit to China in 1974 while studying Chinese in Hong Kong. He was posted to Peking from 1976 to 1978. Subsequent postings included being director of the New Zealand Commerce and Industry Office in Taipei from 1994 to 1997, and as ambassador in Beijing from 2004 to 2009. After retiring from MFAT in 2011, he became chair of both the New Zealand Contemporary China Research Centre and the Confucius Institute at Victoria University of Wellington. He has visited over 70 Chinese cities. When he finally gets to Ningxia, he will have visited every province in China.

Duncan Campbell is a Wellingtonian who spent some years in Malaysia studying Mandarin, after graduating with a degree in English and history from Victoria University of Wellington. Between 1976 and 1978, he was a student in the People's Republic of China. Since then, he has taught (Chinese language, modern and classical; Chinese literature, modern and classical; and aspects of Chinese history and civilisation) at the University of Auckland, Victoria University of Wellington, and the Australian National University in Canberra. In 2015, he was the curator of the Chinese Garden at the Huntington Library, Art Collections and Botanical Gardens in San Marino, USA. His research focuses on the late imperial period of China's long history.

Hilary Chung (1962–2020) taught comparative and Chinese literature in the School of Asian Studies at the University of Auckland from 1999. A graduate of Cambridge and Durham universities, she trained in modern Chinese literature in comparative socialist perspectives. She co-edited and co-translated *Unreal City: A Chinese poet in Auckland* (2006) with

Jacob Edmond. In her last years, before breast cancer took her from us, she was instrumental in the establishment of the cross-faculty Global Studies programme at Auckland.

Paul Clark was one of the first three New Zealand exchange students in Beijing, from October 1974 to July 1976. After completing doctoral studies at Harvard, he worked for 10 years in Honolulu. He returned in 1993 to become chair professor of Chinese at the University of Auckland. His books include works on Māori history, Chinese film, Cultural Revolution culture, youth cultures and (forthcoming) leisure in Beijing since 1949. From 2018 to 2021 he was also director of the North Asia CAPE (Centre of Asia–Pacific Excellence), promoting New Zealanders' engagement with the region.

Jacob Edmond, a professor of English at the University of Otago, is the author of *Make It the Same: Poetry in the Age of Global Media* (2019) and *A Common Strangeness: Contemporary Poetry, Cross-cultural Encounter, Comparative Literature* (2012). He studied Chinese at the University of Auckland, at Wuhan University, and at National Taiwan Normal University's Mandarin Training Center, and he has written about the work of several contemporary Chinese-language poets, including Bei Dao 北岛, Hsia Yü 夏宇, Yang Lian 杨炼 and Yi Sha 伊沙.

Murray Edmond, born in Kirikiriroa in 1949, lives in Glen Eden, Tāmaki Makaurau. Actor, director, writer and critic, he taught drama at the University of Auckland from 1991 to 2014. He has published 15 books of poetry, the most recent being *Shaggy Magpie Songs* (2015), *Back Before You Know* (2019) and *FARCE* (2022); *Time to Make a Song and Dance: Cultural revolt in Auckland in the 1960s* (2021); a book of novellas, *Strait Men and Other Tales* (2015); *Then It Was Now Again: Selected critical writing* (2014); and edited *Ka Mate Ka Ora* (www.nzepc.auckland.ac.nz/kmko). He is the dramaturge for Indian Ink Theatre Company.

Chris Elder trained as a Chinese linguist before serving in the New Zealand Embassy in Beijing when it first opened in the early 1970s. He returned to Beijing as ambassador from 1993 to 1998. Other ambassadorial appointments have been to Indonesia and to Russia. In Wellington, Chris has served as the Ministry of Foreign Affairs and Trade's deputy secretary with responsibility for Asian affairs. He has published a range of papers and articles relating to New Zealand's interaction with China and with Asia, and edited three anthologies on aspects of China: *Old Peking, China's Treaty Ports* and *New Zealand's China Experience*.

Meng Foon was born in Tairāwhiti to working-class migrant parents, but soon immersed himself in a community that didn't look or sound like him. His family's early toil as market gardeners was profitable in a business sense, but more importantly it brought its social benefits, with the Foons connecting with people across the region and from all backgrounds. This grounding, and Meng's interest in te ao Māori, evolved into a talent of building relationships within and between varied and diverse communities. It is this talent which was showcased in 18 years as Gisborne mayor, but has taken on even greater importance with Meng's appointment as Race Relations Commissioner in 2019. Meng uses different languages every day, and is fluent in his Chinese dialects, te reo Rangatira o Te Tairāwhiti and English. Meng's use of language highlights how some of our present race issues can be resolved to create a more harmonious Aotearoa for the future.

Garth Fraser was born in 1943 and grew up in Lower Hutt. His interest in China began through friendships formed with 'old China hands', and they introduced him to the New Zealand China Friendship Society. In 1979, when general secretary of New Zealand's major food industry union, he was invited by the All-China Federation of Trade Unions to lead a delegation to China. This was the beginning of his 30-year-long 'China journey'. Today he is managing director of Asia New Zealand International, a company that handles export licenses for the dairy and general food products industries; it is also involved in the tourism industry.

Esther Fung ONZM is a fourth-generation Chinese New Zealander who grew up firmly ensconced in both Chinese and New Zealand heritages. A diverse professional life has been accompanied by extensive community engagement. Over the years, Esther has served as a trustee for the Poll Tax Heritage Trust, and held executive office in the Wellington Chinese Association, the New Zealand Chinese Association (NZCA), the Wellington Xiamen Association, Multicultural Learning and Support Services, the Wellington Chinese Garden Society, and the Wellington Ethnic Council. A descendant of poll tax payers, Esther and others in the NZCA were instrumental in ensuring that the New Zealand government apologised to the Chinese community for the legislated discrimination that was targeted at the early Chinese settlers in Aotearoa.

Maria Galikowski graduated with a doctoral degree in modern Chinese studies from the University of Leeds. After a three-year junior lectureship at Oxford University, she took up a lecturing position in New Zealand, helping to establish the Chinese Studies programme at the University of Waikato, where she has taught for the past 30 years. Her research interests are in the area of modern and contemporary Chinese visual culture.

Hongzhi Gao is associate professor in the School of Marketing and International Business, Victoria University of Wellington. Dr Gao received his MCom (distinction) and PhD in marketing from Otago University. Before coming to New Zealand, Dr Gao was an analyst of foreign loans and risk management for Jilin provincial government in China. Dr Gao's publications appear in leading marketing and international business journals. Dr Gao has devoted the past 10 years to researching New Zealand firms' marketing and business strategies in China. He is now researching the impact of the US–China trade war on Chinese, American, Australian and New Zealand firms.

Leo Haks (d. 2021), originally from the Netherlands, was a long-time resident of New Zealand. Over the span of four decades, he was an avid collector of, and occasional dealer in, cultural artefacts from several countries, including the People's Republic of China. He also authored a number of works on the objects he collected. The extract included here is from a diary Leo kept of a business trip he undertook to attend the 1977 Canton Trade Fair as the representative of a food-provisioning company. It was his first trip to China, and it ignited in him his lifelong passion for Chinese art and artefacts.

Peter Holmes was born in Palmerston North, and studied traditional European and Oriental ceramics in Australia for two years. His work has featured in a number of exhibitions of ceramic works in New Zealand, and is represented in several private collections. Further study of Fine Arts at the University of Auckland was followed by medieval ceramics research in China for an MA in archaeology and anthropology. Prehistoric ceramics recovered during fieldwork in the USA resulted in several conference papers and published research in the journal *Ceramics Technical*. An archaeologist with 20 years' international experience, Peter now lives in Tauranga.

Amy Holmes-Tagchungdarpa is an associate professor in the Department of Religious Studies at Occidental College in Los Angeles, CA. She is originally from Taranaki, and initially lived in China as a teenager when her parents taught English there. She completed a BA at Victoria University of Wellington, and a PhD at the Australian National University, is the author of *The Social Life of Tibetan Biography: Textuality, community, and authority in the lineage of Tokden Shakya Shri* (2014). She continues to carry out research in China and throughout the Himalayas.

Xiaoming Huang is a professor of International Relations at Victoria University of Wellington, and has taught in the Political Science and International Relations Programme there since 1997. Professor Huang publishes extensively on modern political development in East Asian countries, the political economy of East Asian industrial growth, and the structure, institutions and culture of China's evolving relations with the world. Professor Huang was the founding director of the New Zealand Contemporary China Research Centre, and has been an active participant in and contributor to the development of East Asian studies at New Zealand universities and to public policy debate on East Asia.

Amanda Jack took her first Mandarin class at the University of Auckland in 1988, and ended up with an MSc in cross-cultural psychology from Victoria University of Wellington in 2018. She has worked as a teacher, a lawyer and a counsellor, and has been involved in amateur theatre in Aotearoa, the USA and Japan. Amanda runs a small counselling practice from her current home in Heidelberg, Germany.

Pauline Keating lectured in Chinese history in the history programme at Victoria University of Wellington from 1989 until her retirement in 2013. She first visited China as a tourist in January 1973, less than a month after the New Zealand and Australian governments normalised relations with the People's Republic of China. She taught English in Beijing in 1978–79, then studied Chinese history at Nanjing University in 1981–82. In 1989, she completed a doctoral thesis at the Australian National University on rural co-operatives in the communist base areas during the Sino–Japanese war. She is now making a broader study of 'rural reconstruction' in Republican China.

Joe Lawson is a lecturer in Chinese history at Newcastle University (UK). He grew up in Dunedin and graduated from the University of Otago with a BA in history in 2004. After four years in China, he did a PhD at Victoria University of Wellington, and then spent 18 months in Taiwan. He is the author of *A Frontier Made Lawless: Violence in Upland Southwest China, 1800–1956* (2017), and has published academic articles on various aspects of China's political, social and environmental history. He has also translated Chinese historical scholarship into English, including Mao Haijian's *The Qing Empire and the Opium War* (2016).

Bo Li is the managing director and founder of Asiaworks, a one-stop-shop to help New Zealand businesses maximise their Asian market share and raise awareness by overcoming cultural and language barriers. Bo is a well-known New Zealand-based consultant on Chinese culture and business practice. Before founding Asiaworks in 2010, he led many significant marketing projects for Bananaworks, Brand Works and Maxim Group. He is chairperson of the New Zealand Asia Trust and a committee member of the Auckland Chinese Community Centre.

Phillip Mann is a highly regarded science fiction writer and theatrical director. Born in North Yorkshire, he studied drama and English at the University of Manchester, and has worked extensively in theatre in Europe and North America. He moved to Wellington in 1969, and took up a lectureship in drama studies at Victoria University of Wellington the next year. The drama studies degree programme that he founded was the first of its kind in New Zealand, and celebrated its fiftieth anniversary in 2020. Phillip wrote his first science fiction novel while working as a sub-editor at the China News Agency Xinhua 新华社 in Beijing in 1978–79. He has now written more than 20 novels.

Lewis Mayo grew up on the northern periphery of South Auckland, and studied at the University of Auckland between 1982 and 1984; he was a New Zealand China Exchange Programme student at the Peking Languages

Institute in 1985, and at Peking University in 1985 and 1986, before going to the University of Hawai'i in 1987 to do a Master's on the history of the Song dynasty. Between 1988 and 1989 he taught English (in company with his late partner, Miriam Lang, 1959–2018) at the Southwestern University of Finance and Economics in Chengdu; this period coincided with the protest movements of April to June 1989. He completed a PhD at the Australian National University in 1999, with a thesis on the political history of birds in the oasis of Dunhuang between the ninth and eleventh centuries. In 2000 he took up a position teaching Chinese and Asian Studies at the University of Melbourne, where he still works.

John McKinnon joined the then Ministry of Foreign Affairs in New Zealand in May 1974. From 1975 to 1977 he undertook two years of Chinese language study in Hong Kong, following which he was assigned to the New Zealand Embassy in Beijing as second secretary. His subsequent overseas assignments with the New Zealand foreign service were in Washington, Canberra and New York. John served twice as New Zealand ambassador to China and Mongolia, the first time from 2001 to 2004, the second time from 2015 to 2018. Prior to this last posting, he was executive director of the Asia New Zealand Foundation. John McKinnon is now a senior fellow of the Centre for Strategic Studies, at Victoria University of Wellington. He became the chair of the New Zealand China Council in 2021.

Brian Moloughney was born in Blenheim but grew up mostly in Papatoetoe. After completing a Master's in Chinese history from the University of Canterbury, he had the good fortune to be awarded a CHEP scholarship, which enabled him to live and study for a period in Nanjing. He did a PhD in Chinese history at the Australian National University, and since 1993 has taught at the University of Otago, a position he retires from in 2022.

Philip S. Morrison is professor emeritus at the School of Geography, Environment and Earth Sciences, Te Herenga Waka Victoria University of Wellington. He was a member of the 1971 student delegation to the People's Republic of China. Following degrees at Victoria University of Wellington, Philip secured a Commonwealth Scholarship in 1972 and went on to complete a PhD degree from the University of Toronto. After a post-doc at the University of Pennsylvania, he was appointed to the academic staff of Victoria University in 1982. He was awarded the first Hodge Fellowship by the Social Science Research Fund Committee in 1985. This was followed by an Association of Commonwealth Development Fellowship for research into off-farm employment in Sarawak, Malaysia, in 1987, later supplemented by several Chair of Malay Studies travel grants and an Institute of Southeast Asian Studies (ISEAS) fellowship in 1990. He served as editor of *Asia Pacific Viewpoint* (formally *Pacific Viewpoint*) between 1984 and 2001. Philip initiated the biennial Labour, Employment and Work conferences (LEW) in 1984, which continue to be run by the VUW Centre of the same name. He co-organises the International Conference on Wellbeing and Public Policy, and currently chairs a longitudinal, multi-cohort study of student wellbeing at Victoria University of Wellington.

Mavis Mullins MNZM (Rangitāne, Ngāti Ranginui) began her working life as a wool classer in her family's shearing business, Paewai Mullins Shearing Ltd. That enterprise was founded in the 1930s by her great-uncle, All Black Lui Paewai. Mavis graduated with an MBA from Massey University in 1996. She very soon became a leader in the field of business governance, and an activist committed to the development of strong governance skills in Māori businesses. Among many other awards and honours, she has been made a Member of the New Zealand Order of Merit (2002) and inducted into the New Zealand Business Hall of Fame (2017).

John Needham (1937–2000), born in Yorkshire, taught English literature at Massey University in Palmerston North for many years. Returning in 1995 to Hong Kong, where he had taught in the 1960s, he met up with the Hong Kong poet and scholar Leung Ping-kwan (or PK, 1949–2013), carrying a copy of PK's poetry collection, *City at the End of Time*, the introduction to which had been written by an ex-student of his.

Rebecca Needham is a first-generation Eurasian New Zealander who has spent significant periods of time living and working in China, both as a student and as a New Zealand diplomat. She now works at Te Herenga Waka Victoria University of Wellington.

James Ng MBE, CNZM came to New Zealand from China as a five-year-old, and grew up in the family laundry business in Gore and Ashburton. He later trained to be a doctor at the University of Otago, and worked as a general practitioner. He is a prominent member of the New Zealand Chinese community, and, as such, has forged important cultural links between New Zealand and the PRC. In recognition of his achievements and contributions, he has been awarded an MBE, CNZM and the Medallion of the Dominican Order. He was made D.Litt as the author of *Windows on a Chinese Past* (4 vols, 1993–1999), and his library collection on Chinese New Zealanders has UNESCO recognition. He is now retired.

Thomas Nicholls (Ngāti Huarere rāua ko Ngāti Maru) is a public servant based in Wellington. He began learning Mandarin at the University of Auckland. After graduating with a Bachelor of Arts he went on to complete a Master's in international politics at Fudan University. His China-related work experience includes teaching Mandarin at Queen Margaret College, developing Chinese language learning software, supporting the China–New Zealand Year of Tourism and research for the New Zealand Contemporary China Research Centre.

Ashalyna Noa is a PhD candidate at the Macmillan Brown Centre for Pacific Studies, and works as a Pacific academic lead at the University of Canterbury. Her PhD provides a comparative analysis of New Zealand and China's foreign aid and soft power in the Pacific, with a case study on Sāmoa. Ashalyna is a first-generation New Zealand-born Samoan from Auckland and Christchurch.

Adam Osborne-Smith is a teacher and small commodities trader living in Yiwu, China. Born in New Zealand, he first moved to China when he was 24. Adam has travelled extensively around China and has conducted research on its political system.

Michael Powles, brought up partly in Sāmoa, is a former Aotearoa New Zealand diplomat. Overseas he headed New Zealand posts in Fiji, Indonesia and China, and was permanent representative to the United Nations in New York. In Wellington he became deputy secretary of Foreign Affairs. After retirement, he spent several years in China, founded the Pacific Cooperation Foundation, and worked as a Human Rights Commissioner and as a member of the Council of the National University of Sāmoa. He has spoken and published on foreign relations issues, particularly subjects relating to New Zealand's role in the Pacific, its relations with China and its policies in the United Nations.

Nina Mingya Powles is a prizewinning poet, essayist and zine-maker of mixed Malaysian–Chinese and Pākehā heritage. As a child, she lived for a number of years in Shanghai, a city she returned to as a university student in 2016.

Wen Chin Powles 陈雯 is a New Zealand diplomat with many years' experience working on relations with China, including as New Zealand consul-general in Shanghai in 2006. Wen was born in Malaysia of Hakka

客家 heritage, and traces her ancestry back to the Guangdong border-lands with Hong Kong. Her passion for archaeology and Chinese history, literature and politics continues to kindle an interest in exploring museums and archaeological sites in China and elsewhere. In Wen's whānau are Michael, Nina Mingya, Anna, Jonathan, and other close family in Malaysia, Canada, Singapore and Australia.

Luke Qin 秦瞳 arrived in New Zealand as a teenager from Sichuan, China. He is now an experienced international trade banker, helping established exporters and importers with working capital funding and risk management. Luke currently serves as an elected board member of the New Zealand Institute of International Affairs, executive committee member of the New Zealand China Council, cultural ambassador for the Hurricanes Super Rugby team, panel member of the Ministry for Ethnic Communities Development Fund, and chair of Hutt City Council Community Funding Panel. He is also an elected board director and treasurer of Transparency International New Zealand, serving as chair of the Affiliations Committee and deputy chair of the Audit & Risk Committee. Luke graduated with a Master's in applied finance from Victoria University of Wellington and is currently studying te reo Māori. He is a member of the Institute of Directors, Australia New Zealand Leadership Forum Emerging Leaders Programme, Asia New Zealand Foundation Leadership Network, and has been serving as a justice of the peace since 2012. Luke was awarded a Community Service Award by Multicultural New Zealand in 2020, a Long Service Medal by Fire and Emergency New Zealand for his service as a qualified volunteer firefighter, and successfully completed the Firefighter Sky Tower Stair Challenge to raise funds for charity in 2018.

Michael Radich started his study of China at the University of Auckland. He formerly taught in religious studies at Victoria University of Wellington and is now professor of Buddhist studies at the University of Heidelberg,

Germany. His Harvard PhD thesis (2007) was entitled *The Somatics of Liberation*. He is author of *How Ajātaśatru Was Reformed* (2011), and *The Mahāparinirvāṇa-mahāsūtra and the Emergence of Tathāgatagarbha Doctrine* (2015). He was a Humboldt Fellow in Hamburg (2015), and Shinnyo-en Visiting Professor of Buddhist Studies at Stanford (2019).

Mary Roberts-Schirato was born in Wellington, and undertook her primary and secondary education in Wellington and The Hague. She attended Victoria University of Wellington, where she gained a PhD in linguistics, and she also attended the Peking Languages Institute and Peking University. She has taught adults at all levels, from basic literacy instruction to university level. The institutions at which she has worked include the Peking Languages Institute, Victoria University of Wellington, the University of Otago, the University of Macau and China Women's University in Beijing.

Brenda (Englefield) Sabatier has had an enduring interest in language and culture, teaching in New Zealand, England, Spain and China. The first experience of China was joining a New Zealand China Friendship Society tour when at Wellington Teachers' College in 1978. Since then, she has visited several times, learned some Chinese and studied Chinese politics and literature. Except for the period teaching in China, from 1986 to 2019 she was a lecturer at AUT.

Alex Smith (Ngāti Kahungunu/Pākehā) is a public servant and writer from Wellington. She started learning Mandarin at Wellington Girls' College, and has since studied and worked in Shanghai and New York. She holds a Master of Arts in East Asian regional studies from Columbia University, a certificate in Chinese language from Fudan University, and a Bachelor of Arts (Honours) from Victoria University of Wellington.

Ellen Soullière has taught at the Chinese University of Hong Kong, Victoria University of Wellington, Wellington Polytechnic, and Massey University, where she served as head of school of Language Studies and Wellington Regional Director of the College of Humanities and Social Sciences. She is presently an honorary research associate of the School of Humanities, Media and Creative Communication at Massey University. Her research interests include Chinese history, the history of Chinese women, the history of Chinese art, material culture and literature, oral history, second-language acquisition in English and Chinese, applied linguistics, and translation.

Margaret T. South (1926–2016) taught Classical Chinese and Chinese poetry at the University of Auckland from 1967 until her retirement (as associate professor of Chinese and head of the Department of Asian Languages and Literatures) in 1992. An Australian by birth, she was a graduate of both the University of Sydney and the Australian National University. Her PhD thesis at the latter was on the weird and wonderful Tang dynasty poet Li He 李賀 (ca. 790–ca. 816). The memoir and poems in this anthology arose from time she spent in Xi'an in the 1980s during periods of leave.

Kerry Taylor is a professor of history and head of the School of Humanities, Media and Creative Communication at Massey University Te Kunenga ki Purehuroa. He is a specialist in the history of the Left, especially the history of the Communist Party of New Zealand. He is co-editor, with Pat Moloney, of *On the Left: Essays on New Zealand socialism* (2002). He is currently working on a history of the relationship between the New Zealand and Chinese communist parties, a project he began in 2019 while on a visiting fellowship at the History Department of Peking University.

James To is senior adviser (research and engagement) at the Asia New Zealand Foundation, where he works to grow New Zealanders' connections and understanding of Asia. James is also the national secretary of the New Zealand Chinese Association (Inc), serving to manage the interests of its 14 branches. He has pursued his interests and engagements with China and the Chinese community through these roles, building upon his previous experiences as a political scientist, author and businessperson.

Hone Tuwhare (Ngāpuhi) (1922–2008) was born in Kokewai, Northland. He worked as a boilermaker and welder with New Zealand Railways, and served as a trade union delegate. His writing began to attract attention in the 1950s, and he held Robert Burns Fellowships at the University of Otago in 1969 and 1974. He was the co-organiser in 1973 of the first Māori Writers and Artists Conference at Te Kaha. He participated in the Māori Land March of 1975. He was awarded honorary doctorates in literature by the universities of Otago and Auckland, and occupied the position of Te Mata Poet Laureate from 1999 to 2001. In 2003 the Arts Foundation named him as one of New Zealand's 10 great living artists. Hone relished his mahi, visiting schools and encouraging students over several decades to create their own stories and poems. *Small Holes in the Silence* (2016) is a comprehensive collection of his poetry, and includes Māori translations of the poems. His small crib in Kaka Point, South Otago, was opened in October 2022 as a creative residence.

Andrew Wilford works at the New Zealand Contemporary China Research Centre while concurrently undertaking postgraduate studies in international relations. He moved to China at the age of 17 and joined the New Zealand Contemporary China Research Centre after 10 years of living in Sichuan, in both Chengdu and Xichang. At the time of the 2008 Wenchuan earthquake, Andrew was working at a Chengdu training centre, teaching English to students ranging in ages from six to sixty.

Alison Wong's ancestors first arrived in New Zealand from Guangdong in 1879. She grew up in Hawke's Bay, has lived most of her life in Wellington, and now lives in Geelong, Australia, moving back and forth across the Tasman. In the 1980s she studied in Xiamen on a New Zealand–China exchange scholarship. She spent 1994 in Shanghai, and returned for the 2014 Shanghai Writing Program and the 2016 Sun Yat-sen University International Writers' Residency in Guangzhou. Her novel, *As the Earth Turns Silver* (2009), won the New Zealand Book Award for fiction. She co-edited *A Clear Dawn: New Asian Voices from Aotearoa New Zealand* (2020).

Jason Young is director of the New Zealand Contemporary China Research Centre and associate professor of political science and international relations at Te Herenga Waka Victoria University of Wellington. He studied Mandarin Chinese at Fu Jen University and Tunghai University in Taipei and Taichung, and is a graduate of the University of Otago and Victoria University of Wellington. Jason's research focuses on China's domestic politics and foreign policy and New Zealand–China relations. He is author of *China's Hukou System* (2013) and a number of journal articles and chapters in English and Chinese.

Acknowledgements

First and foremost we would like to express our gratitude to the wider editorial group who worked collectively to produce this anthology: Paul Clark, Chris Elder, Maria Galikowski, Pauline Keating, James To, Andrew Wilford and Jason Young. Pauline's organisational energy sustained the project and Andrew provided much-needed technological support, both of which were critical for the original workshop which helped spark interest in the project. Not all those who participated in the workshop went on to write something, and for reasons of space not every submission could be included, but we are grateful to all who participated in the workshop for their support, and on behalf of the group we thank all those who offered submissions.

In a few instances we have included an essay or poem that has been published before, and we thank the individuals and publishers concerned. These include Rob Tuwhare, for permission to include one of his father's poems, and Colleen Dallimore, Leo Hak's widow, who gave us permission to copy and publish extracts from her husband's 1977 diary. We also thank The Cuba Press for permission to republish a chapter from Nick Bridge's memoir, *The Boat that Brought Me*, as well as Auckland University Press, Cold Hub Press and Otago University Press for permission to republish a selection of Diana Bridge's poems. Auckland University Press and May Needham gave us permission to publish an abridged version of John Needham's 'Hong Kong Revisited', originally published in *The Departure Lounge: Travel Literature in the Post-Modern World*. Emma Wright, of the Emma Press, gave us permission to include Nina Mingya Powles' essay, which was first published in *Tiny Moons: A Year of Eating in Shanghai*. An earlier version of Alison Wong's 'Lost in Shanghai' was published in English with Chinese translation in *The Mother Tongue in a Foreign Land: Tenth Anniversary of the Shanghai Writing Program Collection* in September 2017. We are grateful to Hu Peihua for permission to republish the story. We thank, too, Murray Edmond, editor of *ka mate ka ora: a new zealand journal of poetry and poetics*, for permission to include his own essay and that of Hilary Chung, both first published in that journal, and Hilary's partner Trevor Hardy for his encouragement.

Nicola Legat's enthusiasm for the project came at just the right time, and her suggestions have improved the book in a number of ways. She has been a pleasure to work with, as have her colleagues at Massey University Press, Tracey Borgfeldt, Anna Bowbyes, Emily Goldthorpe and designer Alice Bell. Kate Stone helped shape 50 different contributions into more of a coherent whole, and we are grateful for her guidance. Finally, we would like to thank Stan Chan 陳康渭 for the beautiful calligraphy in a variety of styles that adorns the book.

Index

Page numbers in **bold** refer to images.

2degrees 86, 88

A

Academy of Sciences 105–9
agriculture 89–92, 104–10, 130, 305–8
Albanian Party of Labour 122, 123
All-China Federation of Trade Unions 283–84
Alley, Rewi & family 15, 17, 33, 36, 52, **53**, 67, 111–14, 117, 261, 283, 286, 289–90, 356
Archer, Courtney 283
Asia New Zealand Foundation 276, 278–80, 352
Asiaworks Ltd 145, 146
Ātihau-Whanganui Incorporation 89–90
Atkins, Dick 36–38
Auckland Chinese Community Centre 145–46
Auckland & South Auckland 26–29, 31–32, 254, 273
Austin, Dougal 188–94
Australia 25, 73, 86, 119, 123, 128, 215, 250, 316

B

Bailey, Rona 120–21
Barton, Shirley 356
Beichuan **220**, 221, 232–33
Beida (Peking University) **115**, 116, 117, 248–50, 321–23
Beijing 51, 67–68, 74–76, 111–13, 202–7
Bo Li 16, **144**
Bollard, Ted 105–6, 109

Brady, Anne-Marie 290
Brecht, Bertolt 176
Bridge, Diana **60**
Brown, Lorraine 235
Browne, Tony 237
Buchanan, Keith 355–56
Buddhism 18, 60, 149–50, 160–61, 176–77
Burdett, Councillor 234–35
Burdon, Philip 276

C

Cai Shaoqing 167
Campbell, Duncan 16, 149, 152
Canton 23–24, 43–49
   see also Guangzhou
Cao Yujuan 284
ceramics 179–86
Chan, Stan 244, 245
Chang 46, 48, 49
Chang, Allen 239
Chen Kaige 29–31
Chen Suzi 181, 185, 186
Chen Mingming 239
Chen Weiming 180, 186
Chen Zhengwei 173–78
Chengde **363**
Chengdu & earthquake 218–21, 232–33, 286–89
Chiang Kai-shek (Madame) 114
Chin, Peter 54, 55
China 168, 170–71, 187–94, 357
   & NZ, diplomacy 11–13, 29, 33–42, 54, 67–73, 92–93, 314–17
China Exchange Programme 15–16, 326, **329**
China Import and Export Fair 43–49
China News Agency
   see Xinhua

China University of Political Science and Law 261–63
China Week 52
Chinese, in NZ 50–55, 142–46, 231–45, 275–82
Chinese Bridge Speech Competition 253–59, 361
Chinese Communist Party 26, 27–29, 118–24, 170
   see also communism
Chinese English Poetry Festival 267
Chinese Foreign Ministry (Waijiaobu) 38
Chinese Industrial Cooperatives *see* Gung Ho
Chinese New Year Festival Market Day 146
Chinese People's Association for Friendship with Foreign Countries (Youxie) 33, 277, 284, 286
Chinese Poll Tax Heritage Trust 241, 244
Chongqing 114, 189, 282, 361
Christianity 55, 70, 76, 312, 322
Christie, John 54
Clark, Helen 110, 239, 244
Clark, Paul **301**
Clinton, Hillary 126–27
communism 26–29, 50, 75, 97, 99–100, 118–24
   see also Chinese Communist Party
Communist Party of Australia 123
Communist Party of New Zealand 13, 22, 26–29, 118–24
Confucianism & Confucius Institute 69–70, 166, 196, 237, 258–60, 320
congyou banmian 208–17
Covid 72–73

Cultural Revolution 102,
104–5, 116, 167, 224–27,
229, 285
currency, foreign 196–97,
247–48
Cuthbert, David 358

D
Dai Qing 125–32, **131**
Dao'an 151
Daoism 160, 309, 320, 322
Dazhai 148–50
Democracy Wall 125, 229–30
Deng Mingyan 267
Deng Xiaoping 14, 39–42,
113, 156, 227, 286, 356
dissidents 67–68, 102, 125–
35, 202–7, 300–302
Douglas, Murray 52, 54
Drummond, Sheldon 235
Duan 166–67
Dujiangyan 218, 233
Dunedin 52–55, 206, 215
Dunhuang **60**

E
Edmond, Murray **271**
education 15–16, 114, 283–84,
291–95
Education Commission
284–85
Elder, Chris 38, 290
English First 212–17
English Language Institute
327
environment & sustainability
89–92, 127–30, 287
Evans, Patrick 134
Ewen, Jack & Joyce 124, 286
exports *see* trade

F
Falun Gong 320–21, 322
Fan Ye 171
Fangshan 149–51
Farley, Malcolm 181

Faxian 150–51
Field, Mick 54
food products *see*
agriculture; trade
Forster, E. M. 140
Fotudeng 151
Four Olds 168
Friends of Nature 128
Fudan University 150,
362–64
Fujian Province &
organisations 104, 179–85,
354
Fukuyama, Francis 214
Fung, David 241

G
Gair, George & Mrs Gair 39
Gang of Four 47, 48, 116
gaokao 342
gardens 52, 54, 55
George, H. V. 327
Gim Shan 50
Gisborne 231–38
gold mining, in NZ 12, 50,
52, 55
Gorbachev, Mikhail 248–49
Grant-Mackie, Jack 25
Great Leap Forward 355
Great Mosque, Xi'an 160, 163
Greater Wild Goose Pagoda
(Da Yanta) 162–63
Grocott, Paul 358
Gu Cheng 102, 133–35, 273
Guangdong & Museum 51,
189, 192–93
Guangxi 305–6
Guangzhou 43, 189–91, 354
see also Canton
guanxi 231–38, 280, 317
Guizhou Province 304, 305,
309
Gung Ho 114, 117, 261, 286,
304

H
Haitian 279
Han 99, 103, 160, 171, 214–17,
323, 324
Handan 150
Hangzhou 180–81, 186–94,
188
Hautaki 86
Hayward, Ramai & Rudall 77
He Liliang 107
Hill, Ted 123
Hoe, Jock 326–27
homosexuality 217
Hong Kong 17, 56, 70, 136–41,
294, 364–65
horticulture *see* agriculture
Houjing 184
Hsu Ming-chiang **329**
Hu Fuming 168
Hu Jianzhong 55
Hu Jintao 221, 366
Hua Guofeng **34–35**, 37–38,
299
Huang Hua 106–7
Huang Shan, Yellow
Mountain 267–74
Huawei 86–88, 365
human rights 17, 70–73,
213–15, 314–16, 364–66
Hunan 231, 254–59
Hung, Cheung-Tak 54

I
imports *see* trade
Inner Mongolia 80, 100
Institute of Botany 107–9
Iosefo, Juzzah, art work **334**
Iti, Tame 22, **22**, 99–100, 121

J
jade 187–94, **190**
Jakobson, Roman 270
Japan 29, 36, 50, 104, 236
Jian Zhan Hare's Fur
(*Tenmoku*) **182**
Jiang Weidong 187, 193–94
Jiang Zemin 54

Jiangsu School of Performing
Arts 173–74
Jianyang 183–85
Jianyao kiln site 181–85
Jingwan 149–50
Joint Communiqué, 1972
11–13, 29

K
Keating, Pauline **131**
Key, John 236, 237
King, Jennifer 277–78, 280
Kovrig, Michael 365–66
Kuan Meng Goh 239
Kuang Yaming 167
Kuomintang Party 50–51,
114, 115
Kura Pounamu 188–94, **191**

L
Lancashire, Professor 273
languages & dialects 74–75,
156–57, 165, 234, 276
Cantonese 75, 112, 242
Mandarin (Putonghua)
74–75, 199–200, 215, 234,
237, 253–59
Lantern Festivals 275–82,
281
Larkin, Philip 140
Legge, James 166
Leung Ping-kwan (PK)
136–41
Levine, Stephen 261–65
Li Keqiang 237
Li Lairong 104–10, **107**
Li Qiyang 284–86
Li Xiaolin 284
Li Zhaoxing 110
Liang Congjie 128
Liang Qichao 128
Liangzhu & Museum 187–94
Ling Hunghsiang **329**
Linwood school 349–50
Liu Guozhong 286
Liu Xianhua 332

Loess Plateau 28–30
Lu Wanru 284
Lu Zenkang 235
Luo Ying 268–69

M
MacIntyre, Duncan 39
Mahuta, Nanaia 92–93
Manson, Jack 120–21
Mao Zedong **22**, 26, 69–70,
100, 119–20, 212, 359
Māori 12, 22, 82–93, 96–99,
285, 287–88
& taonga 77, 90, 188–94, 236,
255, 258, 288
land ownership 31, 91–92,
100
market gardens 26, 83, 102,
103, 104, 231
Mason, R. A. K. 27, 97–99
Massey University 328, 332,
355
May Fourth Movement
272–73
McKenzie, Don 105–7
McKinnon, Don 276
McKinnon, John & family 40,
74–81, **78**
Mei Lanfang 173–78
Meister, Barry 235
Mencius 332–33
Meng Foon 15–16
military & martial law 29,
202, 224, 229, 236–37,
249–51, 299–300, 302, 324,
328–32
Minford, John 180, 273
Minhinnick, Robert 269, 270
Moloughney, Brian 18
Moore, Mike 283, 286
Muldoon, Robert & Thea 33,
34–35, 36–42, **108**, 109,
299
Murphy, Nigel 241, 244–45
Museum of the First National
Congress 153–55

N
Nakamoto Family 235
Nanjing & Nanking 167, **169**,
173, 199, 203
Nash, Walter 241
National Day celebrations 51
National Museum of China
188–92
New China News Agency *see*
Xinhua
New Zealand Centre, Beida
302–3
New Zealand China Council
91, 352
New Zealand China
Friendship Society 13, 18,
52, **53**, 124, 195, 286, 304–7,
310, 352, 356
New Zealand China Research
Centre 262
New Zealand China Trade
Association 145, 352
New Zealand Chinese
Association 239, 241–42,
245
New Zealand Communist
Party *see* Communist
Party of New Zealand
New Zealand Contemporary
China Research Centre 19,
237, 260–66
New Zealand Federation of
Ethnic Councils 242
New Zealand Security
Intelligence Service 119,
121, 122
New Zealand Shanghai Trade
Fair 54
New Zealand University
Students Delegation
354–60
New Zealand–China Free
Trade Agreement 145, 236
New Zealand–China Student
Exchange Scholarship
156, 165

New Zealand–China Trade Agreement 36–37
Newnham, Tom 283, 284
Ng, James 53
Ngā Tamatoa 100
Ngāti Konohi 235
NGOs 126–32, 261, 263
Ningbo 339–46
noodles 208–17
North Korean students 197–98
NZAID 304–5

O
Olympic games 198, 215, 232, 234–35, 361
opera 173–78

P
Pacific region 15, 73, 85, 86, 276, 335–38
Pardoe, Anne 231–32
Peking University see Beida
People's Liberation Army 249–50, 299, 328–32
People's Republic of China see China; Chinese Communist Party
Peters, Winston 54, 302
Petit, Pascale 269, **271**
Phillips, Richard T. 25
Plumer, James 181
poetry 56–66, 96–103, 133–37, 161–64, 267–74, 335–38
police 49, 202, 229
poll tax 239–45
pollution 130, 213, 232, 287
pounamu 188–94, 236, 255
Poutama Trust 83–84
poverty reduction 304–10
Powles, Michael **71**, 285
Prakrit 321–23
Probe International 129
protests see dissidents; Tiananmen Square
Pudong area 68

Q
Qian Qichen **71**
Qin, Luke **351**
Quigley, Neil 262

R
racism 17, 96–103, 198–99, 215–16, 239–45
Rathgen, Sonja 245
Rauhihi, Miriama 22, **22**, 99, 121
Red Guards 167, 299
Reform and Opening Up era 75, 168, 290
religions 318–25 see also specific religions
Rewi Alley Scholarship 284–85
Rizhao 231–32
Roberts-Schirato, Mary 15, **115**
Rostow, Walt 355–56
Rowling, Bill 33
Royal Society of New Zealand 105, 109

S
Samoa 335–38
Satyanand, Anand 235
Sciascia, Piri 194
Searle, E. J. 26–27
Sew Hoy, Hugh 51
Shaanxi Province 29, 160, 189, 279, 300, 304, 309
Shandan Bailie School 114, 283–86, 304
Shane English centre 342
Shanghai 52–55, 153–57, 180, 196–201, 208–17, 361–64
Shanghai International Writers' Program 153
Shangnian Production Brigade, Beixiaoying People's Commune 299
Shao Xueping **271**
Sharpe, Bill 287–89
Sharples, Tā Pita 84–85

Shaw, Alister 356–58
Shi Le & Shi Hu 151
Shuiji kiln site 181–85
Sichuan earthquake 68, 304–5, **307**
Smiles, Samuel 140
Song Meiling 114
Song Qingling 111
Soullière, Ellen **329**
South Island Moon Festival 280
Soviet Union 26, 27, 118, 176, 198, 248, 249
stamps **144**, 145
Stanislavski 175–76
studying
  in China 60, 102, 111–17, 130, 147–49, 153–57, 165–68, 173–86, 195–201, 208–17, 260–66, **264**, 298–303, **301**, 361–64
  in NZ 15–16, 52, 143, 284, 313–14, 326–33, 347–50
Su Dongpo 348
Sun Shuqi 167–68, **169**, 171
Sun Yat-sen (Madame) 111
Symmans, Gerry 42
Sze, Arthur 268, 269, **271**, 272

T
Taiwan 51, 214, 344–45
Talboys, Brian 39, 106
Tang, Alex 54
Tao Wuxian 287
Taylor, Ron 122
Te Huarahi Tika Trust 86
Te Maipi, Timi 22, **22**, 99, 121
Te Papa 188–94
te reo 200, 236, 270
tea production 179, 181–83, 186
teaching, in China 125–26, 161, 195, 213–17, 221, 246–49, 262–65, 283–86, 303, 318–21, 339–46, 355
Temple of Flourishing Teaching (Xingjiao) 163–64

Three Gorges Dam 127, 129
Tiananmen Square 67–68,
  126, 168, 180, 202–7, **205**,
  246–52, 273
Tibet 18, 69, 80, 202–3, 204,
  265, 294, 322–24
tourism & tourists 116, 130,
  149, 156, 208, 269, 287
trade 15, 36–37, 43–49, 54, 83,
  105–10, 231, 287, 313–17
trade unions 283–90
Tū Te Mana Maurea 235–36
Tumahai, Lisa 194
Tupara, Nick 235
Tuwhare, Hone 12, 22, **22**,
  23–23, 26–27, 96–103, 121

U
Underground Press Cave 27
United Food and Chemical
  Workers Union of New
  Zealand 285, 288
United Kingdom 14, 36, 196
United Nations 73, 126, 287
United Nations' Fourth
  World Conference on
  Women 126
United States 14–15, 17,
  72–73, 227, 316, 345
University of Auckland 254,
  273
University of Otago 206
Urumchi 212–17
Uyghur people 73, 80, 99,
  213–16

V
Victoria University of
  Wellington 125, 260–62,
  326

W
Waikato 52, 232, 286–89
Walding, Joe 15
Walls, Richard 52
Wang Chih-kao **329**

Wang Dejia 129
Wang Heyong 286–89
Wang Laoshi 177
Wang Li 165
Wang Xinzhong 284
Wang Yu-chiung **329**
Wellington Chinese
  Association 239, 241
Wen Jiabao 110, 219–21, 366
Wen Shifu 321–22
Wilcox, Victor 118–24, 298
Wilson, Karen (Lang) 186,
  283
Wilson, Willie 22, **22**, 99, 121
Wilson family 235
Wolf, Dick 121, 122
Women's Federations 304–5,
  309
Wong, Malcolm 55
Workers' Cultural Palace,
  Shandan 285, 288
Wu, Harvey 241, 244–45
Wu Chucai & Wu Diaohou
  165–66
Wu Hung-po **329**
Wu Tianming 300
Wuhan 96, 102–3
Wuyi Mountain Reserve
  181–83, 184, 185
Wylie, Helen 326–27

X
Xi Chuan 269–70
Xi Jinping 168–70, 236, 292
Xiamen 105, **108**, 109, 156,
  237, 354–55
Xi'an 161, 189, 300
Xiangyang 150–51
Xiaorong 321–22
Xie Ye 133
Xinhua 120, 225–30
Xinjiang 73, 80, 214–16, 294
Xisi, Beijing 300–302
Xuan Zang (Tripitaka)
  163–64

Y
Yan Li 268, **271**, 273–74
Yang Lian 133–35, 268,
  270–73, **271**
Yang Shangkun 67–68
Yellow Earth (*Huang tudi*)
  29–31
Ying Kaoshu 166–67
Young, Bruce 54
Young, Steven 244
Yujia Gong, art work **343**

Z
Zang Di 267–68, **271**
Zhang, James 232
Zhang Dongxun 128
Zhang Heng 299–300, **301**
Zhang Xinhui 284
Zhang Yimou 300
Zhao Ziyang 40–41
Zhejiang Province 278–79
Zheng, Zhuang and Duan,
  states 166–67
Zhou Enlai 299–300
Zhu Rongji 286
Zhuang 166–67
Zigong 279, 282

First published in 2022 by Massey University Press
Private Bag 102904, North Shore Mail Centre
Auckland 0745, New Zealand
www.masseypress.ac.nz

Text copyright © individual contributors, 2022
Images copyright © as credited, 2022

Design by Alice Bell
Cover artwork: Simon Kaan (Ngāi Tahu and Poon Yue), *Tio VIII*, 2018, acrylic and
Chinese ink on board, courtesy of the artist and Sanderson Contemporary Art

Duncan Campbell and Brian Moloughney have asserted the right to be identified as the
Editors of this work

A catalogue record for this book is available from the National Library of New Zealand

Printed and bound in Singapore by Markono Print Media

ISBN: 978-1-99-101615-7
eISBN: 978-1-99-101621-8

Published with the support of The New Zealand Contemporary China Research Centre